THE STORY OF
A Hundred Operas

THE STORY OF
A Hundred Operas

Grosset & Dunlap
PUBLISHERS
NEW YORK

PRINTED IN THE UNITED STATES OF AMERICA

PREFACE

THE Story of a Hundred Operas is not intended in any way to be a serious literary production, but is an endeavor to present to the opera-loving public in clear and concise form, the plots of the operas, with mention of the principal arias as they occur. It includes practically all the grand operas in the repertoire of the leading opera houses of Europe and America, and is submitted with the hope that it will prove thoroughly enjoyable and find an abiding place in the library of the recipient.

FELIX MENDELSOHN

FOREWORD

WHEN Felix Mendelsohn first conceived the idea of writing *The Story of a Hundred Operas*, opera-going was a luxury available only to the "carriage trade" and those with a European background who had learned to love operatic music from the vantage points of low-priced seats in municipal Grand Opera houses. There were a few bold spirits who dared to predict the day when the people of America, popularly supposed to be completely occupied in grubbing for dollars, would become opera-minded.

One is almost tempted to believe an opera-lover such as Mr. Mendelsohn might have been gifted with second-sight, since the radio, the greatest single factor in the phenomenal spread of interest in the opera, was not even dreamed of in those days. Each week, in the season, many millions of Americans listen to the great operas played and sung over the air waves. A generation ago the Ring might have meant the local political set-up of a

Foreword

provincial city. Today Americans discuss the beloved epics of the operatic stage as they discuss books and plays and movies. The growth and spread in appreciation of this longest-neglected of the arts is as amazing as the development of our architecture or our systems of transportation.

It is for these sincere and enthusiastic converts, whose lives have been so immeasurably enriched by contact with the great operatic treasures, that this little book has been prepared. Naturally, it cannot contain all of the outstanding works of the master composers. Perhaps one or two of your favorites have had to be omitted. Something had to be sacrificed for the convenient format which fits so handily in milady's handbag or causes scarcely a bulge in mimaster's coat pocket.

THE PUBLISHERS

MARCH 1, 1940

Index to Operas

Index to Operas

[x]

Index to Operas

L'AFRICAINE

GRAND OPERA IN FIVE ACTS BY MEYERBEER
LIBRETTO BY SCRIBE
FIRST PRODUCTION—PARIS, 1865

CAST

DON PEDRO, Councillor to the King..*Basso*
DON DIEGO, admiral..............*Basso*
INEZ, his daughter..............*Soprano*
VASCO DE GAMA, officer in navy....*Tenor*
GRAND INQUISITORE.............*Basso*
SELIKA.........⎰ Slaves ⎱.........*Soprano*
NELUSKO......⎱   ⎰.........*Baritone*
CHIEF PRIEST OF BRAHMA.......*Basso*

ACT 1

Council Chamber at Portugal. Inez is bewailing (*Romance: "Adieu, dear Tagus"*) the long absence of Vasco de Gama, her betrothed. Her father, wishing her to forget de Gama and marry Don Pedro, tells her he is dead, but she declares she will remain faithful to him. *Terzett: "O childhood's love."* Her father's story is refuted by the sudden appearance of Vasco, who has just returned bringing news of a new and wonderful country, and produces two of the inhabitants, Nelusko and Selika, whom he has captured and brought with him as slaves. Don Diego, displeased at his return, causes

[1]

L'Africaine

his story to be doubted. At this Vasco becomes so enraged that he speaks violently against the injustice, and, together with his slaves, is thrown into prison.

ACT 2

Prison. Vasco lies asleep, tenderly watched by Selika, who loves him. *Aria: "In my lap rest thy weary head."* Nelusko, who is jealous of Selika's love for Vasco (*Nelusko: "Daughter of Kings"*), attempts to stab him, but Selika prevents him from doing so. Upon Vasco's awakening, she tells him the course to the island which is her home. *Duet: "In vain their powerless fury."* Inez, in order to save Vasco, has been compelled to marry Don Pedro, and he attempts to cheat Vasco of his fame. Taking with him Vasco's private papers and maps, also Inez and Selika, whom Vasco has presented to Inez as a wedding gift, he sails in search of the unknown land under the pilotage of Nelusko, who through jealousy of Selika's love for Vasco, offers to guide him. Vasco, who has been released, follows in pursuit.

ACT 3

Don Pedro's ship. Nelusko is guiding the ship toward a dangerous reef. *Nelusko: "Adamastor, Ruler of Ocean."* Vasco, whose ship is following close by, comes on board

[2]

Don Pedro's ship to caution him, but is put into irons by Don Pedro. Just then the ship is attacked by Indians, who kill or take as prisoners all on board with the exception of Vasco. He is saved by Selika, the queen of the tribe.

ACT 4

Temple of Brahma in the country of Selika and Nelusko. *Indian March.* The chief priest of Brahma forces Selika to swear destruction to all the crew, but saves Vasco, who is entranced with the beautiful country, (*Vasco: "O Paradiso"*) by announcing that he is her chosen husband. An elaborate marriage ceremony is arranged, and just as it is about to take place, Vasco hears the voice of Inez and rushes to her.

ACT 5

Selika, convinced that Vasco loves Inez, sacrifices her own feelings and assists them to escape, sending Nelusko to escort them to Vasco's boat. As the vessel disappears from view, Selika, no longer desiring to live, inhales the fumes of the poisonous mancanilla tree. Here she is found dying by Nelusko, who in his grief also inhales the deadly blossoms and dies at her side. *Finale. "What wondrous music."*

AIDA

GRAND OPERA IN FOUR ACTS BY VERDI
TEXT BY GHISLANZONI
FIRST PRODUCED—CAIRO, EGYPT, 1871

CAST

THE KING OF EGYPT............*Basso*
AMNERIS, his daughter.....*Mezzo-Soprano*
AIDA, an Ethiopian slave.........*Soprano*
RADAMES, Captain of the guard....*Tenor*
RAMFIS, high priest...............*Basso*
AMONASRO, King of Ethiopia.....*Baritone*

PLACE—Egypt, in the time of the Pharaohs.

ACT 1

Palace at Memphis. Aida, the daughter of the King of Ethiopia, is in captivity among the Egyptians. Radames, who is in love with her, is delighted by hearing from the High Priest that he has been selected to head the army against the invading Ethiopians. He hopes to gain the honor and lay his triumphs at Aida's feet. *Romanza, Radames: "Celeste Aida."* Amneris, daughter of the Egyptian King, has long loved the young warrior, and, now entering the room, wonders at his joy. *Duet, Radames and Amneris: "In thy visage I trace."* While he tells her of the honor about to be conferred upon him, Aida enters, and, watching them, Amneris suspects the

[4]

truth. *Terzett, Aida, Amneris and Radames:* *"Oh, fate o'er Egypt looming."* The King enters and Radames is formally invested with the command. Aida secretly grieves, as the leader of the Ethiopians is her father. *Aida:* *"Return victorious."*

SCENE 2

The Temple of Ptha. *Chorus of Priestesses:* *"O Mighty Ptha."* Radames enters and is made commander-in-chief by the High Priest and receives the blessing. *Prayer, Ramfis and Chorus: "O Mighty One, guard and protect."*

ACT 2

Amneris' Chamber. *Chorus of women:* *"Our songs his glory praising."* Amneris is being adorned for the festival in honor of the victorious homecoming of Radames. As Aida enters she dismisses her slaves, and tricks Aida into revealing her love for Radames by falsely announcing that he has been killed. *Duet, Amneris and Aida: "The chances of war afflict thy people, poor Aida." Aida: "O love, O joy, tormenting."*

SCENE 2

The return of Radames, victorious. *Chorus, King and people: "Glory to Egypt."* Amonasro, recognized as the Ethiopian King only by Aida, is among the captives, and he signals to her not to betray his rank

(*Amonasro:* "*This dress has told you*"), declaring to the Egyptians that the King has fallen in battle. At Radames' request, the prisoners, with the exception of Aida and her father, whom the King holds as hostages —are released. The King also bestows his daughter's hand upon Radames and proclaims him heir to the throne.

ACT 3

Near the Temple of Isis on the banks of the Nile. *Chorus of priests and priestesses: "O thou who to Osiris art."* Amneris has come to the temple to pay her vows to Isis on the evening before her marriage. Aida secretly follows to meet Radames for the last time. *Aida: "Oh, my dear country."* Her father finds her and persuades her (*Duet: "Once again thou shalt gaze"*) to betray to him the movement of the Egyptian army. He hides upon the approach of Radames, whom Aida urges to flee with her (*Radames and Aida: "Again I see thee"*), and from their conversation learns what he wishes to know, and now appears and reveals his identity, urging Radames to take sides with Ethiopia, pledging Aida's hand as reward, and while they are arguing, Amneris, who has overheard the conversation, comes out of the temple and denounces Radames. Aida and Amonasro flee, but Radames remains to be taken a prisoner. *Terzett, Amonasro, Aida and Radames: "I am dishonored."*

ACT 4

Corridor in the Palace. *Amneris: "My hated rival has escaped me."* Duet, Amneris and Radames: *"Now to the hall the priests proceed."* He is tried and sentenced to be buried alive. *Judgment Scene, Amneris, Ramfis and Chorus: "Heavenly spirit, descend."* Amneris seeks to save him, telling him that if he will denounce Aida, who still lives, she will obtain his pardon, but he refuses. Change of scene; the burial place in the temple; also the temple above. When Radames is entombed, he finds Aida, who has come to die with him. *Duet: "The fatal stone now closes over me."* Radames: *"To die, so pure and lovely."* They perish in each other's arms, while above them the penitent Princess kneels in prayer. *Finale, chorus of priests and priestesses: "Almighty Ptha."*

* * *

L'AMICO FRITZ

OPERA IN THREE ACTS
MUSIC BY PIETRO MASCAGNI
LIBRETTO BY SUARATONI FROM
THE ERCKMANN-CHATRIAN STORY
FIRST PRODUCTION—ROME, 1891

L'Amico Fritz

CAST

FRITZ KOBUS, rich bachelor.......*Tenor*

DAVID, a rabbi..................*Baritone*

FEDERICO, friend of Fritz..........*Tenor*

HANEZO, friend of Fritz............*Tenor*

SUZEL, a farmer's daughter........*Soprano*

BEPPE, a gypsy...................*Soprano*

CATERINA, a housekeeper.......*Contralto*

PLACE—Alsace

ACT 1

Room in Home of Fritz Kobus. Fritz, the wealthy bachelor, is celebrating his fortieth birthday. His friends banter him about his unwedded state and he declares that he never expects to get married. This greatly worries the Rabbi David, who is a famous matchmaker and who determines that a bride shall be found for Fritz. The merrymakers are interrupted by the arrival of pretty Suzel, daughter of the overseer on Fritz's estates. She has brought him some violets for his birthday. *Suzel: "Here are some flowers."* Fritz is much struck by her beauty and sweet, innocent ways and invites her to sit beside him at the feast. The friends begin to predict an early wedding. David, for one, is now sure that Fritz has found a girl that will win his heart. But when Suzel has

gone Fritz indignantly denies that he loves
the girl or that he will ever marry her. He
bets the rabbi one of his vineyards that he will
not marry Suzel.

ACT 2

A Yard on Fritz's Farm. *Suzel and chorus:
"O, beautiful cherries."* Here Fritz, attracted
by the lovely Suzel, listens to the girl sing
while he picks cherries. She helps him gather
them and he is enjoying every moment of the
time he is in her presence. But suddenly
Fritz's friends arrive. They see that he is
fond of Suzel, and the rabbi determines to
find out if an early marriage has not been
agreed on by the sweethearts. When the
girl appears David questions her and persuades her to tell him the story of Rebecca.
Suzel: "Now, Abraham was growing old."
When she finishes the girl realizes that the
rabbi has drawn from her a confession of her
love for Fritz. She is greatly confused and
runs into the house. When the rabbi questions Fritz the young man is much annoyed
and declares that he has no intention of
marrying Suzel. But he realizes that the girl
strangely fascinates him and he determines
to leave at once. *Fritz: "Whence this
strange and troubled feeling?"* Suzel weeps
for him as if heartbroken.

ACT 3

Room in Fritz's Home. Here Fritz, loving Suzel and out of her presence, is miserable. *Fritz and chorus: "Pretty maidens, weave garlands."* The young man's friends arrive and want to know why he is so melancholy. Beppe tells him the cause of the malady. *Beppe: "Courage, my dear friend."* Fritz then muses on love, concluding that it is the light of the world. *Fritz: "Life is love."* The rabbi enters and slyly tells Fritz that Suzel is to wed another. Jealousy now arouses the young man to action. He questions Suzel and urges her to postpone the wedding. Soon he declares his own love for the girl whom he thinks is about to be lost to him. *Fritz: "I love you, O, precious treasure dear."* The girl is even happier than he is. The rabbi finds them joyous. He has won the vineyard from Fritz but he gives it to the bride for her dowry.

* * *

L'AMORE DEI TRE RE

TRAGIC POEM IN THREE ACTS BY SEM BENELLI
MUSIC BY ITALO MONTEMEZZI
FIRST PRODUCTION, LA SCALA, MILAN, 1913

CAST

ARCHIBALDO ....*Basso*
MANFREDO ....*Baritone*

L'Amore dei tre Re

AVITO ....*Tenor*
FLAMINO ....*Baritone*
FIORA ....*Soprano*

A youth (a boy child—voice behind the scenes), a handmaiden, a young girl, an old woman and other inhabitants of Altura.

PLACE—Italian Castle.
TIME—Middle ages, forty years after a barbarian invasion.

Baron Archibaldo, a blind king, once a conquering invader, has secured the hand of Fiora, a native princess, for his son, as hostage of war. She does not love her husband, but loves Avito, a native prince to whom she was betrothed before the war separated the lovers. Manfredo, the husband, goes to war and this gives the lovers an opportunity to enjoy many hours together. Flamino, one of Avito's henchmen, is a guide to the king and so manages to smuggle Avito into the castle. The lovers are often interrupted by the blind king, who suspects his daughter-in-law but is unable to find out the identity of her lover. He accuses her but she denies her guilt.

ACT 2

Terrace on the High Castle Walls. Manfredo, having left his troops in the field, returns to visit his wife. He pleads so passionately with her that she yields to his affection and promises to wave a scarf to him from the castle battlements when he returns to his troops. Avito appears, but she sends him away, determined to be true to her husband, but her resolve falters and she calls him back. Just during the love scene which ensues, the king enters and strangles her when she admits her guilt.

Manfredo, noting his wife has disappeared from the battlements, fears she is in trouble and returns, just as she dies, and learns that she has been killed by his father because of her unfaithfulness.

ACT 3

Crypt in the Castle Chapel. Fiora lies in state. The king has streaked her lips with poison so that he may learn who was her lover. Avito comes for a last look and kiss and as he slowly dies, Manfredo also enters and learns from Avito that he was Fiora's lover. In agony he throws himself on the corpse and kisses his dead wife, and when Archibaldo enters to gloat over his vengeance he finds his son has become the victim. The king throws down his sword and bewails his fate just as his son dies.

ANDRE CHENIER

OPERA IN FOUR ACTS BY UMBERTO GIORDANO
LIBRETTO BY LUIGI ILLICA
FIRST PRODUCTION—MILAN, 1896

CAST

ANDRE CHENIER, a young poet.... *Tenor*
CHARLES GERARD, servant and revolutionary .... *Baritone*
MADELEINE DE COIGNY........ *Soprano*
BERSI, her old servitor...... *Mezzo-Soprano*
MME. LA COMTESSE DE COIGNY *Soprano*
MADELON, an old woman........ *Soprano*
MATHIEU, a sans culotte.......... *Baritone*
THE ABBE......................... *Tenor*
A SPY.............................. *Tenor*
FOUQUIER-TINVILLE .... *Basso*
ROUCHER .... *Basso*

PLACE—Chateau de Coigny, Paris
TIME—French Revolution

ACT 1

Ball room in the chateau. Gerard, a servant and revolutionist, chafes under restraint. *"Thou hast patiently listened."* He is secretly in love with Madeleine, the countess' daughter. Madeleine shows weariness of the life of fashion. *"As in a vice one struggles gasping."* Among the guests at the ball are Andre Chenier, a brilliant poet, and his friend,

[13]

the Abbe, an author. The latter bids the guests be merry. *"What matters that, my friends?"* Shepherds and shepherdesses come and go singing. *"O gentle nymphs, adieu."* Madeleine, in jest, asks the poet for an improvised poem on Love. He, eager to arouse the seriousness in her nature, grants the request. *"Your scorn has touched me here."* He sings feelingly of the wrongs suffered by the poor. The gayety begins again, but Gerard appears with a crowd of ragged men and women. *"Each day, each morrow, brings want and sorrow."* Servants force the intruders out. Chenier and Madeleine know they love each other.

ACT 2

Cafe Hottot in Paris, several years later. Chenier has given offense to the revolutionists by denouncing Robespierre. A spy watches Bersi, Madeleine's old nurse, hand Chenier a letter. The poet has been receiving unsigned letters from a girl who he knows loves him. Now the girl, dogged by spies, begs him to come to her aid and she arranges for a meeting. Chenier's friend Roucher brings him a passport. But the poet declines to flee from the city, saying he must meet a girl whom he does not know but who needs him. *"Do you believe in Fate?"* Roucher sees the letter. *"A truly feminine hand."* Still he begs the poet to escape. Robespierre passes, a mob following. Gerard, now high in the revolutionary party, questions the spy about Madeleine, whom he desires to possess. *"Her eyes are like the sky."* Bersi returns with a final message to Chenier, and the revolutionists sing, *"Let us be merry like Barras."* Night comes on and Madeleine comes to meet the poet. Chenier recognizes the girl; so does the spy. *Madeleine: "In your hour of fame?" Chenier: "Hail, golden hour."* They are about to flee when Gerard, notified by the spy, finds them. Chenier and Gerard fight with swords. The latter is wounded and the lovers escape.

ACT 3

Revolutionary Tribunal. Gerard makes a plea for money. *"Citizens, France is weeping tears of blood." Chorus: "Take them, my ear-rings."* The crowd sings the *Carmagnole.* Gerard learns that Chenier has been captured and that Madeleine is near. He writes the indictment for his rival. Madeleine comes to him and pleads for her lover. Gerard refuses to save him. Now Madeleine promises to give herself if Chenier is spared. *"Ere death had taken my darling mother."* Gerard, moved at last by the girl's love, declares he

[15]

will save Chenier if he can. The blood
thirsty mob comes into the tribunal. *"Mother
Cadet, sit by the barrier there."* Finally the
poet. faces judge and jury. He ably defends
himself. *"I was a soldier and faced death
on the field."* Gerard, true to his promise,
declares that the indictment against Chenier
is false. *"Our country? Justice did you dare
to say?"* But the mob demands Chenier's
death and he is led away.

ACT 4

Prison of Lazare at midnight. Chenier is
writing. *"Like a summer day that closes."*
He bids his friend Roucher goodbye. Madeleine enters with Gerard. She has bribed the
guard to allow her to substitute for another
woman so that she can die with Chenier.
*Chenier: "From thee, beloved, my restless
soul." Madeleine: "I will not leave thee."*
Together they go to the scaffold.

* * *

ARIANE ET BARBE-BLEUE
(ARIANE AND BLUE-BEARD)

OPERA IN THREE ACTS
MUSIC BY PAUL DUKAS
LIBRETTO BY MAURICE MAETERLINCK
FIRST PRODUCTION—PARIS, 1907

CAST

BLUE-BEARD ....*Basso*

ARIANE, wife of Blue-Beard.......*Soprano*

THE NURSE....................*Contralto*

SELYSETTE, wife of Blue-
  Beard ....*Mezzo-Soprano*

YGRAINE, wife of Blue-Beard......*Soprano*

MELISANDE, wife of Blue-Beard....*Soprano*

BELLANGERE, wife of Blue-Beard..*Soprano*

ALLADINE, wife of Blue-
  Beard .... *(Acting Role)*

AN OLD PEASANT................*Basso*

PLACE—Blue-Beard's Castle.
TIME—Middle Ages.

ACT 1

Hall in Blue-Beard's Castle. Ariane is the sixth wife of the terrible Blue-Beard of story book fame. Outside voices of the crowd are heard in warning. Blue-Beard has already murdered five wives. Ariane and the Nurse enter. Ariane has six keys of silver and one of gold. She discards the silver keys and with the gold one will open the forbidden chamber. The Nurse is in terror for the safety of this sixth young and lovely wife of the monster. When Ariane throws down the six silver keys the Nurse picks them up. With one she unlocks one of the smaller doors. Instantly amethystine jewels in every form—diadems, bracelets, rings, girdles—fall down on her. She is beside herself with joy. *"Pick them up; bend you down."* Now the second door is opened and there is a rain of sapphires. The third door opened brings a deluge of pearls. From the fourth chamber pour emeralds. From the fifth come rubies. The sixth brings a shower of diamonds. Ariane is dazzled by this wondrous display. *"O, my diamonds rare."* Now Ariane will open with the golden key the seventh door despite the pleadings of the Nurse. The door swings, revealing a black chasm. From it come the voices of the five lost wives. *"Daughters five of Orlamonde."* Here Ariane is surprised by Blue-Beard. He chides her because she, like the rest, let her curiosity overcome her and thus brought about her fate quickly. He lays hold of her and she struggles with him. Outside the clamors of the crowd are heard. Admitted by the Nurse, the people rush into the castle to kill Blue-Beard. But Ariane calmly tells them that he has not harmed her.

ACT 2

A Subterranean Hall. Ariane descends into the depths with the Nurse. The sixth wife finds the five wives still alive but emaciated and in rags. *"Ah, I have truly found you."*

"O, you have really suffered." She tells the five wives that she, too, has disobeyed—a higher law than Blue-Beard's. They tell her of their duties—to pray, sing, weep and watch. Ariane tells them that outside the birds are singing and the sun is shining. A jet of water extinguishes Ariane's light, but the brave girl is not fearful. She leads the five reluctant ones toward a radiant spot at the end of the vault. Here she comes to a barred wall. The five warn her but she throws herself against it. Finally the wall gives away and the sunlight streams in. The wives are blinded at first by its brilliance, but finally they come out of the vault and go off singing joyously.

ACT 3

Same as Act 1. The wives are adorning themselves with the help of Ariane. She urges them to make the best use of their gifts. News comes that Blue-Beard is approaching and that the people lie in wait for him. The wives watch his capture from the windows. Bound and wounded, he is brought in before the wives. Ariane bandages his wounds and the others help her. Then she cuts the cords and frees him. Now she leaves, though Blue-Beard pleads with her to remain. She in turn implores the five wives to go with her to freedom. But they decline and she leaves them in the castle. It is the eternal story of woman finding freedom and then failing to accept it.

* * *

ARMIDE

ROMANTIC OPERA IN FIVE ACTS
MUSIC BY CHRISTOPHER W. GLUCK
BOOK BY QUINAULT, FOUNDED ON TASSO'S
"JERUSALEM DELIVERED"
FIRST PRODUCTION—PARIS, SEPT. 23, 1777

CAST

ARMIDE, a sorceress............*Soprano*
PHENICE, her friend............*Soprano*
SIDONIE, her friend............*Soprano*
HIDROAT, King of Damascus.....*Baritone*
ARONT, his chief of staff...........*Basso*
RINALDO, Commander of Crusaders..*Tenor*
ARTEMIDOR, a Crusader..........*Tenor*
UBALDO, a Knight...............*Baritone*
A DANISH KNIGHT................*Tenor*
THE FURY OF HATE..........*Contralto*
DEMON AS LUCINDA...........*Soprano*
DEMON AS MELISSA.............*Soprano*
A NAIAD...................*Soprano*

PLACE—Damascus.
TIME—First Crusade, A. D. 1089

ACT 1

Palace of Armide. The beautiful princess Armide, who is also a sorccress, has not wed, though the King desires it. Her mind is fascinated by the deeds of Rinaldo, general of the crusading army of Godfrey de Bouillon, though she hates him for his victories over her people. At last come tidings that the Saracens have defeated the Christians and Armide will wed the victor over Rinaldo. But Aront, for whom a festival is planned, arrives wounded. The report is false—the Christians again being victorious. The populace shouts for vengeance against the invaders.

ACT 2

A wood. Rinaldo is wandering in the forest, for Godfrey de Bouillon is angered at him because of the deed of a brother knight whom Rinaldo will not betray. The power of Armide changes the wood into a beautiful, enchanted garden. Naiads rise before him and sing him to sleep. Armide comes close to him with drawn dagger, ready to slay her country's enemy. But sight of her hero melts her heart and she clasps the crusader in her arms.

[21]

ACT 3

Hall in palace of Armide. The princess is troubled by conflicting emotions. Instead of slaying her enemy she has yielded herself to him. Endeavoring to conquer her passion for the warrior, she summons the Demon of Hate. The demon warns her that Rinaldo will yet escape her wiles. Armide, still irresolute, orders the demon from her. Hate departs, warning Armide she will never return.

ACT 4

The Enchanted Wood. Rinaldo, under the sway of the sorceress, neglects his cause and his army. Ubaldo and a Danish knight are sent to find him. Armide tries to turn them aside, but she is powerless before Ubaldo's consecrated scepter. Armide summons still other visions—the images of the loved ones of both knights—but these also are dissipated by the scepter of Ubaldo.

ACT 5

Palace of Armide. The princess brings Rinaldo to the palace and seeks to give him delight with ballets and tableaux. In the sweetness of her love Rinaldo forgets the past glories of his army. But Armide leaves him alone for an interval, and during her absence Ubaldo and the Danish knight arrive. Their scepter and shield bring back to the warrior a sudden desire to be done with caresses and return to his waiting army. He grasps his sword and bids farewell to Armide. Again she would kill him, but Hate cannot return and she, in her love, is powerless. In despair she summons all the power of her magic, the demons destroy the palace and Armide goes to her death in the ruins.

* * *

THE BARBER OF SEVILLE

COMIC OPERA IN TWO ACTS BY ROSSINI
LIBRETTO BY STERBINI
ADAPTED FROM BEAUMARCHAIS' COMEDY
FIRST PRODUCTION—ROME, 1816

CAST

COUNT ALMAVIVA................*Tenor*
BARTHOLO, physician.............*Basso*
ROSINA, his ward................*Soprano*
BASILIO, music master...........*Basso*
MARCELLINE ....*Soprano*
FIGARO ....*Baritone*
FIVRILLO, servant to the count......*Tenor*

PLACE—Seville.
TIME—The 17th Century

[23]

The Barber of Seville

ACT 1

Count Almaviva, who has fallen in love with Rosina, the ward of Dr. Bartholo, is serenading her at dawn beneath her balcony, and seeking an opportunity of getting into her presence. This is hard because Bartholo guards her carefully, as he is anxious to marry her for her fortune. In this he is assisted by Basilio. Figaro, the town barber, approaches singing: *"I am the factotum of the ladies."* The Count asks Figaro to aid him in meeting Rosina. Duet: *"The shine of gold falls upon me."* He suggests that the Count, who is known to Rosina as "Lindoro, the student," disguise himself as a drunken soldier and gain admittance to the house.

SCENE 2

A room in Bartholo's house. *Rosina's cavatina: "I ask my timid heart."* Rosina has just written a letter to "Lindoro" (the Count) and upon leaving the room meets Bartholo and Basilio. The doctor's suspicions are aroused and he accuses her of writing letters. Basilio suggests making the Count's presence in Seville irksome by a few clever innuendos against his character. *Aria: "Calumny is light as air."* After they leave, Figaro enters and pleads for Lindoro, and Rosina gives him the letter she has just written. Just at this time the Count enters disguised as an intoxicated soldier and gives Rosina a letter. The doctor orders his arrest, but the officer releases him—unknown to Bartholo—when he mentions who he is.

ACT 2

Music room in Bartholo's house. The Count now appears as a music teacher, announcing that Basilio is ill and has sent him in his stead to give a lesson to Rosina. Figaro now insists upon shaving Bartholo, and as he does so Rosina and the Count plan an elopement. *Quintet: "What, Basilio what do I see?"* The music teacher suddenly arrives, but is bribed to feign illness. The keys to the balcony are secured by Figaro, but the lovers' plans are prostrated by the guardian, who hastens away in search of a notary public to draw up a marriage contract in his favor. The stage is vacated while the music describes a thunderstorm. At the hour agreed upon the Count and Figaro enter through a window. When Basilio and the notary arrive, Basilio is again bribed and the contract is made out in the Count's favor. The outwitted Bartholo is appeased by being allowed to retain Rosina's fortune.

THE BARTERED BRIDE

OPERA IN THREE ACTS
MUSIC BY FRIEDRICH SMETANA
BOOK BY K. SABINA
FIRST PRODUCTION—PRAGUE, 1866

CAST

KRUSCHINA, a peasant...........*Baritone*
KATINKA, his wife..............*Soprano*
MARIA, their daughter..........*Soprano*
MICHA, a landowner..............*Basso*
AGNES, his wife................*Contralto*
WENZEL, their son.................*Tenor*
HANS, son of Micha by former marriage ....*Tenor*
KEZUL, a marriage broker..........*Basso*
SPRINGER, a theatrical manager.....*Tenor*
ESMERALDA, a dancer...........*(Silent)*

PLACE—A Bohemian Town.
TIME—Present

ACT 1

Village Square and Inn. A festival is in progress. *Chorus: "See, the buds are opening."* All are happy but Maria, for on this day a suitor chosen for her is to claim her. She loves Hans, who is a poor boy. But her father has selected for her Wenzel, son of the rich farmer, Micha. Maria's mother is on her side and favors her love for Hans.

The Bartered Bride

Kruschina, the father, goes off with Kezal, the marriage broker, to see Micha at the inn. *Trio, Kruschina, Katinka, Kezul: "All is as good as settled."*

ACT 2

A Room at the Inn. Here Wenzel, who stutters, meets Maria and does not know that she is the bride picked for him. She, scheming to defeat the will of her father, warns Wenzel against his bride. *Duet, Wenzel and Maria: "I also knew a dear sweetheart."* The girl finally makes him promise not to go near this Maria person. But meanwhile Kezul, the broker, gets hold of Hans. The greedy, clever boy signs away his claim on Maria for a nice sum of money. But the agreement further stipulates that Maria must marry Micha's son. *Hans: "It must succeed."* Everybody is disgusted with him for thus giving up his sweetheart.

ACT 3

The Village Square. A traveling troupe is performing for the benefit of the residents. Wenzel is much captivated with Esmeralda, a dancer in the show. *Wenzel: "O, what ails me?"* The manager persuades him to play the role of dancing bear. The actor who has been playing the part is intoxicated. Wenzel, delighted to be near Esmeralda, gives a fine performance. Here his parents find him. They want him to marry Maria, but he refuses and runs off. *Quartet: "This comes like a clap of thunder."* Maria is greatly distressed for she has heard of Hans' outrageous bargain and is ready to marry Wenzel. After these misfortunes, she will not make another choice. But suddenly Micha recognizes in Hans his son by a former marriage. This Hans knew all the while and so was playing a clever game when he had the agreement read "Micha's son." Wenzel, as a bear, comes up to declare that he is satisfied. *Wenzel: "Be without fear, all is well."* Hans' stepmother is angry at the joke, but recovers her balance in time to enjoy the young people's happiness. *Duet, Hans and Maria: "My dearest sweetheart." Finale: "Willingly we come."*

* * *

LA BOHEME

OPERA IN FOUR ACTS BY PUCCINI
LIBRETTO FROM GIACOSA AND ILLICA FROM
MURGER'S BOOK "VIE DE BOHEME"
FIRST PRODUCTION—TURIN, 1896

CAST

RUDOLPH, a poet..................*Tenor*
SCHAUNARD, a musician.........*Baritone*

MARCEL, a painter..............*Baritone*

COLLINE, a philosopher............*Basso*

BERNARD, the landlord............*Basso*

MIMI ....,.................*Soprano*

MUSETTE ....*Soprano*

ALCINDORO, a wealthy Parisian.....*Basso*

PLACE—Paris.
TIME—About 1830

ACT 1

Garret. Rudolph and Marcel are burning one of Rudolph's manuscripts in an effort to keep warm in their attic, which is shared by two other Bohemians, Schaunard and Colline, who presently appear with food and fuel, as Schaunard has had the good fortune to dispose of one of his compositions. While they are drinking and eating, the landlord appears to collect the long-overdue rent, but soon forgets his mission in the wine that is given him. He starts telling stories, and they, pretending to be shocked, throw him out. The rent money is divided for a revel in the Latin Quarter and they leave for there, Rudolph, however, remaining to work. He is soon disturbed by Mimi, a pretty neighbor (afflicted with consumption), who comes for a light. She departs, but soon returns, having forgotten her key, and while looking for it both candles go out, but Rudolph finds and keeps the key. They relate to each other their experiences (*"Who am I? Then hear"*; *"They call me merely Mimi"*), and confess their love for one another. *Rudolph: "Your tiny hand is frozen."* They now go out to join their friends, singing of their love. *Duet, Rudolph and Mimi: "Love alone."*

ACT 2

Latin Quarter. It is Christmas Eve and they pass many tradespeople on the street (*Chorus: "Come buy my oranges"*) on their way to join their friends at the cafe. Here they see Musette—an old love of Marcel's—entering with Alcindoro. She attempts to attract Marcel's attention (*Musette: "As through the streets I wander"*) and also to get rid of Alcindoro, whom she sends out for a pair of shoes, claiming that the ones she has are too tight and hurt. *Duet, Marcel and Musette: "Break it, tear it, I can't bear it."* They join the others, and when they find that they are unable to pay the bill, their funds having given out, Musette charges it to Alcindoro and they leave the place. When Alcindoro returns with the shoes, seeking Musette, and is presented with the bill, he sinks in a heap at sight of the amount.

ACT 3

At a customs gate. *Chorus: "Pass the glass! Let each toast his lass!"* Mimi comes, asking for Marcel, who is working near by. When he reaches her she tells him how miserable she is because she truly loves Rudolph, but has quarreled with him, and that he has abandoned her. *Mimi: "O good Marcel."* Rudolph, who has been at the inn, now appears seeking Marcel, and Mimi hides behind a tree. Rudolph tells Marcel of Mimi's fatal malady *(Rudolph: "Love in my heart was dying")*, but Marcel tries to silence him for Mimi's sake, but she has heard and is discovered by her violent coughing. They become reconciled *(Duet: "Adieu, glad awakenings")* and Marcel is joined by Musette, with whom he quarrels, accusing her of flirting. *Duet, Musette and Marcel: "You were laughing, you were flirting."*

ACT 4

Same as first scene. Marcel and Rudolph, thinking of their sweethearts, are at work *(Duet: "Ah, Mimi; ah, Musette")*, when the other two Bohemians arrive with supper. They make merry, pretending it is a banquet. *Quartet: "Now take your partners."* Musette enters, bringing Mimi, who is extremely ill.

La Boheme

They assist her to a cot, and then hasten out and pawn their coats for restoratives for the dying girl. Mimi and Rudolph, left alone, dream of their past happiness (*Duet, Mimi and Rudolph: "Have they left us?"*) and when the others return Mimi dies, with the heart-broken Rudolph at her bedside. *Prayer, Musette: "O Virgin, save."*

* * *

BORIS GODOUNOW
THE OPERA

OPERA IN THREE ACTS. TEXT ARRANGED BY MOUSSORGSKY, BASED ON A HISTORICAL DRAMA BY THE FAMOUS RUSSIAN POET, PUSHKIN. MUSIC BY MODESTE MOUSSORGSKY. PORTIONS OF THE OPERA WERE GIVEN AT ST. PETERSBURG IN FEBRUARY, 1873, BUT THE PRODUCTION OF THE WORK IN ITS ENTIRETY WAS DELAYED UNTIL JANUARY 24, 1874. PRODUCED AT MOSCOW IN 1889. IN 1896 THE ORCHESTRATION WAS SOMEWHAT REVISED BY THE COMPOSER'S FRIEND, RIMSKY-KORSAKOFF. GIVEN AT PARIS IN 1908 BY A RUSSIAN OPERA COMPANY, WITH CHALIAPIN IN THE TITLE ROLES. FIRST AMERICAN PRODUCTION AT THE METROPOLITAN OPERA HOUSE, NEW YORK, NOVEMBER 19, 1913, WITH THE ORIGINAL COSTUMES AND SCENERY PAINTED FOR THE PARIS PRODUCTION.

CHARACTERS

BORIS GODOUNOW, Regent of Russia
XENIA, his daughter   VARLAAM
THEODORE, his son   MISSAÏL
THE NURSE   TCHEKALOFF
MARINA   PIMENN
CHOUISKY   SIMPLETON
DIMITRI   POLICE OFFICER
TWO JESUITS

TIME AND PLACE—About 1600; Russia

The prologue is before the Novodievitchi Convent, Moscow. Boris Godounow is regent for Czar Feodor, son of Ivan the Terrible. In an ambitious moment, Boris has murdered his nephew, Dimitri, Ivan's younger brother to whom the throne would have passed, upon the tyrant's death; but seized with remorse, he has fled to the Novodievitchi Convent to expiate the sin. He has a wide following among the people, who are unaware of the murder. And they have thronged, with nobility at their head, to beg him to take the throne.

ACT 1

The scene changes to a cell in the Convent of Miracles. Pimenn, an old monk, reveals to Gregory, a young monk, the story of Dimitri's death. Gregory, learning that Dimitri was of his own age, resolves to spread the

[33]

report that Dimitri was never slain, and to usurp the Russian throne. Again the scene changes; Boris, amid great pomp, consents to take the throne as regent.

ACT 2

The second act in the opera, as usually given, opens in an inn on the Lithuanian border, whither Gregory, with two companions, has escaped from the Convent. He hopes to cross the frontier and raise an army, but is prevented by a Government order issued after escape. He just misses arrest, by making a soldier believe one of his companions the offender, then leaping off through a window.

Meanwhile, Boris, in the Czar's palace in the Kremlin, a prey to fear and remorse, is talking with his young son, Theodore, when an old accomplice, Chouisky, appears, to bring the news that people are in revolt under the belief that Dimitri still lives. They are actually at the Russian border; and if they once enter the country, the country must fall. Boris, a superstitious mystic, actually wonders if the ghost of Dimitri has risen to appear against him.

———

Gregory awaits the lovely Marina, a Polish Lady who serves the interests of Poland by helping him play Dimitri. He lurks in her garden during a great banquet. When this is ended, Marina appears, to stir up together his ambition for the throne and his love for herself. This is the remarkable "Garden Scene," with its wonderful slow-swinging, se ductive rhythm and melody, like nothing else in music.

ACT 3

The next phase of the work is in the Forest of Kromy, where peasants are making sport of a nobleman who has fallen into their hands. The scene, written years ago, is a prophecy of what since has happened in Russia. Gregory, as the false Dimitri, enters, and the people, dissatisfied with Boris, join him in revolt. As they disappear, a village Fool sits alone in the snow, singing a heart-rending ditty on the hopeless condition of the empire. The simple irony of this touch is unsurpassed in opera.

Finally, the Duma gathers in the Imperial Palace to meet Boris. Chouisky plans treachery, and hints to the assembled boyars, or nobles, something of the real truth regarding Dimitri. Boris, entering, is confronted by Pimenn, who tells how a blind man has been restored to vision at the tomb of the murdered youth. Boris listens with horror, and finally interrupts with a cry. He is dying, and he asks for Theodore. He passes away begging the son to rule wisely and to protect Xenia, his sister. The opera ends abruptly, leaving the inference that Gregory's rebellion must perish, the true facts of Dimitri's death being known.

* * *

CARMEN

OPERA IN FOUR ACTS BY BIZET
TEXT BY MEILHAC AND HALEVY
AFTER THE NOVEL BY PROSPER MERIMEE
FIRST PRODUCTION—PARIS, 1875

CAST

ZUNIGA, lieutenant................*Basso*
JOSE, sergeant.......................*Tenor*
MORALES, sergeant................*Basso*
ESCAMILLO, a bull fighter............*Basso*
DANCAIRO, a smuggler...........,*Tenor*
REMENDADO, a smuggler........*Baritone*
CARMEN, a gipsy girl............*Soprano*
FRASQUITA, a gipsy..............*Soprano*
MERCEDES, a gipsy..............*Contralto*
MICAELA, a peasant girl.........*Soprano*

PLACE—Seville, Spain.
TIME—1800

ACT 1

A group of soldiers, waiting for the guard to be changed, are lounging about the guard-house, which faces the cigarette factory. The gentle Micaela appears searching for Jose, bringing a message from his mother. Lieutenant Zuniga asks her to wait for Jose, but she declines. He comes with the relief of the guard, and the square is crowded. The factory girls emerge from the factory, among them being Carmen the gipsy, who is the most admired. She repulses all except Jose, who is indifferent to her charms. *Habanera: "Love is a bird."* She hurls her flowers at him trying to win him. This arouses Jose and he is under the spell of Carmen's fascination. Micaela, who loves Jose, now returns with his mother's letter. *Jose: "Tell me what of my mother."* Touched by the girl's devotion, he is about to fling the flowers away when a tumult is heard in the factory. Carmen has wounded one of the girls in a quarrel and is arrested, but through the intervention of Don Jose escapes, and he promises to meet her. *"Near to the walls of Seville."*

ACT 2

Evening at the smugglers' inn. The gipsies and smugglers are singing and dancing. *"The rattling, ringing tambourine."* The bull fighter, Escamillo, is loudly welcomed. All sing: *"To the fight, Torero."* The Captain, who is enamored with the beautiful Carmen, pleases her by telling her Don Jose's imprisonment for aiding her to escape is ended. Jose arrives. *"Halt! who goes there?"* Carmen tempts him to desert and join the smugglers, but he refuses, but when Zuniga appears and orders him out, swords are drawn. Carmen screams for aid. The Lieutenant is overpowered by the smugglers, and Carmen, Don Jose and the smugglers escape to the mountain. *Duet and dance, Carmen and Don Jose: "I will dance in your honor."*

ACT 3

Haunt of the smugglers. Fickle Carmen's love for Jose is waning. Escamillo, not recognizing Jose, confesses to him his devotion for Carmen. This causes a fight over cards. *Trio over cards: "Shuffle, shuffle, cut them, cut them."* The rivals are separated by Carmen and the smugglers. *Duet: "I am Escamillo."* Escamillo departs after inviting all to the approaching bull fight. Micaela appears (*Aria: "Here is the smugglers' stronghold"*), urging Jose's immediate return to his dying mother. He hesitates, but his better self conquers and he goes with Micaela.

ACT 4

Outside of bull-fighting arena. The fight is about to commence. Escamillo leaves Carmen to enter the arena. Carmen has promised herself to him if he is victorious. Carmen's friends warn her that Jose is looking for her. Jose, still desperately in love (*Duet, Carmen and Jose: "Is it thou? It is I"*), meets Carmen. Upon her refusal to bestow her love and fidelity upon him, and when she shows her delight in Escamillo's victory, he stabs her and she expires just as the victorious Escamillo returns.

* * *

CAVALLERIA RUSTICANA

OPERA IN ONE ACT BY MASCAGNI
LIBRETTO ADAPTED BY TARGIONI TOEZETTI AND
MENASCI FROM THE BOOK OF VERGAS
FIRST PRODUCTION—ROME, 1890

CAST

SANTUZZA, a young peasant.......*Soprano*
TURIDDU, a young farmer..........*Tenor*
LUCIA, his mother...................*Alto*
ALFIO, a carter..................*Baritone*
LOLA, his wife.............*Mezzo-Soprano*

PLACE—A Sicilian Village.
TIME—The Present

[39]

Cavalleria Rusticana

The scene is a Sicilian village square, on Easter morn. At one side is the church. Turiddu is heard singing *"Oh, Lola, lovely as the spring's bright blooms,"* as the curtain rises. He has been in love with Lola, but returning from the army found her wedded to Alfio. He then turns to Santuzza, who loves him, but she now fears he has discarded her and returned to Lola. The churchgoers appear and enter the church. *Chorus from church:* "Queen of Heaven." Santuzza now arrives and meets Lucia, Turiddu's mother, to whom she tells her sad story. *"Well do you know, good mamma."* Lucia, much distressed, but unable to help the poor girl, enters the church, but Santuzza waits for Turiddu, who arrives presently. *"You, Santuzza."* She implores him not to forsake her, but he scorns her and enters the church with Lola. *Duet:* "Ah, what folly"; *Lola:* "My king of roses." Santuzza becomes despondent and when Alfio arrives she tells him of the faithlessness of his wife. *Duet:* "God has sent you, neighbor Alfio." He departs with Santuzza, threatening vengeance and determining to kill Turiddu. The stage remains unoccupied while the orchestra plays an exquisite intermezzo. Turiddu, Lola and the other villagers now come out of the church. Turiddu sings a drinking song ("Hail the

red wine, richly flowing") and invites Alfio,
who has just returned, to drink. He declines
and challenges Turiddu to a duel by biting
his ear, which is the Sicilian fashion. Turiddu accepts. He bids his mother farewell,
asking her to take care of Santuzza, whom
he regrets having so wronged. Turiddu and
Alfio repair to the field, and soon the peasants
rush upon the stage, with the news that
Turiddu has been killed. Upon hearing this
Santuzza falls to the ground in a deadly
swoon.

* * *

LE COQ D'OR

THE OPERA IS A PANTOMIME IN THREE ACTS, BY
BIELSKY, BASED ON FAIRY TALE BY PUSHKIN;
MUSIC BY RIMSKY-KORSAKOFF. FIRST
PERFORMANCE AT ZIMIN'S PRIVATE
OPERA HOUSE AT MOSCOW,
SEPT. 24, 1909

THE PRINCESS	THE PRINCE
THE KING	THE GENERAL
AMELIA	A KNIGHT
THE ASTROL-OGER	VOICE OF THE GOLDEN COCK

*Boyars, Court ladies and Nobles, Soldiers,
Oriental Dancers, Giants, and Dwarfs.*

[41]

Le Coq d'or

ACT 1

SCENE

Palace of King Dodon. The aged King Dodon holds conference with his boyars (princes). Satiated with his duties and with warfare, he is offered no council by the assembly. General Polkan objects to the suggestions of Girdon, the crown prince, that the troops he concentrated at the capital. The astrologer appears offering to Dodon a golden cockerel which will always give warning of approaching danger. With great ceremony the bird is put to bed. The doubting King accepts the gift promising that, should the cockerel prove worthy, he will give the Astrologer anything he should see fit to demand. The bird soon warns the monarch of an invasion at his borders. The blood-princes then depart to repulse the attacking forces.

ACT 2

SCENE

A narrow gorge in a mountain pass. The Cock warns the King to go to the help of his sons. Finding their bodies he sheds tears over them, when a beautiful woman emerges from a tent on the hillside, singing, in the opera, the odd *"Hymn to the Sun,"* causing him to forget his sorrow. In a peculiar, wailing hymn, embellished with strange chromatic

[42]

scales and modulations, asks if in her own "dear land" the roses yet grow in splendor and the "lilies burn in fiery sheaves"; if in the evenings, the maidens come with soft songs to the fountains of mystical water.

The venerable King Dodon, enamoured of the queenly creature sings to her in his ancient, querulous voice, and dances a clumsy and strange dance. The queen returns the love of this unprepossessing old man, and promises to marry him.

ACT 3

SCENE

Outside Dodon's palace. The populous awaiting the King and his bride see the pair arrive in great splendor. Dodon, seeing the Astrologer passing by, asks him to name his reward. When the Astrologer demands the Queen, Dodon strikes him dead. A storm comes up, and Dodon, terrified goes to his Queen, who scorns him. Above the thunder, the Golden Cock is heard crowing. Flying at Dodon, he pecks him on the skull, killing him. When the storm breaks, the Queen and bird have vanished, and the people chant a fantastic lament over the corpse.

CRISPINO E LA COMARE
(THE COBBLER AND THE FAIRY)

OPERA BOUFFE IN THREE ACTS
MUSIC BY LUIGI AND FEDERIGO RICCI
LIBRETTO BY PIAVE
FIRST PRODUCTION—VENICE, 1850

CAST

CRISPINO, a cobbler.............*Baritone*
ANNETTA, his wife, a ballad
      singer ....*Soprano*
COUNT DEL FIORE...............*Tenor*
FABRIZIO, a physician.............*Basso*
MIRABOLANO, an apothecary.......*Tenor*
DON ASDRUBALE, a miser.........*Basso*
LA COMARE, a fairy........*Mezzo-Soprano*

PLACE—Venice.
TIME—Seventeenth Century

ACT 1

Crispino and his wife are in sore straits. The cobbler cannot sell his shoes and nobody cares for his wife's songs. Don Asdrubale, their landlord, is about to put them out for non-payment of rent. Crispino mends shoes while the apothecary's apprentices across the street mix drugs. *Chorus: "Beat, beat, pound, pound."* The miser and the Count are drinking coffee in the cafe. The Count loves the miser's daughter but the miser re-

fuses his consent. *Count: "Lovely as an angel
art thou."* The cobbler tries to drive off
the blues. *"Once upon a time an humble
cobbler."* Annetta comes selling her songs.
"Pretty stories, fine to read." Nobody buys
and the rent money is demanded. *"Pay what
you owe."* The cobbler, in desperation, runs
away, followed soon by his wife. The poor
man is about to drown himself in a well when
a fairy appears to him. She gives him money
and tells him that he will be a famous doctor,
performing marvelous cures. His wife meets
him and they rejoice. *Duet: "Yes indeed, O
husband mine."*

ACT 2

The Cobbler's Home. The cobbler nails
up a physician's sign while his wife sings,
"No longer am I poor Annetta." The neighbors, curiosity aroused, stare and rail at the
sign and the cobbler is furious. But soon a
mason is brought in severely hurt. The doc-
tors fail to bring him around, but Crispino
cures the man. *Duet: "Many kisses, dearest
fairy."* The neighbors are amazed. *Chorus:
"Long live Crispino."*

ACT 3

Crispino has acquired overbearing airs
since his good fortune. The apothecary de-

clines to fill the braggart's prescriptions, but
Fabrizio, the physician, makes peace between
them. Annetta, entertaining her friends, tells
them of Crispino's unkindness since he has
become rich and prominent. She is the same
as ever and sings a ballad: *"Dearest Pietro,
here is a cake."* Crispino comes in and drives
out the friends. The fairy appears again and
he forgets himself and berates even her. But
with a blow the fairy takes him down into
a deep cavern. Here he sees figures of Time
and Judgment and many candles (human
lives) burning away. His own candle is
nearly gone but Annetta's will burn for a
long time. Crispino, terrified, sees that the
wonderful fairy has the face of a skull. He
makes his will, then learns from the fairy that
he must remain where he is. Utterly humbled and in terror, he begs for another
glimpse of his wife and children. *"Dear
fairy, not much I ask."* Soon he loses consciousness. But the fairy has heard his
prayer and has forgiven him. The cobbler
awakes to find himself with his family once
more. Annetta in rapture sings, *"Ne'er have
I known so joyous a moment."*

THE DAMNATION OF FAUST

DRAMATIC OPERA IN FOUR ACTS BY HECTOR BERLIOZ

BOOK BY BERLIOZ, GERARD AND GANDONNIERE.

FIRST PRODUCTION—PARIS, 1846

CAST

MARGUERITE, a peasant girl.....*Soprano*
FAUST, a philosopher...............*Tenor*
MEPHISTOPHELES, the tempter.....*Basso*
BRANDER, a convivial friend........*Basso*
Peasants, Troopers, Roysterers, Students, Sylphs, Fiends, Angels

PLACE—A German Village.

TIME—18th Century

ACT 1

The Fields. Faust wanders, meditating upon Nature, at dawn. *"Now ancient winter hath made place for spring."* A throng of peasants are making merry. Hungarian troops appear, marching to music, and the peasants show great enthusiasm. Faust wonders at the outburst. *Chorus: "The shepherd early dons his best."* The troops step to a Hungarian march.

ACT 2

Faust's Study. Faust can find no satisfaction in Nature or his books. His heart

[47]

The Damnation of Faust

empty, he resolves to end his life. But as he is about to drink poison an Easter hymn is heard. *"Christ is risen."* His hand is stayed, and soon his friend Mephistopheles tempts him with the pleasures of earth. Faust succumbs, and they go to a tavern together. They find companions and all sing, *"Fill up again with good red wine."* Faust becomes disgusted with this hilarity, and Mephistopheles takes him to a beautiful garden. Here he is lulled to sleep by the music of a chorus of sylphs. *"Dream, dream."* He dreams of a lovely peasant girl, Marguerite. Awakening, the sylphs dance about him, and he is filled with a desire to find the girl of his dreams. Soldiers, joyous, pass him returning from the war. *Chorus: "Towns with their battlements."* Students join them and all sing, *"Gaudemus igitur."* Faust feels the lure of worldly things again.

ACT 3

Marguerite's Chamber. Faust, led by Mephistopheles, hides in Marguerite's room. *Faust: "O welcome, gentle twilight."* She has dreamed of Faust and is musing on the dream as she arranges her hair. She sings a ballad, *"There dwelt a king in Thule."* Mephistopheles, outside, sings a mocking serenade, *"Dear Katherine, why, to the door of thy lover."* Faust appears and Marguerite is startled. But so ardent is his plea that the girl finally consents to give herself to him. Mephistopheles enters to tell the lovers that the villagers are coming to warn Marguerite's mother of the maiden's danger. The girl is terrified, but reluctantly parts from her lover, who is dragged off by his triumphant friend. The villagers approach threateningly. *Trio and chorus: "Angel of light."*

ACT 4

Marguerite's Chamber. The girl is stricken with grief over her sin, her mother's death and the absence of her lover. Soldiers pass singing of the glories of battle. The next scene shows Faust in his study. In Nature he has found a heart balm. *"Majestic spirit, calm and resistless."* Mephistopheles breaks in on him to tell him that Marguerite is in prison. She is charged with the murder of her mother, to whom Mephistopheles gave too strong a sleeping potion. To free her Faust must sign a paper. This he does, but instead of liberating Marguerite, he consigns his own soul to perdition. Mephistopheles now takes his victim off on a wild ride for the depths of hell. Terrible shapes close around them. Faust sees it rain blood, and he is finally hurled into the abyss from whence there is no escape. A triumphant chorus of demons celebrates his fate. The final scene is a cell in the prison. A chorus of angels is heard, the prison walls fade away, and Marguerite is lifted to heaven.

* * *

DINORAH

OPERA IN THREE ACTS BY GIACOMO MEYERBEER
LIBRETTO BY BARBIER AND CARRE
FIRST PRODUCTION—PARIS, 1859

CAST

HOEL, a goatherd....................*Basso*
DINORAH, betrothed to Hoel......*Soprano*
CORENTIN, bag-piper ....*Tenor*
HUNTSMAN ....*Basso*
FIRST SHEPHERD BOY.........*Soprano*
SECOND SHEPHERD BOY..*Mezzo-Soprano*

PLACE—Brittany.
TIME—Early Middle Ages
FIRST PRODUCTION—Paris, 1859

On the day that Hoel and Dinorah are to be married a terrific thunderstorm destroys Dinorah's house. Hoel, to comfort the sorrowing Dinorah, determines to rebuild the house. The old wizard Tonick tells him that there is gold way off in a glen guarded by goblins. To secure this gold to rebuild the house he must remain in the glen and keep silent for a year. Then the first person who touches the gold will die. After this the goatherd will be able to get all he needs. Hoel departs and Dinorah thinks that she has been deserted. So great is the shock that she becomes half demented.

ACT 1

Dinorah appears in the woods in bridal robes looking for her pet goat. Finding him she sings a lullaby, *"Yes, my beloved one."* Wandering on she finds a bag-piper, Corentin, who has just returned from uncanny regions where he saw gnomes and elves and other terrifying creatures. He thinks that the girl is one of these phantoms who makes people dance until they die. In fun Dinorah does make the bag-piper dance—until he is exhausted. *"Blow, blow lively."* The girl sings to the accompaniment of the dance. Hoel, back from his year of silence in the glen, suddenly appears. Dinorah is frightened at the stranger, once her sweetheart, and she flees in terror. Hoel, wanting somebody to touch the magic gold first, schemes to get the bag-piper to go with him. He tells Corentin that he lived with a wizard for a year and that this wizard told him to find a white goat which would guide him to the treasure. Hearing

[51]

the bell on Dinorah's goat, Hoel rushes out taking the bag-piper with him.

ACT 2

Wood by moonlight. This act begins with the beautiful shadow dance. Dinorah sees her shadow in the moonlight, thinks that it is a friend, and sings and dances to it. *Shadow song: "Light flitting shadow, companion gay."* Hoel and Corentin reach the wild district in which the gold is to be found. A female voice is heard singing the legend of the gold—he who touches it first shall die. Upon hearing this the bag-piper, already scared at the surroundings, determines to get out as fast as possible. This determination leads to an altercation between him and Hoel. Dinorah appears pursuing her goat. Hoel thinks she is a supernatural messenger sent to warn him against causing the death of the bag-piper and he regrets his murderous intentions. The demented girl, in crossing a bridge, loses her balance and falls into the river below. Hoel plunges in after her and brings her to shore unconscious.

ACT 3

Ideal country landscape. Hunter's song, *"On, on to the hunt."* Hoel enters bearing the senseless Dinorah. He is heartbroken for he has recognized her as his lost sweetheart. *"You are avenged by my remorse."* The girl recovers consciousness, and, due to the shock of the fall and finding her lover again, her reason suddenly returns. The song of the pilgrims is heard, and Hoel gives up further thought of treasure. Instead he goes with Dinorah to the church to marry her.

* * *

DON CARLOS

OPERA IN FOUR ACTS
LIBRETTO BY MERY AND DU LOCLE
MUSIC BY VERDI
FIRST PRODUCED AT PARIS, MARCH 11, 1867
IN LONDON, AT HER MAJESTY'S THEATRE, JUNE 4, 1867
ALTHOUGH IT WAS REVISED AND IMPROVED BY VERDI IN 1883, IT IS SELDOM GIVEN NOWADAYS

CHARACTERS
(Original Paris Cast)

PHILIP II ....*Bass*
DON CARLOS ....*Tenor*
MARQUIS DE POSA ....*Baritone*
GRAND INQUISITOR ....*Bass*
ELIZABETH DE VALOIS ....*Soprano*
PRINCESS EBOLI ....*Soprano*

Don Carlos, son of Philip II, King of Spain is in love with Elizabeth de Valois, daughter

[53]

of Henry II of France. His affection is deep and sincere, and it is returned in equal measure. For reasons of state, however, Elizabeth is wedded not to Don Carlos but to Philip II, and the young prince therefore finds himself in love with his own stepmother. He confides in Rodrigo, Marquis de Posa, who entreats him to leave the Spanish court. The two pledge friendship in the beautiful *"Dio che nell alma infondere"* (*Infuse Friendship Into Our Souls, O Lord!*). Carlos therefore begs the Queen to obtain Philip's permission to join the Flemings in the struggle against the Spaniards. But the King is secretly in favor with the Spanish tyrants, the request only angers him and further estranges father and son.

Don Carlos has a dangerous admirer in Princess Eboli, who learns that the Queen has by no means ceased to love Don Carlos though married to his father. Princess Eboli allows jealousy to get the better of her and she informs King Philip of the condition of affairs. This maddens the King still further, and, on the advice of the Grand Inquisitor, Don Carlos is thrown into prison. Rodrigo visits the Prince there, and is shot by the King's friends, who suspect him of aiding the Flemings. He bids farewell to earth in a beautiful aria, *"O Carlo, Ascolta"* (*O Carlos,*

Hear Me) repeating a theme of the friendship duet. And even before this, filled with the idea of sacrificing his own liberty for that of Don Carlos, he has a noble aria, the *"Per me giunto e il di supremo"* (*The Supreme Day*). Carlos is freed, and goes to the monastery of St. Just to keep tryst with Elizabeth. The King surprises them there, and his anger once more aroused, he hands over Don Carlos to the Officers of the Inquisition, who bear him away to death as the curtain falls.

* * *

DON GIOVANNI

OPERA IN TWO ACTS
MUSIC BY WOLFGANG AMADEUS MOZART
LIBRETTO BY LORENZO DA PONTE
FIRST PRODUCTION—PRAGUE, 1787

CAST

DON GIOVANNI (JUAN) a Cas-
tilian nobleman ....*Baritone*
DON PEDRO, the Commandant......*Basso*
ANNA, his daughter..............*Soprano*
OCTAVIO, fiance of Anna..........*Tenor*
ELVIRA, former sweetheart of
Juan ....*Soprano*
LEPORELLO, servant of Juan........*Basso*
MASETTO, a peasant................*Basso*
ZERLINA, his betrothed.......... .*Soprano*

Don Giovanni

PLACE—Seville.
TIME—Seventeenth Century

ACT 1

Courtyard of the Commandant's Mansion. Don Juan, notorious as an enticer of women, comes to Seville by night and enters the apartments of Anna. The girl screams for succor and her father comes to her rescue. He and Don Juan fight and the Commandant is killed. Don Juan and his servant Leporello escape. Anna charges her betrothed, Octavio, to avenge her father's death. The next scene shows an inn just outside Seville. Here Don Juan meets by mistake a former sweetheart, Elvira. She upbraids him for his desertion of her but he escapes and leaves Leporello to make explanations. This the servant does, telling of the hundred and one ladies with whom Don Juan has had affairs. *Leporello: "This list, gentle lady."* Elvira is nonplussed by the story of Don Juan's amours, and she decides to avenge herself. The Don now meets a wedding party. Masetto, a peasant, and Zerlina are to be married. The gay nobleman is fascinated by Zerlina and invites the whole company to his palace to partake of refreshments. Meanwhile he makes love to Zerlina. *Duet, Don Juan and Zerlina: "Thy little hand, love."*

Elvira, who has been watching, follows to
the palace. She meets Anna and Octavio bent
on revenge. Anna tells Octavio that by his
voice she thinks she recognizes Don Juan as
the murderer of her father. All three will
keep watch at the ball. Don Juan is still
happy, despite impending complications, and
sings: *"Wine, flow a fountain."* In Don
Juan's garden Masetto calls Zerlina to account for her flirtation with the Don. *Duet:*
"Scold me, dear Masetto." Partly pacified,
the bridegroom goes to the dance. Anna,
Elvira and Octavio are masked. They rush
in to rescue Zerlina when she cries for help.
But Don Juan, defending himself with his
sword, escapes from the palace.

ACT 2

Square Showing Elvira's Home. Zerlina is
Elvira's maid and Don Juan comes wooing
again. He sings below the window and Elvira answers. He pretends to repent of his
deeds and Elvira comes out. Don Juan makes
Leporello impersonate him and the servant
and Elvira go off together. Now Don Juan
sings to Zerlina: *"Open thy window, love."*
He is surprised by Masetto and his friends.
Quickly the Don pretends he is Leporello
and offers to aid them in capturing the noble
himself. They do capture Leporello, thinking

he is Don Juan. Anna, Octavio and Elvira are now convinced that Don Juan is the one who murdered Anna's father. In the next scene Don Juan and Leporello are near the statue of the slain Commandant. The statue speaks to them and Leporello is terrified. But Don Juan, still defiant and looking forward to more conquests, invites the statue to come to a banquet at the palace. Later the statue does come to the banquet hall. Lights are extinguished and the marble figure strikes terror to all hearts. Marble hands lay hold on Don Juan, flames appear, and the young nobleman is carried down into infernal regions.

* * *

DON PASQUALE

COMIC OPERA IN THREE ACTS
MUSIC BY GAETANO DONIZETTI
BOOK BY CAMERANO FROM OLDER ITALIAN OPERA
"SER MARC ANTONIO"
FIRST PRODUCTION—PARIS, JANUARY 4, 1843

CAST

DON PASQUALE, an old bachelor....*Basso*
DR. MALATESTA, a physician....*Baritone*
ERNESTO, nephew of Pasquale......*Tenor*
NORINA, a young widow.........*Soprano*
A NOTARY ....*Basso*
Citizens, Trades People, Servants

ACT 1

Don Pasquale's Apartments in Rome. The old bachelor is angry because his nephew, Ernesto, does not wed the woman picked out for him instead of becoming enamored of a fascinating widow, Norina. Don Pasquale's physician, Dr. Malatesta, proposes that the uncle have revenge by marrying himself. He describes to the bachelor a very beautiful girl who he says is his sister. *"O, like an angel of beauty."* The old man is elated with the idea. *Don Pasquale: "O, how I feel the glow of fire in my heart."* The nephew comes in again and his uncle urges him to give up the gay widow. Ernesto again refuses and then Don Pasquale says that he himself will marry and disinherit the young man. The poor boy is in despair. *"Sweet holy dreams I loved to cherish."* Ernesto begs his uncle to consult Dr. Malatesta for advice. Don Pasquale then informs him that it was the doctor who proposed the plan and offered his sister as the bride. Ernesto is still more astonished for he thought the physician his friend. There is a change of scene and a room in Norina's house is shown. The girl is reading a romance: *"Glances so soft."* Dr. Malatesta enters just as the widow receives a despairing note from Ernesto. The doctor tells her that he has concocted a

Don Pasquale

scheme to make Don Pasquale consent to a
marriage between her and Ernesto. She is to
impersonate the physician's sister, go through
a mock ceremony with Don Pasquale and
then lead him a wild goose chase. Persuaded
that she will finally wed Ernesto by this
somewhat roundabout method, she consents.
Norina: *"I'll play my part."*

ACT 2

Don Pasquale's Apartments. Norina enters
with the Doctor. A Notary, who is in the
plan, arrives with the papers. Ernesto enters
and is astonished. But he is quickly informed
of the facts. Pasquale, in his eagerness, signs
over half his property to his mock bride. As
soon as the signature is on paper the widow
changes her demeanor. She will not let the
bridegroom even kiss her. The nephew
laughs at him and is ordered out. But the
bride chooses the nephew for a shopping expedition and Don Pasquale is thunderstruck.
She orders an alarming array of costly things.
Don Pasquale: "I am betrayed." The curtain falls on the utter dismay of the bridegroom.

ACT 3

Don Pasquale's Apartments. Furniture and
costly bric-a-brac are piled everywhere. So
are bills. Norina decides to go to the theatre

for diversion. *Duet: "My lady, why this haste."* As she departs she drops a note in which a night rendezvous is mentioned. Dr. Malatesta enters and pretends to sympathize. He declares that they will watch Norina that night. Don Pasquale gloats over his forthcoming triumph. *"Wait, wait, dear little wife."* The next scene shows a balcony at night. There is a lovely serenade, *"Soft beams the light."* Norina joins Ernesto and happy together they sing, *"Tell me again."* Don Pasquale, carrying a lantern, rushes out to denounce the young people. He is enraged. Now Dr. Malatesta reveals the plot and the mock marriage. The old bachelor is so glad to be let out of his bargain that he sanctions the match and all ends joyously.

* * *

DON QUICHOTTE

OPERA IN FIVE ACTS
MUSIC BY JULES MASSENET
LIBRETTO BY HENRI CAIN AND LE LORRAINE
FIRST PRODUCTION—MONTE CARLO, 1910

CAST

LA BELLE DULCINEE..........*Contralto*
DON QUICHOTTE..................*Bass*
SANCHO ....*Baritone*

Don Quichotte

PEDRO (Travesti) ....*Soprano*
GARCIAS (Travesti) ....*Soprano*
RODRIGUEZ ....*Tenor*
JUAN ....*Tenor*
TWO VALETS...................*Baritone*
THE CHIEF OF THE BANDITS— FOUR BANDITS

ACT 1

Square in front of the house of Dulcinee. A fete is in progress and the people praise in song the beauty of Dulcinee. Among the throng are several admirers of this professional beauty—Juan, Pedro, Garcias and Rodriguez. Into the midst of the crowd come the comical Knight, Don Quichotte, and his still more comical companion, Sancho. The Knight serenades Dulcinee, and this arouses the jealousy of Juan. The two are about to fight a duel, but Dulcinee prevents them. She is greatly interested and amused by the avowals of Don Quichotte, and promises him that she will be his loved one if he will recover for her a necklace stolen from her by brigands. Don Quichotte vows that he will recover the necklace and claim her love.

Act 2 finds the Knight and Sancho on their way to the camp of the brigands. The latter rides his donkey. The former has tested his valor in several ways—once by charging some hogs, and again by attacking a wind-mill. The latter tosses him about quite roughly. Sancho is disgusted with the Knight for his weak sentiment and such foolish deeds of valor. But Don Quichotte is bent on braving death for the lady of his dreams.

In the third act the two meet the brigands in the mountains. Don Quichotte bravely attacks them, while Sancho retreats and makes his escape. The Knight is captured and expects to be put to death. But he finds comfort in dreaming of the beautiful Dulcinee. His courage and his love for his lady deeply impress the bandits. Their hearts are so touched that they give him the necklace and his liberty.

The fourth act shows a fete at Dulcinee's. The beautiful girl grows weary of the compliments and admiration of the men about her. There is much astonishment when the Knight and Sancho put in their appearance. Dulcinee, overjoyed at recovering the necklace, affectionately embraces the Knight. He begs her to marry him at once. Deeply touched by his devotion, Dulcinee tells him that she is far from being the kind of woman he thought she was. Don Quichotte is grateful to her for her frankness and he declares that his love for her will never end.

The last act takes place in a forest. The

Knight is dying. Sancho proclaims his gallantry and his goodness. Don Quichotte tells Sancho that he has given him the island he promised him in their travels; the most beautiful island of all—the Island of Dreams.

* * *

ELEKTRA

MUSIC DRAMA IN ONE ACT
MUSIC BY RICHARD STRAUSS
LIBRETTO BY HUGO VON HOFMANNSTAHL
FIRST PRODUCTION—DRESDEN, 1909

CAST

QUEEN KLYTEMNESTRA..*Mezzo-Soprano*
AEGISTHUS, her lover..............*Basso*
ORESTES, the Queen's son.........*Tenor*
ELEKTRA, the Queen's daughter...*Soprano*
CHRYSOTHEMIS, the Queen's
daughter ....*Soprano*

PLACE—Greece. TIME—Antiquity

SCENE

Interior Court Formed by the Rear of the Palace. The Queen and her paramour, Aegisthus, have murdered the noble King Agamemnon. Wishing not to be bothered with him when he should become old enough to think and act for himself, the Queen has

sent her boy Orestes off into exile. Her two
daughters, Elektra and Chrysothemis, she
treats shamefully, making them live with the
servants and perform all sorts of humiliating
duties. The story begins with the comments
of the servants on Elektra's hardships which
they deeply deplore. Elektra appears, thinking of her noble father. She sings of his
glory and predicts the day of vengeance. *"All
alone, all alone."* *" 'Tis the hour, yours and
mine."* Elektra's gentle sister comes to tell
her that the Queen and her lover have
plotted to throw Elektra into prison. Elektra
is defiant, but the sweet Chrysothemis says
that it is better to die than live as she is
living. Elektra rebukes her. Soon the Queen
appears and converses with Elektra. The
latter hides her bitterness under sweet words.
The Queen confesses that she is miserable.
"Where art thou, O truth?" At night she
cannot rest because of terrible dreams. She
hopes that Elektra can tell her of some cure.
The daughter does tell her of a cure—the
spilling of a woman's blood. All anxious,
the Queen demands to know what woman
should be slain. But Elektra is evasive. She
declares further that the rite shall be per-
formed by a man, a stranger, yet of their
house. Then she turns on the mother and
boldly predicts her murder. *"Thine own*

[65]

throat when the hunter hath taken thee."
The Queen is terrified by this sinister outburst from her daughter. Now Chrysothemis
comes to Elektra weeping. An old man and
a youth have arrived at the palace with news
of the death of their brother Orestes. Elektra will not believe the tidings. But she
determines that now she and her sister must
be the avengers of their father's murder.
The gentle sister, however, refuses to aid
Elektra in killing her mother. Elektra now
launches into a wild, unholy praise of her
sister that frightens the girl. The youth who
has brought the tidings of Orestes' death
comes upon the passionate Elektra creeping
around the wall. Elektra denounces him for
not giving up his life to save that of Orestes.
But soon she discovers that the youth is
none other than Orestes himself. Elektra is
beside herself with joy. *"Orestes, Orestes!"*
In a sudden burst of passion she tells how
the crime of her mother has obsessed her.
Orestes is eager to avenge the crime. Elektra
joyously awaits the final moment. *"Happy
he who comes to end the work."* The youth
enters the palace and there is a scream from
the Queen. She has gone to her death at the
hands of her son. Meeting Aegisthus, Elektra,
with mock courtesy, leads him to his doom.
Inside the palace the servants and retainers

who side with Orestes battle with the sup-
porters of Aegisthus. Orestes is victorious
and his mother's lover is slain. Elektra
dances wildly in her joy and passion and
falls senseless as the curtain falls on the
horrible, unholy tragedy.

* * *

L'ELISIR D'AMORE
(THE LOVE POTION)

COMIC OPERA IN TWO ACTS BY GAETANO
DONIZETTI
BOOK BY OTT FROM ITALIAN OF ROMANI
FIRST PRODUCTION—MILAN, 1832

CAST

ADINA, rich young landowner.....*Soprano*
NEMORINO, a young peasant......*Tenor*
BELCORE, sergeant..............*Baritone*
DULCAMARA, a quack.............*Basso*
GIANETTINA, a peasant..........*Soprano*

ACT 1

The scene is an Italian village. Adina, a
well-to-do girl, flirts outrageously with two
men, Nemorino, a young farmer, and Belcore,
a recruiting sergeant from the next town. The
peasant boy is particularly ardent. *"What
loveliness and grace."* But Belcore is more

persistent. She treats both badly, but the young farmer cannot leave her. *"Ask the winds of spring."* Trouble takes another angle when Dulcamara, a quack from a neighboring village, arrives in town. His coming creates a stir. *"Hear and be astounded, you peasants."* He has what he declares is the elixir of love. It is only a bottle of wine, but Nemorino, hopeful of winning Adina, buys the bottle and drinks the contents. *Duet: "Take courage."* He promptly gets drunk, and Adina is so astonished and shocked that she pretends she will marry Belcore. Next day the contract will be signed. *Terzett: "Now must it be done quickly."* Nemorino is so disheartened that he desires another bottle of the love medicine. As before, the quack sells him a bottle of wine. All his money is gone, but he enlists under Belcore and thus gets the coin to pay for the second bottle. The result is that he gets drunker still.

ACT 2

The Wedding Feast. The peasants are rejoicing over the feast, but Adina suddenly announces that she is not ready to sign the marriage contract with Belcore. The quack doctor grows enthusiastic over the girl. *"Dear child, you are beautiful and I am rich."* Soon the village maidens arrive with the astounding news that Nemorino's rich uncle has died and made the boy sole heir. *Chorus: "Can it be possible."* Naturally the girls all begin to show attention to the peasant who does not even know that he is rich. He thinks that his magnetic powers are due entirely to the love potion. *Quartet: "The dose has done me good."* Adina is sad now for she believes that the youth will be won away from her and she really loves him. *Duet: "O, how cruel, this warm love."* The quack, feeling sorry for the girl, tells her that it was only wine her sweetheart drank. Adina feels now that to go to such lengths for her really indicates true love and she is willing to wed Nemorino. But the sergeant Belcore says that the lad has enlisted, has received money which he has spent and that he will have to remain enlisted. But the girl buys his release and the sergeant sees that his suit is lost. The girl and lad plight their troth amid general rejoicing. The peasants, thinking that the quack's potion did the work, buy liberally of his liquid wares.

ERNANI

DRAMATIC OPERA IN FOUR ACTS
MUSIC BY GIUSEPPE VERDI
BOOK BY PIAVE AFTER HUGO'S "HERNANI"
FIRST PRODUCTION—VENICE, 1844

CAST

DON CARLOS, King of Spain......*Baritone*
DON RUY GOMEZ DE SILVA, a
    grandee ....*Basso*
DONNA ELVIRA, his niece........*Soprano*
JOHANNA, her nurse............*Contralto*
ERNANI, an outlaw..............*Tenor*
DON RICCARDO, royal armor
    bearer ....*Tenor*
IAGO, armor bearer to Gomez.......*Basso*

SCENES—Aragon, Aix-la-Chapelle and
    Saragossa TIME—1519

ACT 1

A Mountain Retreat. Ernani, son of a
Spanish duke, has been outlawed by the
King. He goes to the mountains and becomes chief of a robber band. The bandits
regard him highly. *Chorus: "To you we
drink."* But they notice now that he is
morose. *"Why, O strong one, does care sit
on your brow?"* Ernani tells them that he
loves Donna Elvira who is betrothed to
old Gomez de Silva, her uncle. He begs the

bandits to help him abduct her. The next scene shows Donna Elvira's apartments. The wedding presents are brought in, but the girl is in despair. *"Ernani, save me."* King Carlos, in disguise, enters and makes love to Donna Elvira. He is attempting to use force when Ernani suddenly arrives. *Terzett: "A friend comes quickly to your aid."* Ernani recognizes the King and the latter recognizes him. They are about to fight when Silva, the grandee, comes in. *Finale: "Dreadful night."*

ACT 2

Hall in Silva's Palace. Disguised as a pilgrim, Ernani now comes to stop the wedding. *Terzett: "The pilgrim may appear."* Silva, not knowing him, grants him shelter from the King, who is hunting him down. Elvira, not recognizing Ernani, tells him that she believes her lover is dead and that she will kill herself at the altar. Ernani reveals himself. *Duet: "Ah, false one."* Silva surprises them but cannot have vengeance on the pilgrim because of the laws of hospitality. *Terzett: "Shameless ones, ye shall rue it."* King Carlos arrives to find the castle barred. Silva, true to his promise, will not surrender Ernani. *Carlos: "Let us see, thou prater of virtue."* The King withdraws his troops

Only when Elvira is given to him as a hostage. *'Choose thy sword and follow."* Silva now releases Ernani from the castle and challenges him to a duel. But both postpone the battle until they have freed Elvira from the King. Ernani owes his life to Silva and will forfeit it to him when Silva shall blow the bugle that he gives him.

ACT 3

Charlemagne's Tomb. The King visits the great Emperor's tomb. *Cavatina: "Ye golden dreams of youth."* Behind the vault he overhears a plot to assassinate him. *Chorus: "O noble Carlos."* Among the conspirators are Silva and Ernani. The King summons his attendants and orders all the conspirators executed. Then, awaiting death, Ernani tells the King that he is the proscribed Don Juan of Aragon and that he has been driven by wrongs to attempt rash deeds. Elvira pleads to the King for her lover. Carlos, experiencing a sudden change of heart, grants the girl's request and reunites the lovers.

ACT 4

Castle of Ernani. *Chorus: "Hail bright hour of gladness."* The happy sweethearts have just been married. They are joyous in each other's love and their possession of ancestral estates. But suddenly the sound of a bugle cuts the air. It is Silva before the gates, come to recall to Ernani his pledge. He hands Ernani a dagger and the young bridegroom stabs himself to the heart. *Terzett: "Cease, O music, put out the lights."*

* * *

FALSTAFF

COMIC OPERA IN THREE ACTS
MUSIC BY GUISEPPE VERDI
BOOK BY BOITO AFTER "THE MERRY WIVES OF
WINDSOR," BY SHAKESPEARE
FIRST PRODUCTION—MILAN, 1893

CAST

SIR JOHN FALSTAFF, heavyweight
  knight ....*Baritone*
FORD, a citizen of Windsor........*Baritone*
MISTRESS ALICE FORD, his wife..*Soprano*
ANNE FORD, their daughter......*Soprano*
MISTRESS PAGE................*Soprano*
MISTRESS QUICKLY...........*Contralto*
FENTON, affianced of Anne.........*Tenor*
DR. CAIUS, a citizen..............*Tenor*
BARDOLPH, follower of Falstaff.....*Tenor*
PISTOL, follower of Falstaff.........*Basso*
  PLACE—Windsor. TIME—15th Century

ACT 1

Room at the Garter Inn. Falstaff, the fat knight who boasts of his prowess in battle,

now decides to try his fortune in the lists of
love. The objects of his attention are Mistress Page and Mistress Ford, two highly regarded ladies of Windsor. He prepares two
notes, one for each of the ladies, but his followers balk on delivering the tender missives.
Falstaff in anger sends the letters by a page.
He kicks his two followers out. A change
of scene shows the Ford garden. Mistress
Ford and Mistress Page receive the notes and
they compare them. With the willing aid of
Mistress Quickly, they plan to have some fun
at the fat knight's expense. Ford himself
gets an inkling of part of the plot and is to
meet Falstaff under another name. Meanwhile Ford has planned to marry his daughter, Anne, to Dr. Caius. But the girl loves
young Fenton, who loves her.

ACT 2

Room at Garter Inn. Bardolph and Pistol,
who are in on the plan of the ladies and are
anxious to be revenged for the kicking they
have received, announce the arrival of Mistress Quickly. The lady comes with a nice
note from Mistress Ford, who makes an appointment with the knight for that very
afternoon. Ford is introduced under another
name. He appears to love Mistress Ford and
offers Falstaff money to intercede with the

lady in his behalf. Falstaff agrees declaring
that he has an appointment with her in the
afternoon. This appointment is more than
Ford expected and he is beside himself with
jealousy. Another scene brings the actors
to a room in Ford's home. Mistress Ford
has a large clothes-basket ready. Mistress
Quickly announces Falstaff. He meets Mistress Ford and makes violent love to her.
But he is interrupted by the arrival of Mistress Page, and is concealed behind a large
screen. Soon the angry Ford and his friends
who are in dead earnest, arrive looking for
Falstaff. In self-protection he is now hidden
in the large clothes basket. Fenton and Anne,
the lovers, take advantage of the screen to do
a little love-making of their own. Ford, hearing a kiss behind, thinks he has Falstaff. He
is disgusted when he finds only the lovers,
and orders Fenton out. The men continue
the search while poor Falstaff nearly suffo-
cates in the basket. To save him and themselves the women order the basket taken out.
It and its entire contents are dumped into
the river.

ACT 3

At the Inn. Falstaff, though humbled, again
receives overtures from Mistress Quickly. Mistress Ford is to meet him that night under

Herne's Oak in Windsor Park. This plot is overheard by the men and they plan real vengeance this time. Meanwhile Dr. Caius is promised Anne's hand by Ford who tells him to come disguised as Anne and fool Fenton. This side-plot is overheard by Mistress Quickly who warns the lovers. The finale takes place in the park at night. Mistress Ford meets Falstaff and he again begins making love. But the men, disguised as witches and elves, bear down on him and beat him unmercifully. Dr. Caius' disguise avails him little for he is badly fooled and Anne appears with Fenton. Ford, satisfied with vengeance on Falstaff, consents to the wedding of the two young people.

* * *

FAUST

OPERA IN FIVE ACTS BY CHARLES GOUNOD
LIBRETTO BY BARBIER AND CARRE
FOUNDED ON GOETHE'S TRAGEDY
FIRST PRODUCTION, PARIS, 1859

CAST

FAUST, a philosopher.............*Tenor*
MEPHISTOPHELES ....*Basso*
MARGUERITE, a village girl......*Soprano*
VALENTIN, brother of Mar-
   guerite ....*Baritone*

BRANDER, a student............*Baritone*
MARTHA, Marguerite's servant...*Contralto*
SIEBEL, a student...............*Soprano*

PLACE—A German Village.
TIME—18th Century

ACT 1

Faust's Study. The aged philosopher despairs of solving all the mysteries of Nature. There is nothing much left to live for and he is about to take poison, when the sound of Easter music strangely stays his hand. Of a sudden Mephistopheles, the Evil One, appears to him. He shows him a picture of a lovely young girl. He promises to make Faust young again and give him this girl if he will sign away his soul. *"The pleasures of youth."* Faust, eager to experience love again, signs the agreement. *"Heavenly vision."*

ACT 2

The City Square. A festival of soldiers and citizens is in progress. Valentin looks intently at his sister's picture. *"O holy emblem."* He fears to go to war leaving her alone. But the lad Siebel says he will protect her. Mephistopheles and Faust arrive and the former mingles with the throng and sings, *"Gold rules the world."* He then tells fortunes—

that Brander will die soon; that the flowers
Siebel carries to Marguerite will wither.
Mention of Marguerite's name arouses Valentin, and with drawn sword he rushes at
Mephistopheles. But the jeering fiend draws
a magic circle about him that protects him.
Then Valentin and his friends hold their
swords like crosses and he cowers in fear.
Everybody begins dancing again. Marguerite
appears. Faust offers his arm, but is repulsed.

ACT 3

Marguerite's Garden. Siebel brings a bouquet for Marguerite, but it fades. *"In the
language of love."* Siebel departs as Mephistopheles and Faust appear. The latter is
greatly taken with the garden and sings, *"All
hail, thou dwelling pure and holy."* Mephistopheles, knowing every phase of woman
nature, removes Siebel's bouquet and substitutes for it a casket of jewels. Marguerite,
watched by the intruders, comes out and sits
at the spinning wheel singing to herself,
"Once there lived a King in Thule." Soon
she notices the jewel-box and her curiosity
overcomes her. She is astonished with the
gems and begins to place them on her head,
hands and neck. *Jewel song: "Saints above,
what lovely gems."* Martha, Marguerite's
matron companion, finds her gorgeously ar-

rayed. Mephistopheles and Faust now appear. The former tells Martha that her husband has been killed in battle. She gives way to grief, but soon takes hope again when Mephistopheles flatters her and leads her off into the garden. This leaves Faust to woo the girl. *Quartet: "Why so lonely."* He pleads passionately and wins her heart. Mephistopheles invokes the aid of night. *"O night, draw thy curtain."* The lovers are enraptured. *Duet: "Forever thine."* Faust bids Marguerite farewell, but his path is blocked by Mephistopheles, who chides him for his modesty. Marguerite throws open her window. Faust cries out to her. He rushes back to her and Mephistopheles leaves them as she faints in his arms.

ACT 4

City Street. The soldiers return from the war singing the thrilling *"Soldiers' Chorus."* Valentin learns that his sister has been betrayed. Mephistopheles mockingly serenades her. *"Thou who here art soundly sleeping."* Valentin, desperate, rushes out of the house. *Trio: "What is your will?"* He fights Faust a duel in the darkness. Mephistopheles with his sword aids the latter and Valentin is killed. He curses Marguerite with his last breath. The next scene is the interior of a church. Marguerite, driven insane by remorse, falls senseless while praying for forgiveness.

ACT 5

The Walpurgis Revel. Mephistopheles shows to Faust all the horrors of the underworld, among them being Marguerite in chains. The scene changing shows the demented Marguerite in prison. *"My heart is torn with grief."* Faust, coming to her, now realizes the consequences of his own sin. He urges her to escape with him. But her mind does not grasp his meaning. Mephistopheles, seeking to end the drama, drags off Faust to regions under the world forever. But Marguerite is borne to heaven by angels.

* * *

LA FAVORITA
(THE KING'S FAVORITE)

OPERA IN FOUR ACTS
MUSIC BY GAETANO DONIZETTI
LIBRETTO BY ROYER AND WAETZ
FIRST PRODUCTION—PARIS, 1840

CAST

ALFONSO XI, King of Castile......*Baritone*
FERNANDO ....*Tenor*
BALTHASAR, prior ....*Basso*

GASPARO, an officer.............*Tenor*
LEONORE, the King's favorite......*Soprano*
INEZ, her companion............*Soprano*

PLACE—Castile.   TIME—1340

ACT 1

Monastery of St. James. Fernando, a novice in orders at the monastery, confesses to the Prior that he is not altogether true to his vows. He says, that though he tries to banish it, there comes to him again and again a vision of a beautiful girl. *"Like an angel."* The good Prior is astonished, but sees that Fernando is sincere in his confession. He releases him from his vows and the young man goes out into the world again. Circumstances take him blindfolded to the beautiful island of Leon. Here Leonore, the King's favorite, her friend Inez and other lovely maidens, gather flowers and sing. *"Ye Beams of Gold."* Here Fernando recognizes Leonore as the maiden of his dreams and tries ardently to win her. The girl, fearful lest he will discover who she is, gives him a parchment that will insure him success, and declares he must depart. *Duet: "Fly from thee."* As Leonore leaves Fernando finds that the parchment is a commission in the army. He determines to win glory and come back to claim the woman who is his ideal.

ACT 2

Gardens of the Alcazar Palace. The King greatly admires the palace which has been captured from the Moors by the victories of Fernando. But a disquieting message comes from Balthasar, declaring that the King is offending the Church party by his life with Leonore. Leonore is wretched and begs the King to release her. *"From my father's halls."* Balthasar enters with a message from the Pope excommunicating the King if he does not release Leonore in a day. *"The wrath of Heaven!"* Leonore is overcome with shame at deceiving Fernando.

ACT 3

An Apartment in the Palace. The King decides to give the girl up. He receives Fernando with great honors and asks him to name his reward for victories won. The unsuspecting Fernando requests the hand of the beautiful Leonore. The King grants the request and says the wedding will take place in an hour. Leonore, knowing that she must confess now, gives Inez a message to Fernando which tells him everything. But almost immediately Inez is detained by order of the King. Fernando appears and Leonore is enraptured that her message has made no difference with him. Fernando is given a title and the wedding is celebrated. But when presented at court the couple are coldly received. Fernando, not understanding, is angered. Balthasar appears and is horrified that Fernando has married Leonore. Then the soldier finds that the girl is the King's mistress. He denounces the King, who becomes remorseful. *"Stay. Hear me, Fernando."* Leonore faints as Fernando rushes off, never to return.

ACT 4

Cloisters of the Monastery. Fernando returns and is welcomed by the monks. *Chorus: "In heavenly splendor."* One look backward and Fernando muses on the dead love *"Spirit so fair."* But Leonore, disguised as a novice, comes to the Monastery. She tells Fernando that she sent him a message by Inez which he never received. She never meant to deceive him. He forgives her for everything. *"As merciful as God."* But he has given up the world forever, and the girl swoons as he rejoins the monks in procession

* * *

FEDORA

OPERA IN THREE ACTS

MUSIC BY UMBERTO GIORDANO

LIBRETTO BY COLAUTTI FROM THE SARDOU DRAM

FIRST PRODUCTION—MILAN, 1898

CAST

PRINCESS FEDORA...............*Soprano*
COUNT LORIS...................*Tenor*
COUNTESS OLGA...............*Soprano*
DE SIRIEX, a Diplomat...........*Baritone*
GRECH, a Police Officer............*Basso*
DMITRI, a Groom................*Contralto*
CYRIL, a Coachman.............*Baritone*
BOROV, a Doctor................*Baritone*
BARON ROUVEL..................*Baritone*

PLACE—St. Petersburg, Paris and Switzerland. TIME—Present

ACT 1

Home of Count Vladimir. The servants discuss the approaching marriage of the Count and the beautiful Princess Fedora. The Princess enters to await the coming of her betrothed. She gazes lovingly at his photograph: *"O, eyes, filled with truth."* Soon the Count is brought in by De Siriex, who has found him mortally wounded. Suspicion for the murder falls on Count Loris, who occupies the home opposite, and who is supposed to be a Nihilist. The officers go in search of the murderer. The Count breathes his last in the presence of Fedora. The Princess, taking a Byzantine jeweled cross from her breast, swears that she will avenge the assassination of her betrothed.

ACT 2

Salon of Fedora. Here Fedora, supposedly a political exile, works diligently to obtain evidence that will lead to the capture of the Count's slayer. Loris, who is suspected, is entertained by Fedora in order that she may get proof of his guilt. She uses all her arts to fascinate him and he falls desperately in love with her. *Loris: "My love must make you love me."* Soon she draws from him a confession of the murder of her betrothed. Fedora informs Grech, the officer, and he plans to take Loris after all the guests have left. When the reception ends and all depart, Loris returns as Fedora has asked him. He tells her that he killed the Count because he betrayed his young wife and brought about her untimely death. Fedora realizes that the murder was justified, forgives the assassin and takes him into her arms. But the officers wait outside—the trap for Loris is ready to be sprung. Fedora's only thought now is to save her lover. *"Behold I weep not for mine own grief."* In this her efforts are successful.

ACT 3

Loris and Fedora are married and are living happily in Switzerland. *Duet: "Spring is come, the birds are trilling."* But Loris' footsteps have been followed by a persistent spy.

Fedora

Fedora now learns that, owing to Loris' act, his brother has been thrown into prison and has died there. The shock of this has caused the death of Loris' mother. *Fedora: "O, God of justice."* Loris is heartbroken at the news. *"O, my dear mother."* He wildly curses the spy who has brought this grief upon him. Fedora cringes before his anger and sorrow. Loris now discovers that it was Fedora who manipulated the machinery of justice. In rage, he is about to kill her although she pleads that her work as a detective ceased the night she saved him. In her despair at the terrible culmination of events she swallows poison. Loris, coming to his senses, pleads with her to live and continue to love him. But it is too late. *Fedora: "Darkness is falling."* She dies in Loris' arms.

* * *

FIDELIO

OPERA IN TWO ACTS BY LUDWIG VON BEETHOVEN
LIBRETTO BY SONNLEITHNER FROM BOUILLY'S
"LEONORE"
FIRST PRODUCTION—VIENNA, 1805

CAST

DON FERNANDO, minister........*Baritone*
DON PIZARRO, governor of
    prison ....*Baritone*

DON FLORESTAN, a noble prisoner.. *Tenor*
LEONORE, his faithful wife........ *Soprano*
ROCCO, jailer...................... *Basso*
MARZELLINE, his daughter........ *Soprano*
JACQUINO, gatekeeper.............. *Tenor*
CAPTAIN OF THE GUARD........ *Basso*
LIEUTENANT .... *Basso*

PLACE—Spanish State Prison Near Seville

ACT 1

Courtyard of the Prison. Don Florestan, who has incurred the hatred of Don Pizarro, governor of the prison, is thrust into a dungeon. Here the governor expects him to die by starvation so as to make violent murder unnecessary. *Pizarro: "Fateful moment. My revenge is near."* In order to complete the plan he circulates the report that Dan Florestan is dead. But his faithful wife does not believe it. Disguising herself as the boy, Fidelio, she enters the service of Rocco, the jailer. She discovers that her husband is not dead but is to be starved to death. Marzelline, the jailer's daughter, falls in love with the handsome "youth" Fidelio. *"Would I were wed to thee."* Fidelio agrees to wed Marzelline because she must keep near her husband. Word soon comes that Don Fernando, minister of state, is coming to inspect the prison. Don Pizarro is alarmed for he does not want the minister to find the imprisoned Don Florestan, who has been hurled into a dungeon purely from personal vengeance. So he decides to have Don Florestan murdered and buried at once. Rocco declines to murder the prisoner but consents to dig the grave. The faithful wife, overhearing this is in despair. *Aria: "O, wicked one."* Fidelio gets permission for the prisoners to come out into the court for a little fresh air. *Chorus: "O, what joy in Heaven's fresh air."* She hopes to get a message to her husband this way, but he does not appear with the rest. Despairing she goes with Rocco to dig the grave in the dungeon.

ACT 2

Dungeon of Florestan. *Aria: "God, how dark, this dreadful quiet."* As Fidelio and Rocco come in to dig the grave, Florestan sinks down exhausted, not recognizing his wife. Work begins. *Duet: "Be brisk and dig cheerily."* Florestan partly revives and Fidelio gives him bread. *Terzett: "May a better world reward you."* Pizarro, who has decided to murder Florestan himself, now enters the dungeon. He is about to kill Florestan when Fidelio hurls herself between them crying, "First kill his wife!" With a pistol she menaces the cowardly governor who retreats. Trumpet calls are heard announcing the arrival of Don Fernando, the minister. Florestan and Fidelio, clasped in each other's arms, sing of their happiness. *Duet: "O, endless joy."* The jailer Rocco is nonplussed at the turn in events and the revelation of Fidelio as a woman. The next scene takes place in the courtyard. Fernando commends Don Florestan on his narrow escape and warmly praises the faithfulness of Fidelio. *Chorus: "Hail the day; hail the hour."* The minister orders that Don Florestan's chains be put on the murderous governor. Marzelline is comforted in the loss of her "sweetheart" by finding another—a real boy—in Jacquino, the gate-keeper.

* * *

THE FLYING DUTCHMAN

ROMANTIC OPERA IN THREE ACTS
MUSIC AND LIBRETTO BY RICHARD WAGNER
FIRST PRODUCTION—DRESDEN, 1843

CAST

THE DUTCHMAN...............*Baritone*
DALAND, Norwegian sea captain.....*Basso*
SENTA, his daughter.............*Soprano*
ERIC, a huntsman..................*Tenot*

The Flying Dutchman

MARY, Senta's nurse.............*Contralto*
DALAND'S STEERSMAN...........*Tenor*
PLACE—The Coast of Norway

Wagner founded the text of the opera on Heine's legend that is told wherever seamen sail. A Dutch captain, buffeted by storms in trying to round the Cape of Good Hope, swears a sacrilegious oath that he will get around the Cape if it takes him an eternity. So through centuries his phantom ship, manned by demons, sails the seas—a terror to sailors everywhere.

ACT 1

A Norwegian Bay. Daland, a Norwegian captain, is driven into port by a storm. Going ashore, he finds he is not far from his own home, but cannot sail nearer until the weather moderates. The crew are at rest, a steersman on watch. *Steersman: "Through thunder and wars of distant seas."* He finally falls asleep too. Then comes The Flying Dutchman with her blood-red sails and black masts. She slips in and drops anchor by the Norwegian ship. Another seven years is up. The captain may now go ashore. If he finds a woman who will give up everything for him the awful curse will be raised. *"The*

The Flying Dutchman

term is past." Daland, the Norwegian, is astonished to see the strange craft hard by his own. The strange Dutch captain in black asks Daland for shelter in his home and offers him a big sum. The Norwegian is delighted. When the phantom captain finds the Norwegian has a daughter he proposes marriage. The Norwegian, dazzled by the gold, agrees to the proposal. *Chorus: "Through thunder and wars of distant seas."*

ACT 2

Daland's Home. Girls are happily spinning and singing. *Chorus: "Spin, spin, fair maiden."* But Senta, the Norwegian's daughter, is pensive. She is again musing on the familiar legend of the Flying Dutchman. *"Saw ye the ship on the raging deep?"* She longs to meet the Dutchman and by her fidelity raise the curse. The girls are surprised at her earnestness. Eric, who loves her, tells her he dreamed the Dutchman came and carried her off to sea. Instead of being frightened at this Senta is delighted. Soon Daland arrives with the Dutchman. Senta is struck with his resemblance to pictures of the Flying Dutchman. The two are soon enamored of each other. Daland is pleased and invites the Dutchman to a gala fete to celebrate the safe arrival of the Norwegian ship. Senta pledges to the stranger her love until death. The Dutchman is exultant, for the hour of freedom, he thinks, has come.

ACT 3

The Harbor. The Norwegian ship is aglow with lanterns. The Dutchman lies black and silent beside her. The Norwegian sailors gladly partake of the food brought by the girls. But to their invitations to invisible Dutch sailors there is no reply. Soon weird lights glow on the Dutchman and the sea is troubled. The onlookers are in terror at this phenomenon. Eric, coming down to the shore with Senta, is desperate, passionately begging her not to follow the Dutch captain. The captain, coming on them suddenly, believes Senta is false to him and all is lost. *"All is lost, Senta, farewell!"* He treaches the deck of his ship, the bloody sails swell, and the Flying Dutchman sets sail. But Senta runs to the top of the highest rock. She cries, "I am faithful unto death!" and flings herself into the sea. The Flying Dutchman sinks, but in the waves are the forms of Senta and the captain. Love has triumphed and the curse is lifted at last.

LA FORZA DEL DESTINO

OPERA IN FOUR ACTS

BOOK BY PIAVE; MUSIC BY GIUSEPPE VERDI. PRO-
DUCED FIRST AT ST. PETERSBURG,
NOVEMBER 11, 1862

CAST

MARQUIS OF CALATRAVA.........*Bass*
DONNA LEONORA, his daughter..*Soprano*
DON CARLO, his son............*Baritone*
DON ALVARO......................*Tenor*
ABBOT OF THE FRANCISCAN
  FRIARS ....*Bass*
MELITONE, a friar...............*Baritone*
CURRA, Leonora's maid..........*Contralto*
TRABUCCO, muleteer, afterwards
  a peddler........................*Tenor*
A SPANISH MILITARY SURGEON..*Tenor*
AVE ALCADE........................*Bass*
Muleteers, Spanish and Italian peasants and
  Soldiers, Friars of the Order of St. Francis,
  etc.

SCENE and PERIOD: Spain and Italy about
  the middle of the eighteenth century.

ACT 1

Drawing room of the house of the Marquis of Calatrava. Don Alvaro, a noble youth
from India, has fallen in love with Donna

La Forza del Destino

Leonora, daughter of the Marquis of Calatrava, who is strongly opposed to an alliance
between them. Knowing of her father's
aversion, Leonora determines to escape with
Alvaro, with the aid of Curra, her confidante.
As she is about to elope, her father appears,
and is accidentally slain by her lover. Hor-
rorstricken, Leonora rushes to her father and
is cursed by him with his dying breath.

ACT 2

SCENE 1

An inn at Hornacuelos. Don Carlo, son
of the defunct Marquis, is disguised as a
student, to aid him in avenging his father.
Leonora, travelling in male costume, is terrified, upon arriving at the inn, to see her
brother, who has sworn to kill Alvaro and
herself. She flees to the convent of Hornacuelos, arriving at night.

SCENE 2

The convent of Hornacuelos. Kneeling in
the moonlight, she prays to the Virgin for
protection. (*Holy Mother have Mercy.*)

Leonora is admitted to the convent by the
abbot, to whom she confesses. Procuring her
a nun's robe, he directs her to a cave, assur-
ing her that a curse will fall upon anyone who
seeks to find her out. In her gratitude she

sings the second great air. (*May angels guard thee.*)

ACT 3
SCENE

A military camp near Velleti. In this act we meet Alvaro in Italy, where he has enlisted in the Spanish army. He appeals to Heaven for pity recounting his misfortunes. (*Thou heavenly one.*)

In the next scene he saves the life of Don Carlo, who has wandered hence in search of vengeance. Both having assumed fictitious names, neither is aware of the other's identity; they swear eternal friendship. Shortly afterward, Don Alvaro is wounded, and is brought in on a stretcher. Believing himself to be dying, he sends away his attendant soldiers, and is left alone with Don Carlo. These two then render the great duet, the finest number of the opera. (*Swear in this hour.*)

Alvaro confides a case of letters to Don Carlo to be destroyed, first exacting a promise that their contents should not be examined. Carlo swears and the pair bid each other a last farewell. Alvaro, however, does not die, and in the next scene his identity becomes known to Don Carlo, who challenges him. They fight, and Alvaro, under the impression that he has killed his enemy, resolves to end his days in a monastery.

ACT 4

SCENE

The Inn at Hornacuelos. Five years have elapsed. Alvaro, now Father Raphael, is discovered by Don Carlo, who with great persistence revives the feud. They finally agree to renew the combat. A fiery duel ensues. (*In vain, Alvaro.*)

Carlo demands that Alvaro renew the feud, but the priest at first refuses, saying that vengeance is with God. But at last, taunted past endurance he consents to fight. (*Thy menaces wild.*)

Alvaro, recovering his poise appeals to his foe's reason, showing the futility of reopening the feud.

ACT 5

SCENE

A wild spot near Hornacuelos. The scene is in the vicinity of Leonora's cave. Pale and haggard, the wretched woman emerges from the cave, and implores heaven to let her die, as she is unable to forget her lover. (*Mercy, O my Lord.*)

A storm then breaks and Leonora retires within the cave just before the two combatants arrive on the scene. Alvaro recognizes the spot as accursed, but declares it to be a fitting place for so deadly a duel. Don Carlo falls mortally wounded and asks Alvaro to confess him, but the monk is under the curse of the cave and cannot. He goes to summon the friar, who inhabits the cave, when Leonora rushes forth and embraces her wounded brother. He, true to his vow, stabs her to the heart. The trio then render a dramatic number. (*Swear not, be humble.*)

Don Alvaro gives a fitting end to the tragedy by throwing himself from a cliff as the monks arrive singing the Miserere. The curtain then falls.

* * *

FRA DIAVOLO

LIGHT OPERA IN THREE ACTS
MUSIC BY DANIEL FRANCOIS E. AUBER
LIBRETTO BY SCRIBE
FIRST PRODUCTION—PARIS, 1830

CAST

FRA DIAVOLO, a bandit chief.......*Tenor*
LORD COCKBURN, an English
tourist ....*Basso*
LADY PAMELA COCKBURN, his
wife ....*Mezzo-Soprano*
LORENZO, an officer of the guard....*Tenor*

Fra Diavolo

MATTEO, tavern keeper............*Basso*
ZERLINE, his daughter...........*Soprano*
FRANCESCO, a miller...........*Baritone*
GIACOMO, a bandit................*Basso*
BEPPO, a bandit...................*Tenor*

PLACE—A Terracine Village
TIME—Nineteenth Century

ACT 1

Matteo's Tavern. Lorenzo, an officer, together with a company of guards, arrives to capture the celebrated bandit, Fra Diavolo, for whom a large reward is offered. The officer not only wants to win this reward but the hand of the inn-keeper's daughter, Zerline. Soon English visitors arrive. They are Lord and Lady Cockburn and their traveling companion, one Marquis of San Marco. The latter has been paying a great deal of attention to the lady. In addition to this grievance, Lord Cockburn declares that they have been robbed. Soon the Marquis appears. He is of course, none other than Fra Diavolo himself. He orders a dinner and listens to Zerline tell of the exploits of the celebrated bandit. *"On yonder rock reclining."* Again he pays suit to the English lady and manages to steal from her a valuable locket. Then Lorenzo, the officer, appears again. He has broken up the gang of bandits, recovered the jewelry stolen from the travelers and has won a big reward. Now he hopes to win Zerline also. *Finale: "I hear the marchers coming."*

ACT 2

Zerline's Bedroom. Zerline conducts Lord and Lady Cockburn to their apartments which join hers. She is happy over her coming union with Lorenzo. *"What luck I breathe again."* Terzett: *"Dear wife, let us go to sleep."* Meanwhile Fra Diavolo and his two followers conceal themselves in Zerline's room. *Cavatina: "Tomorrow, tomorrow, what joy."* They observe Zerline undressing. *Quartette: "What a pretty child."* The girl retires and falls asleep. Then the three bandits proceed to rob the Englishman and his wife. But the victims awaken and an alarm is given. Lorenzo and his guards rush in. Fra Diavolo, still the Marquis and traveling companion of the English couple, saves himself from suspicion of robbery by covering the retreat of his two confederates. But he is still in a bad position, for being in the sleeping rooms, he arouses the jealousy and suspicion of both Lorenzo and Lord Cockburn. Lorenzo challenges Fra Diavolo to a duel and the latter accepts.

ACT 3

In the Forest. Fra Diavolo, a bandit undisguised now, awaits Lorenzo. *"My friend I hear."* Zerline is to wed against her will the peasant Francisco. In the wedding procession are Fra Diavolo's two followers, who are immediately arrested by Lorenzo, who is sad at losing Zerline. *"Forever I will think of thee."* He compels the bandits to lure Fra Diavolo into a trap and the celebrated robber is shot. *"Away, away to new strife."* But before dying the bandit declares that Zerline is innocent. Lady Cockburn is astounded to find that the Marquis was none other than the desperado. The story ends with the uniting of Lorenzo and Zerline.

* * *

DER FREISCHUTZ
(THE MARKSMAN)

ROMANTIC OPERA IN THREE ACTS
MUSIC BY CARL MARIA VON WEBER
LIBRETTO BY FRIEDRICH KIND FROM OLD LEGEND
FIRST PRODUCTION—BERLIN, 1821

CAST

OTTAKAR, Duke of Bohemia.....*Baritone*
KUNO, his head game-keeper........*Basso*
AGNES, game-keeper's daughter.....*Soprano*

Der Freischutz

ANNA, her friend.. ....*Mezzo-Soprano*

MAX, a ranger.....................*Tenor*

CASPAR, a ranger..................*Basso*

KILIAN, a wealthy peasant.........*Tenor*

A HERMIT......................*Basso*

ZAMIEL, THE EVIL ONE...... (*Speaking*)

PLACE—Bohemia
TIME—The Middle Ages

ACT 1 '

The Target Range. Kuno, the head ranger of the Duke, is growing old and his successor must be chosen. Max, the ranger, who loves Kuno's daughter, is a candidate for the position, which is won in sharp-shooting contests. The preliminary contest is on. Max loses to Kilian, the peasant. *Chorus:* "Victory, long live the master." Kilian mockingly sings, "*Let him gaze on me as King.*" Longing to change his bad luck, Max falls under the influence of Caspar. This individual has sold himself to the Evil One, but hopes to regain his freedom by bringing in another victim. *Trio:* "O, the sun." Max is much dejected. "*Through fields and woods.*" Caspar tries to put courage into him. "*Here in this vale of tears.*" He gives him a gun loaded with magic bullets and Max is astounded at bringing down an eagle from an unusual height.

Caspar tells him that in the Wolf's Glen is a magician who can mould for him seven magical bullets that will hit any mark. Max, hopeful of winning the prize and Agnes, agrees to go, though it will cost him his soul. Caspar is triumphant. *"Silence, let no one warn him."*

ACT 2

Agnes' Room. The girl is awaiting Max and is much alarmed when he does not come. She is fearful, because a hermit has warned her of impending danger. But he has also told her that her bridal wreath will protect her. Her friend Anna tries to cheer her. *Air: "Comes a gallant youth."* She tries to persuade Agnes to retire. But the girl says she will wait for her lover. She parts the curtains and prays. *"Softly sighing, day is dying."* Max soon comes. He says that he has not been the victor in the preliminary contests, but that he has shot a stag in the Wolf's Gorge and that he will bring her the deer. Agnes and Anna beg him not to go, fearing evil, but he is determined and departs. *Trio: "What horror there in the Wolf's Gorge?"* The next scene shows the gorge at night. Caspar comes and tells Zamiel, the Evil One, of his suc-

cess with Max. The latter is warned by
the spirit of his mother to turn back. But
Zamiel shows him Agnes drowning herself
because of his failure in the contest. So
Max enters the gorge and, amid lightnings
and terror, the seven magic bullets are
moulded.

ACT 3

Agnes' Room. The girl prays again.
*"Through clouds obscure still shines the sun
in the radiant sky."* She is ready to wed
Max and the bridesmaids arrive with the
bridal wreath. *Chorus: "We wind round
thee the bridal wreath."* When she opens
the box she beholds a funeral wreath. She
is greatly dejected, but the old hermit's
promise to her comforts her. The second
scene is the Duke's camp. The contest is
on and all are amazed at the skill of Max.
He has shot six of his magic bullets. The
course of the last one will be directed by the
Evil One. The Duke orders him to shoot
at a dove. He fires and the bullet strikes
Agnes. But she is saved from death by the
bridal wreath the old hermit blessed. Caspar knows now that he has failed, and
Zamiel seizes him and he expires. Max now
confesses to the Duke the story of the magic

bullets moulded by the Evil One. The Duke imposes a year's penance on Max, at the end of which time he will marry Agnes.

* * *

LA GIOCONDA

OPERA IN FOUR ACTS

IBRETTO BY GARRIO BOITO, FOUNDED ON HUGO'S TRAGEDY, "ANGELO"

MUSIC BY AMILCARE PONCHIELLI

FIRST PRODUCTION—MILAN, 1876

CAST

LA GIOCONDA, a ballad singer....*Soprano*
LA CIECA, her blind mother.....*Contralto*
ALVISE, one of the leaders of the Inquisition ....*Basso*
LAURA, his wife............*Mezzo-Soprano*
ENZO GRIMALDO, a Genoese noble..*Tenor*
BARNABA, spy of the Inquisition..*Baritone*
ZUANE, a boatman..................*Basso*
ISEPO, a letter-writer...............*Tenor*
A PILOT.............................*Basso*

PLACE—Venice.
TIME—Seventeenth Century

ACT 1

Court of the Ducal Palace. "The Lion's Mouth." Here the letters for the Inquisition are received. Men and maidens are in holi-day attire and sing, *"Sports and Feasting,"* while Barnaba looks on. He plans to win La Gioconda, the ballad singer, who now arrives leading her blind mother. La Cieca is grateful to her daughter. *"Daughter, my faltering steps."* Gioconda is going to seek Enzo, whom she loves, but Barnaba stops her and declares his love. The girl escapes him and flees. The regatta over Zuane, the defeated entrant, is told by Barnaba that Cieca has thrown a spell of ill-luck over him. Thus Barnaba hopes to have revenge for Gioconda's repulse. Zuane attacks the old woman but she is saved by the arrival of Enzo. Alvise, a leader of the Inquisition, also arrives with his wife, Laura, who is loved by Enzo. Alvise, through the pleading of his wife, agrees to protect Cieca, and the blind woman voices her gratitude. *"Angelic voice."* Barnaba, the spy, notices the glances between Enzo and Laura. He tells Enzo that Laura is planning a visit to his ship that night. Enzo, aroused by the thought, hurries off to his ship to receive her. Barnaba then informs Alvise that his wife is to meet Enzo on the latter's vessel. Gioconda overhears this and is heartbroken at the faithlessness of Enzo. The act closes with the famous dance, *the Furlana.*

[105]

La Gioconda

ACT 2

Enzo's Vessel. "The Rosary." Barnaba, disguised as a fisherman, sings to the sailors. *"Fisher boy, thy bait be throwing."* Barnaba leaves after sending for police galleys. Enzo arrives and is royally greeted. He is happy. *"Heaven and ocean."* Laura reaches the ship and the lovers embrace and plan to set sail at dawn. But Gioconda comes and denounces Laura. Each declares that she loves Enzo. *"I adore him."* Gioconda would stab Laura but is prevented by a rosary the latter wears—the gift of Gioconda's blind mother. Laura's husband is approaching and Gioconda generously aids her to escape. She tells Enzo, who shrinks before her scorn, that police galleys are coming to capture him. Enzo, in despair, sets fire to his ship to keep it from being taken by Barnaba.

ACT 3

Hall in the Palace of Alvise. "The House of Gold." Alvise decides that the unfaithful Laura shall die. *"To die is her doom."* He orders her to drink poison and departs. But Gioconda, remembering how Laura befriended her mother, substitutes a narcotic for the poison. Laura drinks and goes off into deep slumber. Alvise thinks she is dead. He now gives a grand ball, the great number of which is the *Dance of the Hours*. Barnaba whispers to Enzo that Laura is dead. Enzo unmasks and denounces Alvise. *"I behold thee."* Alvise has him arrested. But now the murderous husband draws aside the curtain showing the supposedly dead Laura. He declares that he did kill her. All are horrified. Enzo tries to kill Alvise but is prevented. Barnaba is placed over him as guard. Gioconda tells Barnaba if he will release Enzo she will give herself to him. To this Barnaba agrees.

ACT 4

A Ruined Palace on the Adriatic. Gioconda is alone with the unconscious Laura. She persuades the men to search for her mother. Suicide is her only course now. *"Suicide only remains."* Enzo arrives and Laura revives. The lovers are in a heaven of delight, and Gioconda generously aids them to escape. Gioconda is about to swallow poison when Barnaba appears. He declares she has broken her promise to him. She appears to yield to the spy. *"Now Thou art mine."* But she carries a dagger, and with this stabs herself. Barnaba still has his revenge for he cries into her ears that he has murdered her mother.

THE GIRL OF THE GOLDEN WEST

ROMANTIC OPERA IN THREE ACTS
MUSIC BY GIACOMO PUCCINI
DRAMA BY DAVID BELASCO
FIRST PRODUCTION—NEW YORK, 1910

CAST

MINNIE, the Girl................*Soprano*
JACK RANCE, sheriff and gambler..*Baritone*
DICK JOHNSON, alias Ramarrez, an
    outlaw ....*Tenor*
NICK, bartender of the Polka........*Tenor*
ASHBY, Wells-Fargo agent...........*Basso*
BILLY JACKRABBIT, Indian........*Basso*
WOWKLE, Billy's squaw.....*Mezzo-Soprano*
JAKE WALLACE, minstrel........*Baritone*
JOSE CASTRO, greaser from Ramarrez'
    gang ....*Basso*
SONORA, TRIN, SID, HANDSOME
    HARRY, JOE, HAPPY, LARKENS..*Miners*

PLACE—Cloudy Mountain, California
TIME—1849

ACT 1

Interior of the Polka Saloon. Here Minnie,
an orphan, keeps a saloon and acts as a little
mother for the boys—all rough pioneers come
to seek for gold. She is beloved by the
whole camp, every man of whom considers

himself her protector. The miners are congregated in the saloon for the night and a wandering minstrel enters. He sings *"Old Folks at Home"* and arouses the emotions of all in his audience. Jack Rance, the Sheriff, appears on the scene. He loves Minnie and again plies her with questions as to her feelings for him. But she does not nor cannot love Rance. Suddenly to the Polka comes a dashing, devil-may-care man by the name of Johnson. He is none other than Ramarrez, the outlaw, for whom a large reward is offered. He comes to rob the Polka. The boys all receive him gladly but Rance is sullen, seeing how fascinated Minnie is with the stranger. The girl and Johnson dance together. Castro, one of Ramarrez's gang, is caught and brought in. Seeing his master's saddle he knows Ramarrez is near. By a clever ruse he lures the miners off to a spot where he declares Ramarrez is in hiding. Late in the night Minnie and Johnson are alone. The girl recognizes in him a man different from the men of the camp. She trusts him and Johnson secretly resolves he will not rob the Polka. Johnson, in a beautiful number, tells her something of himself and his emotions. *"I myself hardly know what I am."* He promises to meet the Girl in her cabin that night.

The Girl of the Golden West
ACT 2

Interior of Minnie's Cabin. Billy Jack-rabbit and Wowkle await the Girl's coming. When she arrives she begins to adorn herself for Johnson. The outlaw arrives and she receives him gladly but coyly. She tells him of life in the mountains. *"You've no idea how exciting my life is."* The Indians leave and Johnson makes ardent love to the Girl. She is won and allows him to embrace and kiss her while a violent storm rages outside. The Girl says she will give him shelter. She undresses behind the screens and in her night-robe lies down before the fire. Johnson is given Minnie's bed in which to rest. Suddenly the miners arrive at the cabin, searching for Ramarrez who they have now found out is Johnson. Minnie convinces them they were wrong in thinking that he is in her cabin. They depart and now Minnie bitterly denounces Johnson for his deception. He is humbled and departs into the night. *Johnson: "Let me say just one word."* But a shot is heard and he stumbles back wounded. Desperate now, Minnie conceals him in the little garret. Rance enters and discovers him by the dripping blood. He is about to shoot him when Minnie declares she will play cards for her lover's life. If Rance wins he is to shoot Johnson and take Minnie. *Minnie:*

"*My stakes in the game.*" They play and Minnie, cheating, wins. Rance stoically departs, pledged to secrecy.

ACT 3

Foothills of the Sierras at Dawn. Johnson, nursed back to health by Minnie, is escaping. But he is caught by the miners. They give him only a few minutes for his farewell words. He asks that his death be kept from Minnie. *Johnson: "Let her believe I have gained my freedom."* The miners are about to hang Johnson when Minnie appears. The Girl declares that she loves the outlaw and the boys must spare him. Finally they are moved to pity, and Minnie and the outlaw start their journey eastward to begin a new life. *Minnie and Johnson: "My mountains, my Sierras, good-bye."*

* * *

DIE GOTTERDAMMERUNG
THE TWILIGHT OF THE GODS
MUSIC DRAMA IN THREE ACTS AND A PRELUDE
MUSIC AND DRAMA BY RICHARD WAGNER
FIRST PRODUCTION—BAYREUTH, 1876

CAST

SIEGFRIED	.... *Tenor*
GUNTHER	.... *Basso*

Die Gotterdammerung

HAGEN ....*Basso*
BRUNNHILDE ....*Soprano*
GUTRUNE ..../...*Soprano*
WOGLINDA, Rhine-nymph ....*Soprano*
WELLGUNDA, Rhine-nymph.......*Soprano*
FLOSSHILDE, Rhine-nymph......*Contralto*

Prelude. The Walkuere's Rock. Here
Brunnhilde had lain during her magic sleep
which ended by the coming of Siegfried, the
hero. He weds her and they live in a cave.
But now Siegfried decides to go forth in
search of new adventures. He gives Brunnhilde as a pledge the ring of the Nibelung.
This ring he obtained when he slew Fafner,
the dragon, but it carries an everlasting
curse with it. In return for the ring Brunnhilde gives to Siegfried her Valkyrie steed
Grane to carry him to victory. *"Did I not
send thee, sweetest hero."*

ACT 1

Hall of King Gunther on the Rhine. Here
with the King lives his sister Gutrune and
their half-brother Hagen. The latter is
the son of Alberich, the dwarf, and knows
the history of the ring which he longs to restore to his father. He plans to give Siegfried a drink that will make him forget
Brunnhilde and love Gutrune. Then King
Gunther will be free to woo Brunnhilde.

Siegfried is warmly greeted, and accepts the drink. Immediately he loves Gutrune. *"Thou fair one."* The King promises him the maid if he, the King, can win Brunnhilde. In order to deceive Brunnhilde, Siegfried changes himself into the physical form of Gunther and departs from the castle. A change of scene brings the hero back to the rock of Brunnhilde. Siegfried appears, but Brunnhilde is startled for his is not the form of her hero. She cannot comprehend how a stranger penetrated the circle of fire that surrounds the rock. She holds up the ring, thinking that it will protect her. But Siegfried takes the ring from her finger and draws her into the cave.

ACT 2

The Banks of the Rhine. Hagen and his father Alberich plan to win back the ring. Siegfried now in his own physical form, comes and is greeted in a friendly way. He tells Hagen that he has won Gunther's wife for him, and they are returning. Gutrune greets Siegfried lovingly and they go to prepare the feast for the coming of Gunther and Brunnhilde. When the bridal couple arrive, Brunnhilde is stricken with grief at seeing Siegfried with Gutrune. She also sees the ring on the hero's finger and demands an

explanation. Siegfried, still not remembering
his relations to her, cannot give a satisfactory
reply. Then Brunnhilde denounces him and
arouses the suspicion of Gunther, who has
been deceived by Siegfried. The hero defends himself by taking the oath of the spear.
"Haft of war, hallowed weapon." But Brunnhilde still denounces him, and Siegfried
thinks that she has lost her mind. Hagen
assures Brunnhilde that he will avenge her
wrongs, and she tells him that Siegfried is
vulnerable only in the back. His back is not
protected by magic because he would never
retreat. Gunther, Brunnhilde and Hagen
decide that Siegfried must be slain for his
treachery.

ACT 3

Wild Valley and Forest by the Rhine.
Siegfried rests after his hunt. The Rhine
maidens rise to the surface and sing of the
Rhinegold. They try to persuade him to give
them the ring. But he refuses. *"Alike on
land and water woman's ways I've learned to
know."* The maidens, indignant, declare he
will die that day. Horns are heard and
Siegfried gayly receives Gunther and Hagen.
They eat and drink and the hero tells them
of his adventures. He drinks a magic drink
that Hagen gives him and immediately his

memory of Brunnhilde returns. He begins to tell of his quest for her when Hagen plunges a spear into his back. The hero falls dying. *"Brunnhilde, heavenly bride."* The final scene takes place in a hall in the castle. Siegfried's body is borne in and Gutrune is beside herself with grief. Hagen demands the ring off Siegfried's finger. This Gunther refuses to give up. The two fight and Hagen kills Gunther. Then Hagen tries to remove the ring from the dead man's finger, but the arm of the hero rises threateningly. All are struck with terror. But Brunnhilde, sadly beholding the dead hero, orders a funeral pyre built for him on the banks of the Rhine. She now summons two ravens to notify Loki, god of fire; and tell him to destroy the power of the gods by burning Valhalla. *"Draweth near in the gloom the twilight of the gods."* Brunnhilde sets fire to the pyre and summons her steed. Mounting, she rides straight into the flames. The Rhine rises and quenches the fire. The Rhine daughters, riding on the surface, snatch the ring from the embers. Hagen rushes in to seize it but is drawn down into the flood by the maidens. In the distance Valhalla is burning and the gods calmly await their doom.

HAMLET

OPERA IN FIVE ACTS
MUSIC BY AMBROISE THOMAS
LIBRETTO BY BARBIER AND CARRE FROM
SHAKESPEARE'S "HAMLET"
FIRST PRODUCTION—PARIS, 1868

CAST

HAMLET, Prince of Denmark.....*Baritone*
CLAUDIUS, King of Denmark........*Basso*
POLONIUS, Chancellor..............*Basso*
LAERTES, Polonius' son...........*Tenor*
GHOST OF HAMLET'S FATHER....*Basso*
GERTRUDE, Hamlet's mother.......
.... *Mezzo-Soprano*
OPHELIA, daughter of Polonius....*Soprano*

PLACE—Elsinore in Denmark

ACT 1

Hall in the Palace. The Queen is holding a court reception and is worried because her son Hamlet absents himself. As in the tragedy of Shakespeare, the young prince does not know that his father was murdered, but he is angry at his mother for having married his uncle so soon after his father's death. Ophelia appears and wonders if Hamlet has ceased to love her, for she has heard that he is going to leave the kingdom. The Prince tells her never to

[116]

doubt his love. *"Celestial maiden, 'tis not thee I chide."* The principals next appear on a rampart of the castle. It is night and Hamlet's friends tell him of the appearance of the ghost of his father, the late King. Hamlet awaits his father's spirit, which appears at the appointed hour. The spectre speaks. *"I am thy father's ghost doomed for a certain term to walk at night."* It tells of the murder by the present King and urges Hamlet to avenge the crime, leaving his mother's punishment to Heaven.

ACT 2

Garden of the Palace. Hamlet, distressed by Ophelia's despair, feigns melancholia. The Prince, hopeful of entrapping the King into a confession of crime, wishes to employ strolling players to present a play. The King and Queen gladly assent, hoping that this will cheer Hamlet. The Prince explains to the players the plot he wants presented—a duplicate of the murder of his father. He cheers them with wine. *"Wine, this gloom dispel."* Scene two takes place in a hall arranged for the play. The actors, well instructed by the Prince, reenact the murder of Hamlet's father. The King, terrified by what he beholds, cannot conceal his dismay. Hamlet, in a frenzy, now denounces him as the murderer of the noble King. But the court thinks that his accusations are the ravings of a man who is losing his reason.

ACT 3

The Queen's Apartments. The famous soliloquy: *"To be or not to be, that is the question."* The Queen and Ophelia appear and bid him cease his strange musings. He tells Ophelia she should be in a convent and accuses his mother of being an accomplice in the murder. But his father's ghost, suddenly appearing to Hamlet alone, bids him spare his mother.

ACT 4

Near a Lake. Ophelia, deserted by Hamlet, has lost her reason. In this, the Mad Scene, she toys with a garland of flowers. She imitates the lark and sings a wild melody that is broken by laughter and weeping. At the end she hurls herself into the lake and floats down to her death with the flowers.

ACT 5

The Churchyard. Here Hamlet comes to see Ophelia buried. He muses on her grave. *"As a lovely flower."* The funeral procession arrives. Again his father's ghost appears to Hamlet. Desperate now, he attacks and kills the King. The people, now convinced of the dying King's guilt, proclaim that Hamlet shall be King. In the ending, of course, the opera differs materially from the drama in which Hamlet also dies.

* * *

HANSEL AND GRETEL

FAIRY OPERA IN THREE ACTS BY
ENGELBERT HUMPERDINCK
TEXT BY ADELHEIT WETTE, FROM GRIMM'S
FAIRY TALES

CAST

PETER, Broom-Maker.............*Baritone*
GERTRUD, his wife........*Mezzo-Soprano*
HANSEL ⎰ their children ⎱ ...*Mezzo-Soprano*
GRETEL ⎱　　　　　 ⎰ ....*Soprano*
THE CRUNCH WITCH....*Mezzo-Soprano*
THE SANDMAN..................*Soprano*
DEW MANNIKINS...............*Sopranos*
FOURTEEN ANGELS

FIRST PRODUCTION, MUNICH, 1893

ACT 1

The home of Hansel and Gretel. The children are alone and working. They soon leave their tasks, trying to forget their hunger by dancing and singing. *Gretel: "Suse, dear Suse, what rattles in the straw?" Hansel.*

[119]

Hansel and Gretel

"Eia, popeia, what poverty!" The Mother returns and is angry and scolds them for neglecting their work. *"Do you call that work to yell and sing?"* To punish them she sends them into the woods to pick strawberries. *"If you bring not the basket full, I will whip you and your hair pull."* Shortly after they leave, the Father returns carrying a basketful of food. He has been drinking and is in good spirits, having sold his brooms at a good price. *"Oh, we poor, poor people."* He inquires for the children and, when hearing that they have been sent into the woods to pick berries, is greatly alarmed, for at Ilsentein lives the wicked Crunch Witch, who lures children with her magic cakes. *"A witch of hoary age roams in the forest."* The Father and Mother hurry out in search of Hansel and Gretel.

ACT 2

The woods where the children have been picking berries. While Hansel is seeking berries Gretel binds a wreath. *"A little man is in the woods."* When the cuckoo calls they begin to play cuckoo with the berries, and while he is calling they devour them. Night has fallen; they are afraid and in the dark Hansel cannot find the way. Their terror is increased by seeing faces of wood monsters staring at them. Out of the mist appears the Sandman. *"A little Sandman and I-st."* He throws sand in their eyes and they go to sleep after praying to the angels. *"When at night I go to sleep, fourteen angels watch do keep."* From the mist a shining ladder is seen and fourteen angels descend from the sky and surround the children, keeping watch over them while they sleep.

ACT 3

The Crunch Witch's hut. The scene is the same, but the angels have disappeared and mist conceals the background. The children are awakened by the Dream Man and tell each other of the angels they have seen in their dreams. The mist vanishes and they see the Crunch Witch's hut on the Ilsentein. There is a bake oven on the left, on the right a cage, and the hut is surrounded by a wall of gingerbread girls and boys. The children commence to nibble at the hut, which is made of gingerbread. *The voice of the Witch: "Nibble, nibble, who nibbles at my hut?"* They answer: *"The wind, the wind, that heavenly child."* The Witch rushes out, captures Hansel and locks him in the cage and sends Gretel into the house for almonds and raisens with which to fatten Hansel before baking him into gingerbread.

Hansel and Gretel

She looks in her oven and in glee sings: "*Hurr, hopp, hopp, gallop, gallop.*" Hansel warns Gretel on her return: "*Sister dear, be careful.*" The Witch asks Gretel to look into the oven. Gretel acts clumsily and wants the Witch to show her how it is done. The Witch peers into the oven, and with the help of Hansel, who has managed to escape from the cage, Gretel pushes the Witch into the oven. All the children who have been turned into gingerbread become children again and voice their thanks. *Gingerbread children:* "*Thanks, thanks, forever and ever.*" With the arrival of the parents, the Witch, who has been baked to gingerbread, is taken from the oven. *Father:* "*Children, look at the miracle.*" Final chorus: "*When misery is at its lowest ebb, God, the Lord, stretches forth His hand.*"

* * *

HERODIADE

OPERA IN FOUR ACTS
MUSIC BY JULES MASSENET
LIBRETTO BY MILLIET AND GREMONT
FIRST PRODUCTION—BRUSSELS, 1881

CAST

JOHN THE PROPHET.............*Tenor*
HEROD, King of Galilee..........*Baritone*

PHANUEL, a Chaldean.............*Basso*
VITELLIUS, Roman proconsul....*Baritone*
THE HIGH PRIEST.............*Baritone*
A VOICE IN THE TEMPLE........*Basso*
SALOME ....*Soprano*
HERODIAS ....*Contralto*

PLACE—Jerusalem.
TIME—30 A.D.

ACT 1

Courtyard of Herod's Palace. The servants are working under direction of Phanuel, the Chaldean, when Salome enters. The Chaldean is astonished to see her and wonders if she knows the Queen Herodias is her mother. The girl is looking for the prophet John of whom she is strangely enamored. She declares that he is wondrously good and kind and that he saved her from the desert when she was but a child. *Salome: "He is kind; he is good."* Herod finds Salome and now Herodias appears. The Queen is raging at the denunciations of the Prophet and demands of Herod his execution. But Herod, fearing an uprising, cautions Herodias against violence. The Prophet enters and denounces both the King and Queen. Salome receives him joyfully and is eloquent in her love, but he repulses her.

[123]

ACT 2

Herod's Chamber. Herod lies on a couch while the maidens dance before him. But Salome is not there and he is despondent. He drinks a love potion and now the face of Salome appears to him. *Herod: "Fleeting vision."* He declares that he madly loves his wife's daughter and that he would give the world and his soul to possess her. In this condition he falls asleep. The next scene shows a square in the city. Herod, urged on by Phanuel, denounces the Romans and pleads with the people to throw off the yoke of the conquerors. But the sound of trumpets announces the arrival of the victorious general Vitellius. The people are terrified but the Roman is lenient. He agrees to restore the Temple to the Jews. The Prophet and Salome now appear on the scene. The former is received with unusual acclaim. Vitellius is surprised at this, and Herodias, hating John, tells the Roman that the Phophet is thirsty for power. This, of course, instantly arouses resentment in Vitellius. But the Prophet courageously denounces the Roman and declares that all power comes from God.

ACT 3

In Phanuel's Home. The Chaldean is
gazing at the stars. *"O shining stars."* He
seeks to learn what manner of man John is.
Herodias comes to him and tells him that
another (Salome) has stolen Herod's love.
She longs to know, too, about her lost child.
The Chaldean consults the stars and sees
blood. He looks out of the window and beholds Salome. Herodias is horrified to find
that her daughter is her rival. The next
scene takes place in the Temple. Salome is
in despair because John has been imprisoned.
Herod pleads for her love but she denies him.
Vitellius, the Roman, turns the whole case
over to Herod. John is brought forth.
Salome hurls herself at his feet ready to die
with him. Herod, finding that Salome is
wildly infatuated with the Prophet, orders
John put to death.

ACT 4

A Dungeon. Salome comes to John here
and he is touched by her devotion. But
he does not return her earthly love. He
declines to accept pardon on condition that
he help overthrow Roman authority. Salome
is dragged away. The final scene shows an
audience hall in the palace. A feast is being
given in honor of the Roman, Vitellius.

Herodiade

Salome, dancing before Herod, pleads for the life of John. While she pleads the dripping head of the Prophet is brought in. Salome, desperate, tries to kill Herodias. Then the Queen reveals herself as the girl's mother. Horrified, Salome stabs herself and dies.

* * *

THE HUGUENOTS

DRAMATIC OPERA IN FIVE ACTS
MUSIC BY GIACOMO MEYERBEER
LIBRETTO BY SCRIBE AND DESCHAMPS
FIRST PRODUCTION—PARIS, 1836

CAST

COUNT DE ST. BRIS............*Baritone*
COUNT DE NEVERS............*Baritone*
RAOUL DE NANGIS, a Protestant nobleman ....*Tenor*
MARCEL, his servant................*Basso*
MARGARET OF VALOIS, betrothed of Henry IV......................*Soprano*
VALENTINE, daughter of St. Bris..*Soprano*
URBANA, page to Queen Margaret.....
.... *Mezzo-Soprano*

PLACE—Touraine and Paris.
TIME—1572

The night of St. Bartholomew, celebrated in history, is the subject of the plot. While

[126]

The Huguenots

peace exists, still the Catholic party with St.
Bris at its head, determines to murder the
Huguenots. Margaret and De Nevers, how-
ever, are for permanent peace.

ACT 1

Home of De Nevers. The Count is entertaining Catholic friends. But among the
guests comes Raoul, the Protestant, who De
Nevers hopes will be pleasantly received.
The other guests are friendly and he is
urged to tell of some adventures. He assents
and relates the rescue of a lady from revelers.
She is St. Bris' daughter, though he does not
know it. He only knows she deeply impressed him. *"Fairer than the lily."* Marcel,
Raoul's servant arrives, and is chocked to
find his master with Romanists. He warns
him in a fiery Huguenot song: *"Old Rome
and her revelries."* As he finishes a veiled
woman calls to see De Nevers, the others
thinking she is his mistress. Raoul sees the
lady's face and is shocked to recognize the
girl he rescued. She, Valentine, loving her
rescuer, Raoul, has come to De Nevers to
be released from their betrothal. He sadly
grants her request. Meanwhile a page
brings a note to Raoul summoning him on
a strange errand. He accepts and departs.

ACT 2

Gardens of Margaret. The Queen, on her throne, sings of beautiful Touraine. *"Fair land of Touraine."* Valentine arrives to tell the Queen that De Nevers has released her. Valentine retires and Raoul enters blindfolded. When the bandage is removed he is astounded to find himself before the Queen. He pledges himself to her service. She declares, that hoping to reconcile the Catholics and Protestants, she has arranged a marriage in which she hopes the entire court will rejoice. *"Swear that by the marriage vow."* Valentine is brought in and presented to Raoul. The Protestant recognizes her as the veiled woman who called on De Nevers. He is astounded. *"I her husband—never!"* St. Bris immediately challenges Raoul for insulting his daughter. The Queen orders him arrested and the Catholics are raging. Only Marcel is glad—that his master has not married a Catholic.

ACT 3

Square in Paris. Catholics and Protestants drink. The Huguenots sing. *"He took the sword in his hand."* Valentine is now married to De Nevers. By his permission, she is to spend a day praying in a chapel. Here she overhears a plot to assassinate Raoul.

She finds Marcel and tells him of his Master's danger. *Duet: "Here by night alone I wander."* Marcel hurries to rescue his master, and there is about to be a general conflict between Catholics and Protestants. It is prevented by the arrival of the Queen, who tells Raoul that Valentine is innocent. Raoul, now realizing his mistake, is overcome by remorse. But it is too late for Valentine is married. The girl and De Nevers sail away in a beautifully decorated boat.

ACT 4

Apartments in De Nevers' Palace. Valentine is sad, because she loves only Raoul. *"He alone fills my heart."* But suddenly he appears, having forced his way into the castle. The girl, hearing her father and his friends coming, hides Raoul behind tapestries. St. Bris and the others plan to slay all the Protestants that night. But the noble De Nevers declines to join them in murder. He breaks his sword and is led away. But the others consecrate their swords to the wholesale assassination. *"Will ye all join me the traitors to destroy."* The Benediction follows: *"On Heaven's just cause relying"* and after this the fanatical chorus—*"Strike them down, men and children."* The nobles depart and Raoul comes out, horrified

The Huguenots

at what he has heard. He wishes to rush off and warn his friends but Valentine detains him by words of love. *Duet: "Speak those words again."* Suddenly the signal bell sounds the beginning of the slaughter. Raoul rushes to the window while Valentine clings to him desperately. But he frees himself from her arms and is shot as he leaps into the street.

(In some productions the long opera ends here. In others the last scene of the fifth act is given.)

ACT 5

Last Scene. Raoul arrives at a quay mortally wounded. Valentine is with him. Soldiers heedlessly fire on them and the lovers are united in death.

* * *

IRIS

OPERA IN THREE ACTS

MUSIC BY PIETRO MASCAGNI

LIBRETTO BY LUIGI ILLICA

FIRST PRODUCTION—ROME, 1898

CAST

CIECO, a blind man.................*Basso*
IRIS, his daughter.................*Soprano*
OSAKA, a rich young man..........*Tenor*

KYOTO, keeper of a resort........*Baritone*
A GEISHA.....................*Soprano*
A PEDDLER.....................*Tenor*
A RAG-PICKER.................*Tenor*
PLACE—Japan

ACT 1

The Garden of Iris. It is dawn and the rising Sun proclaims himself the god of the universe. *"I am I. I am Life."* Iris, the beautiful innocent young woman, plays with her doll in the garden. *"Silence, O flowers."* She salutes the golden Sun and her father comes calling. *Duet, Iris and Cieco: "Pure and sweet, gay and bright."* The girl is all innocence, but she has attracted and aroused the passions of the rich young Osaka. He plans with a procurer, Kyoto, to secure the maiden for himself. In order to attract Iris' attention they arrange a puppet show in the street. The girl comes out of the garden to see the geishas dance, and she is seized and carried off. Her father calls for her distractedly. But the neighbors tell him that she has gone to a notorious resort kept by Kyoto. Poor Cieco thinks that she has gone willingly and he curses her memory. *"O, beloved home."*

ACT 2

Iris sleeps in the richly furnished resort. Osaka comes and Kyoto tells him how beautiful she is. He must have much money for such a prize as this. Iris awakens and is lost in wonderment at the luxury of her surroundings. She thinks that she has been transported to Paradise. *Iris: "Visions, always visions."* In her delight she paints a flower with a brush. It turns to a snake. Osaka now comes with fine presents for her. He woos her ardently. *"Your hair so long and thick."* But the girl is absolutely innocent and does not divine his meaning. This childlike quality finally cools the man's desire for her. He tells Kyoto to take her away. The resortkeeper now robes her in finest apparel and sends her out to be displayed for the admiration of the crowds in the streets. All admire her beauty. *Chorus: "Wonder of wonders."* Now the blind Cieco comes searching for his daughter. Iris answers him and the crowd becomes angry. But Kyoto appears and declares that he has purchased the girl from the father. Old Cieco, expressing unutterable contempt for Iris, throws mud on her. This drives the innocent girl to distraction and she hurls herself into one of the flooded drain-pipes in the street.

[132]

ACT 3

Ragpickers fish in the sewers with hooks, hoping to recover something of value. Suddenly they come on the body of Iris. Quarreling over the division of the spoils, they tear the rich gown off the body. But when Iris moves they run off in superstitious terror. The Sun partly warms the girl back to life. Hanging between Life and Death, she beholds the egos of her father, Kyoto and Osaka, all trying to justify their existence in the universe. Iris cannot comprehend her own destiny and wonders why everything is. *"The little world of my cottage why destroy?"* She turns toward her one friend, the golden Sun—God of Day— and lovingly greets him. Now beautiful flowers bloom around her and the Sun draws her spirit to him upward into the glorious heavens of light. The opera ends with the exultant chorus of the Sun. *"I am I. I am Life."*

* * *

JEWELS OF THE MADONNA

TRAGIC OPERA IN THREE ACTS
MUSIC BY ERMANNO WOLF-FERRARI
LIBRETTO BY ZANGARINI AND GOLISCIANI
FIRST PRODUCTION—BERLIN, 1911

Jewels of the Madonna

CAST

GENNARO, a blacksmith............*Tenor*

CARMELA, his mother......*Mezzo-Soprano*

MALIELLA ....*Soprano*

RAFAELE, leader of the Camorra..*Baritone*

BIASO, a scribe..............*Buffo-Tenor*

CICCILLO, a Camorrist............*Tenor*

ROCCO, a Camorrist................*Basso*

STELLA, SERENA AND CONCETTA,
   friends of Camorrists...........*Sopranos*

GRAZIA, a dancer.........*(Dancing Part)*

TOTONNO, a peasant..............*Tenor*

PLACE—Naples.

TIME—Present

ACT 1

Square in Naples near the Sea. It is the festival day of the Madonna, and the street is filled with merrymakers. Gennaro, the blacksmith, appears when the rest are gone. *Gennaro: "Madonna, tears and sighing."* He prays from relief for his love for Maliella, a lovely girl who has been reared by his mother, Carmella. Maliella comes on the scene. She is rebellious and defiant, hating her life of quietude. She sings the Canzone di Cannetella: *"Thus sang poor Cannetella."* Chorus of distant Camorrists: *"Soft and low the waters sing."* In merriment Maliella runs off when the others appear. To his mother Gennaro confesses his passion. The mother tells him that when young he lay near death. She promised the Madonna that if she would save him she, Carmela, would adopt a daughter born of a sin. She chose Maliella whom she now wants to marry off so as to prevent her son from loving her. Maliella returns, followed by Rafaele and his band of Camorrists. The girl and Rafaele have a mock duel in which the latter is stabbed in the hand. He makes passionate love to the wilful girl. The procession of the Madonna passes and all for the moment think only of the beautiful statue borne through the square. Rafaele renews his love-making. *"Must I kneel?"* Gennaro warns Maliella against Rafaele but she loves him and does not care.

ACT 2

Garden of Carmela's House. Maliella longs for life. *"I long for mirth and folly."* She packs her clothes and prepares to leave. But Gennaro, beside himself, blocks her path. In response to his urging, she declares that she will love him if he will dare all for her—dare to steal the sacred jewels of the Madonna. Ignorant and religious, he shudders in terror. But as Maliella goes back to her room, the temptation seizes on Gennaro. He secures his skeleton keys while a distant chorus is heard: *"How hard and bitter."* Rafaele comes serenading. *"Yield and surrender, lovely defender."* Through the locked gate he reaches for Maliella. She declares she is his and tomorrow will come to him. *Maliella: "I love you, yours now and forever."* When he has departed Gennaro comes—he has stolen the jewels! In a burst of religious and physical passion Maliella places the sacred jewels on her own person, and thus arrayed, gives herself to Gennaro.

ACT 3

Den of the Camorrists. Here men and maidens make merry. Rafaele arrives. *Chorus: "Welcome, most gallant of lovers."* The women tempt him but he thinks only of Maliella. *"Like a rosebud is Maliella."* Women and men now dance in wild abandon. In the darkness Maliella comes. Gennaro is following her. She confesses to Rafaele that Gennaro possessed her. When Gennaro comes Rafaele is restrained from killing him. Gennaro tells how Maliella forced him to steal the jewels of the Madonna. The men and girls are in terror. As they slink away Gennaro is left alone with his sin. Before a statue of the Madonna he plunges a knife into his breast. *"Beloved mother mine."* He dies just as the first beam of dawn comes through the window.

* * *

THE JEWESS

OPERA IN FIVE ACTS

MUSIC BY JACQUES FRANCOIS HALEVY

LIBRETTO BY SCRIBE

FIRST PRODUCTION—PARIS, 1835

CAST

LEOPOLD, young Prince............*Tenor*
EUDOXIA, his fiancee and niece of
the King......................*Soprano*
ELEAZAR, a Jewish goldsmith......*Tenor*
RACHEL, his daughter............*Soprano*
KING OF GERMANY........(*Silent Part*)
CARDINAL BROGNY, president of
the Council......................*Basso*
RUGIERRO, chief bailiff.........*Baritone*

PLACE—Constance.
TIME—1414

Cardinal Brogny lived in Rome and there was very active in the persecution of the Jews. That was before he entered the church. In the capture of Rome by Napoleon his palace was burned and his wife and baby daughter thought to have perished. But the child was rescued by a Jew named Eleazar, who is now a prosperous jeweler in Constance.

The Jewess

ACT 1

Before the Cathedral. There is a general holiday to celebrate the victories of Prince Leopold. The Jew, Eleazar is arrested because he refuses to quit work and celebrate. Cardinal Brogny, coming out of the cathedral, recognizes him as a Jew from Rome. The Jew in turn recognizes the Cardinal for the latter had his sons put to death. Eleazar curses the Cardinal, but the latter frees him from arrest. *Chorus: "When hate and vengeance."* Prince Leopold, when the street is quiet, appears in simple attire. He loves Rachel, the supposed daughter of Eleazar, and he disguises himself as a young Jew, Samuel. He tells of his love for the girl. *"Far from thee, loved one."* The festival begins and there is dancing and singing throughout the square. Eleazar and Rachel mount the steps of the cathedral to get a better view of the throng. Seeing them the people rush at them, but Prince Leopold saves them from violence. The imperial procession goes by.

ACT 2

In Eleazar's House. Eleazar, Rachel and Leopold sit at the table. *Prayer: "Visit us, O God of our fathers."* Of a sudden the Princess Eudoxia arrives to buy some jewels.

She is the betrothed of Prince Leopold and knows nothing of his infatuation for the Jewish girl. Leopold successfully conceals himself from the Princess who buys a beautiful present that she intends to give him. But Rachel sees that something is wrong and is troubled. Leopold says he will return later and tell her everything. *Rachel: "How my heart beats."* When Eleazar retires he comes back to confess. *Leopold and Rachel: "When my heart I gave to thee."* He tells the girl he is a Christian, but still she is ready to flee with him. Eleazar suddenly comes in. *Trio: "Where do you go?"* When Eleazar finds Leopold is not a Jew he attempts to kill him. Unsuccessful, he finally relents. Leopold, however, knows that the King will never consent to such a union. Rachel is overwhelmed with grief.

ACT 3

Banquet Hall in the Palace. The dancers are performing before the King and his guests. Among the onlookers are Eleazar and Rachel. The Princess Eudoxia declares her willingness to marry Prince Leopold. The Jewish girl recognizes in the Prince her lover Samuel. Infuriated, she steps forward and denounces him. This creates a sensation. Eleazar demands that the nobles pass judgment on Leopold. Cardinal Brogny does sentence the Prince to death and with him Eleazar and Rachel.

ACT 4

Court of Justice. Eudoxia has Rachel brought in and begs her to save Leopold's life by retracting her charges against him. *Duet: "You alone can save him."* The Jewess magnanimously consents. Eleazar refuses to turn Christian to save himself. Determining revenge, he tells the Cardinal that he knows what became of the lost child. But he will not tell the prelate until after Rachel's execution. Though she is the daughter of a Cardinal, he loves Rachel as his own child and does not know whether to allow her to be sacrificed. *Aria: "God directs my acts."*

ACT 5

A Street. The people are assembled for the execution. Leopold's sentence is commuted to banishment. But Eleazar and Rachel will be thrown into boiling oil unless they turn Christians. The girl refuses to turn Christian and she is hurled into the cauldron. As she disappears the Jew cries to the Cardinal, "Behold your child!" His vengeance is complete.

LE JONGLEUR DE NOTRE DAME

MIRACLE PLAY IN THREE ACTS BY MASSENET

TEXT BY LENA

FIRST PRODUCTION—PARIS, 1903

CAST

JEAN, a juggler.....................*Tenor*
BONIFACE, the cook.............*Baritone*
THE PRIOR.......................*Basso*
THE POET........................*Tenor*
THE PAINTER.....⎱Monks⎰.....*Baritone*
THE MUSICIAN....⎰   ⎱.....*Baritone*
THE SCULPTOR....................*Basso*
TWO ANGELS..*Soprano and Mezzo-Soprano*

APPARITION OF THE VIRGIN

MONKS, CAVALIERS, TOWNSPEOPLE, ANGEL
VOICES

PLACE—Cluny.

TIME—Fourteenth Century.

ACT 1

Market place. The first of May, Market Day. *Chorus: "Let us dance."* Jean, a young juggler, wandering hungry and miserable, tries to gain the attention of the people, but they deride his performance. *Jean: "Give place to the king of jugglers."* *Chorus: "Gentle king, choose thy queen."* When.

[141]

however, he sings a ribald song (*Jean: "Alle-
luia to wine"*) they applaud him. Jean, who
is a good Christian, turns to the image of
Our Lady and asks pardon of her for singing
an evil song. In the midst of his song the
Prior appears. *Prior: "Hence, infamous
band."* Jean, who is about to be excommuni-
cated for his blasphemy, asks forgiveness.
Prior: "He weeps, he shall be pardoned."
The Prior tells him that to obtain pardon he
must give up his freedom and enter their
brotherhood. This he feels it is very hard
to do, but hunger overcomes him, and, being
tempted by the rich food of the abbey, re-
linquishes his freedom. *Jean: "O Liberty, it
is Thou!"* *Boniface: "For the Blessed Virgin."*

ACT 2

Study at the abbey, where the monks are
at work. It is the morning of the Assump-
tion, and they are chanting praises of the
Virgin (*Chorus: "Ave rosa, speciosa"*), but
Jean does not take part, for, although he
loves the Queen of Heaven, he does not
understand Latin. The monks tell Jean of
their talents—the songs in praise of the Virgin, the statues—but he has nothing to show.
Jean: "Each one in this holy house." They
leave him with Brother Boniface, the cook,

Le Jongleur de Notre Dame

who consoles him (*"Ah, envy them not"*; *"The Virgin with the Infant Jesus"*), telling him the story of how Mary sought to hide Jesus from Herod, and the sage brush opened her leaf, wherein the child was placed, although the rose refused, pointing out to Jean that every humble trade is acceptable to the Virgin. This comforts him and he resolves to serve the Virgin in his own way. *Jean: "O Virgin, Mother of Love."*

ACT 3

Chapel of the abbey. Jean appears in his juggler's costume and slowly approaches the image of the Virgin, deciding to sincerely offer to her the only gift he possesses—his singing and dancing. In his excitement he does not notice the entrance of the monks (*Chorus of monks: "Ave Celeste Lilium"*), but continues dancing and singing (*"Adorable Mother of Jesus"*). The Prior is about to stop him when a miracle takes place. The image raises its hands, placing them in benediction over the head of Jean. *Angel chorus: "Hosanna!"* The monks acclaim him a saint and sing (*"Sancta Maria, ora pro nobis"*), and Jean is in ecstasy because he understands Latin. *"At last I understand Latin."* Overcome with joy, he sinks to the ground and dies. *Jean: "Radiant vision."*

KOENIGSKINDER (KINGLY CHILDREN)

OPERA IN THREE ACTS
MUSIC BY ENGELBERT HUMPERDINCK
LIBRETTO BY ERNST HOSMER FROM A
FAIRY TALE BY ELSA BERNSTEIN
FIRST PRODUCTION—NEW YORK, 1910

CAST

THE KING'S SON..................*Tenor*
THE GOOSE GIRL.............*Soprano*
THE WITCH....................*Contralto*
THE FIDDLER....................*Baritone*
THE WOODCUTTER..............*Basso*
THE BROOM-MAKER..............*Tenor*
THE INNKEEPER.................,....*Basso*
INNKEEPER'S DAUGHTER *Mezzo-Soprano*
THE COUNCILLOR..............*Baritone*
A STABLE-MAID................*Contralto*
A CHILD........................*Soprano*

PLACE—In the Mountains of Germany
TIME—Middle Ages

ACT 1

Witch's Hut in the Mountains. Here the old Witch keeps the lovely Goose Girl a prisoner. She makes her work at scouring, kneading the magic bread that will some days poison the eater, and tending her flock of geese. She tells her nothing of her origin

[144]

Koenigskinder (Kingly Children)

or the world. *"Were but your wits."* As the girl minds her geese she is surprised by the appearance of the King's Son—the only man she has ever seen. Weary of the rounds at court, he seeks romance and freedom in the mountains. The young man is deeply impressed by the maiden's innocence and charm. *"Are you as lovely as you seem?"* He tells her that he is a King's son and declares that he loves her. She returns his affection and they are locked in each other's arms. But the girl's wreath of flowers is blown off and is broken. The King's Son offers her his golden crown instead, but she does not wish it. He urges her to go with him. She assents but her feet, by magic power, are held to the ground. The King's Son, thinking that she is untrue and fickle, rebukes her in anger and sorrow. *King's Son: "Kings are not for such as thou."* Now come the Fiddler, the Woodcutter and the Broom-maker from Hellabrun to consult the Witch. The King has died and they wish to know who will succeed him. The Witch tells them that the person who first enters the city gates next day at noon should rule. The Fiddler now recognizes in the Goose Girl a maiden of really royal descent. The girl places the golden crown on her head, the crown that the King's Son discarded. *"Father, mother,*

Koenigskinder (Kingly Children)

here will I bow." A shooting star falls into a lily, freeing her from the Witch's power.

ACT 2

Gates of Hellabrun. All are awaiting the appearance of the new ruler. In the throng is the King's Son, in rags and unrecognized. The Inn-keeper's daughter loves him but he rejects her. A little child sees in him a king and becomes his friend. The Councillors hear the story of the pilgrims' visit to the Witch. When the hour of twelve strikes there enters the gates a Goose Girl, surrounded by her geese. The King's Son recognizes his queenly bride and acclaims her with joy. But the people mock him and the Goose Girl. Only the old Fiddler recognizes the Kingly Children, who are driven outside the gates by the derisive populace.

ACT 3

Witch's Hut. It is winter. The Witch has been burned by the people because of their disappointment. Here lives the old Fiddler. To him comes the child who made friends with the King's Son and also other children searching for the kingly ones. *Children: "We're certain they must have been."* The Fiddler goes with them to find the lovers. *"O, whither shall we wander."* The King's

Koenigskinder (Kingly Children)

Son and the Goose Girl now appear cold and utterly fatigued. But the Woodcutter, in the hut, refuses them food. In despair the King's Son barters the golden crown for bread. The Kingly Children then eat—the poisoned bread that the Witch and the Goose Girl herself kneaded. They die together in the snow. *"Let us rest."* Here the Fiddler and the children find them wrapped in each other's arms. *Fiddler, "O, children." Chorus: "Kingly children, kingly children."*

* * *

LAKME

OPERA IN THREE ACTS BY DELIBES
TEXT BY GOUDINET AND GILLE
FIRST PRODUCTION—PARIS, APRIL, 1883

CAST

FREDERICK....Officers of the....*Baritone*
GERALD...British Army in India...*Tenor*
NILAKANTHA, a Brahman priest....*Basso*
LAKME, his daughter...........*Soprano*
MALLIKA, her slave........*Mezzo-Soprano*
HADJI, a Hindoo slave.............*Tenor*
ELLEN......The Governor's......*Soprano*
ROSE ....Daughters.........*Soprano*
MRS. BENSON, their govern-
ess ....*Mezzo-Soprano*

SCENE—India.
TIME—Present

Lakme

ACT 1

Sacred Garden in India. *Hindoo Chorus: "May our prayers ascend."* Lakme and Mallika go into the jungle to gather flowers. *Duet: " 'Neath the dome."* During her absence Gerald and Frederick, accompanied by Ellen, Rose and Mrs. Benson, enter, and are charmed with the garden. *Quintet: "If a maiden's young and charming."* They soon depart. Gerald, however, remains to sketch, in spite of the warnings of his friends. *Gerald: "Idle Fancies."* Lakme returns in a boat, having come by the river (*Lakme: "Why love I thus to stray?"*) and encounters Gerald (*Lakme: "Whence come you?"*) and they fall in love with one another. Gerald departs, just as Nilakantha enters, swearing vengeance upon the intruder. A thunderstorm prevents Nilakantha following Gerald, but he declares to kill this foreigner.

ACT 2

Market place in nearby city. Nilakantha is here with his daughter, both disguised as beggars. He hopes in this way to attract the attention of the Englishman. *Chorus: "Come, old, young, large and small."* Nilakantha orders his daughter to sing (*Lakme: "Where goes the maiden straying"*), accompanied by bells. This is sometimes called the *Bell Song.*

[148]

Gerald, who is in the crowd, recognizes her voice (*Gerald:* "*Lakme, I see but thee*"), and in coming up to her is stabbed by her father. He is believed dead, but Lakme has her servant carry him away.

ACT 3

A hut in the forest. Here Gerald has been nursed back to health by Lakme. *Lakme:* "*'Neath the starry heavens.*" Lakme, fearing that his love may not be constant, goes forth for magic water, which, according to a Hindoo superstition, will render the drinker eternally constant in love. During her absence, his friend Frederick finds him and urges him to return to his duty. *Gerald:* "*Lakme, ah come.*" She returns, and, finding that he desires to go back, poisons herself with the juice of a flower and dies in his arms. *Lakme:* "*Love, thou hast given me beauteous dreams.*"

* * *

LINDA DE CHAMOUNI

OPERA IN THREE ACTS
MUSIC BY GAETANA DONIZETTI
LIBRETTO BY ROSSI
FIRST PRODUCTION—VIENNA, 1842

CAST

ANTONIO, a Farmer................*Basso*
MADALINA, His Wife......*Mezzo-Soprano*

Linda de Chamouni

LINDA, Their Daughter..........*Soprano*
CARLO, a Painter.................*Tenor*
MARCHIONESS DE SERVAL, Mother
   of Carlo..................*Mezzo-Soprano*
THE MARQUIS.................*Baritone*
PIEROTTO, a Poor Savoyard........*Alto*
THE PARISH PRIEST.............*Basso*
PLACE—Chamouni and Paris
TIME—1760

ACT 1

Antonio's farm at Chamouni. The old farmer and his wife have been overtaken by misfortune. The Marchioness de Serval, who owns their farm, threatens to evict them. Antonio and Madalina. *"We were both in this valley nurtured."* Their daughter, Linda, a lovely girl, has met and fallen in love with Carlo, a young painter from Paris, who has come into the valley to sketch. She also has as an admirer, the Marquis of Boisfleury. The latter offers to help the aged couple out of their difficulty, thinking thereby to take possession of the beautiful Linda. But the prefect of the village suspects the designs of the Marquis and advises the old couple to send Linda to Paris where she will be under the care of his aged brother. Linda sets out to Paris under protection of the faithful Pierotto. Linda: *"O, stars that guide my fervent love."*

[150]

ACT 2

Linda gets separated from Pierotto and reaches Paris alone. She finds that the prefect's brother is dead. But Carlo, the painter, has followed her. He reveals himself as the Viscount Serval, son of the Marchioness, who wanted to evict her parents from their farm. Carlo wants to marry her. Duet: *"O, Linda, at thy happy fate."* Meanwhile he installs her in luxuriant apartments. Here the faithful Pierotto finds her. Here also her father, now a beggar, finds her and she gives him money. But thinking that she is an abandoned woman, living off the bounty of some rich lover, he hurls her gold at her and bitterly denounces her. The Marchioness finds her son Carlo about to marry Linda. She declares that the wedding shall never take place and that if Carlo does not wed the girl she has chosen for him, Linda will be thrust into prison. Carlo pretends to grant his mother's wish, in order that he may carry through his plan to marry Linda. Linda: *"Ah, go, my love."* Linda, thinking that Carlo has deserted her, becomes insane from grief and disappointment.

In the last act Pierotto has taken Linda back to her native village again. Carlo finds her here. *"If from heaven the bolts should reach me."* Linda does not remember him.

But Carlo sings to her an old familiar love song, hoping that this may partly restore her reason. *"Hear the voice that softly singing."* His hope is realized, for the song completely restores Linda to her right mind. The lovers are overjoyed. Carlo's mother now favors the wedding with Linda, the farm is restored to the girl's parents, and all ends happily.

* * *

LOHENGRIN

ROMANTIC OPERA IN THREE ACTS
TEXT AND MUSIC BY RICHARD WAGNER
FIRST PRODUCTION—WEIMAR, 1850

CAST

HENRY I, King of Germany..........*Basso*
LOHENGRIN ....*Tenor*
ELSA OF BRABANT.............*Soprano*
FRIEDERICH TELRAMUND, Count
   of Brabant.....................*Baritone*
ORTRUD, his wife..........*Mezzo-Soprano*

TIME—Tenth Century.
Scene on the Scheld

ACT 1

King Henry has arrived at Brabant to assemble the tribes against the invading Hungarians, but finds it in a state of anarchy.

Gottfried, the son of the late Duke, has
disappeared, and Telramund—who has been
acting as regent for Gottfried (he being a
minor), incited by his wife, Ortrud—claims
the dukedom, accusing Elsa of having murdered her brother. The King sends for Elsa,
who denies the charge and declares that she
is willing to submit to the judgment of God
and the ordeal of combat. She chooses as her
defender a Knight she has seen in her dreams.
"Elsa's Dream." Not until the second call of
the herald has gone out and Elsa has fallen
to her knees in prayer does the Knight appear in a boat drawn by a swan. He steps
out (*"Thanks, my trusty swan"*) and announces that he has come to defend Elsa,
but asks her not to question him as to who
he is or where he has come from. He overcomes Telramund, but grants him his life,
and asks Elsa's hand in marriage. She consents, and all rejoice except Ortrud and Telramund, who have been banished.

ACT 2

The Courtyard and Cathedral. The night
before Elsa's wedding. Ortrud and Telramund appear in ragged garments. Telramund is overwhelmed by his misfortunes, but
Ortrud urges him to make another trial to
regain what he has lost. Ortrud now calls

to Elsa, who has just come out on the balcony of the Palace, and, feigning repentance, is forgiven by Elsa, who promises to obtain pardon for Telramund. *Elsa: Thou unhappy one."* Ortrud now schemes to make Elsa ask her betrothed the forbidden questions. Day breaks and the herald announces that the King has made the stranger Duke of Brabant. When all is ready for the ceremony and Elsa and her attendants are about to enter the church, Ortrud, magnificently dressed, steps forth and accuses the Knight of being a magician, and Telramund declares he has gained his victory unfairly. The Knight refuses to reveal his identity. Elsa declares her confidence in him and they enter the church.

ACT 3

The Bridal Chamber in the Palace. The *Wedding March* is played. The bridal party enter, singing the *Bridal Chorus*. The guests depart, leaving the couple alone. Elsa, unable to forget Ortrud's taunts, and despite her promise and her husband's warnings, asks the forbidden questions. Before he has time to reply, Telramund, heading a band of conspirators, rushes into the room to attack the Knight, who easily defeats them all, killing Telramund. Turning sorrowfully to Elsa, he tells her that he will now explain all to the King.

SCENE *2*

Banks of the Scheld. The King and court are gathered waiting for the new Knight, who is to accompany them to battle. He now appears with the nobles who bear Telramund's body, and explains that he is Lohengrin, son of Parsifal, and Knight of the Holy Grail, whose Knights are only permitted to be absent on good deeds as long as they remain unknown, and, having been questioned by Elsa, must now return. The swan reappears, and Lohengrin bids Elsa farewell. *"Lohengrin's Farewell."* Ortrud now declares that the swan is Elsa's brother whom she (Ortrud) has transformed by magic. Lohengrin overhears this and kneels in prayer. A dove descends from Heaven, and the swan dives into the water, reappearing as Gottfried. As Lohengrin is led back to the castle of the Holy Grail by the dove, Elsa dies in her brother's arms.

LOUISE

ROMANTIC OPERA IN FOUR ACTS
MUSIC BY GUSTAVE CHARPENTIER
LIBRETTO ALSO BY CHARPENTIER
FIRST PRODUCTION—PARIS, 1900

CAST

LOUISE .... *Soprano*
THE FATHER.................... *Baritone*
THE MOTHER................. *Contralto*
JULIEN, an artist................. *Tenor*
IRMA, sewing girl............... *Contralto*
THE KING OF THE FOOLS...... *Baritone*
ERRAND GIRL............. *Mezzo-Soprano*
FOREWOMAN .... *Contralto*

PLACE—Paris.
TIME—Present.

ACT 1

Top Room in Paris Tenement. Louise, hurrying through her work, runs to the window to see Julien the artist, who has a studio across the alley. It is spring and the girl's heart is filled with romance. Julien sings of his passion, *"O, loving heart."* The Mother, who despises Julien for his shiftlessness, catches the two love-making from window to window and sets the girl to her tasks. The Father comes in to inquire if the evening meal is ready. Julien has written him a note that he hopes will win his daughter. While supper is being set, Louise's Father talks to her about Julien. He is mild-tempered and sensible on the subject. But the girl's mother declares the artist is not the right sort. Mother and daughter quarrel. Then the father, in a kindly way, reasons with the girl. She promises to try to forget the artist.

ACT 2

A Street in the Montmartre District. It is early morning and strange characters, peculiar to Paris, appear—rag-pickers, scavangers, and the like. Julien and some of his friends come to await Louise who works in a dressmaker's shop nearby. *Bohemian song: "Bohemia's sons are we."* When the girl arrives the artist tries to persuade her to elope with him. She refuses and goes into the shop. The next scene is the inside of the shop. The girls are all working hard and singing. *Chorus: "La, la, la, la."* They chide Louise with being in love. Irma sings, *"A voice of mystery breathing of joy."* Outside Julien's voice is heard. *Julien: "In the city afar."* The girls applaud, but when the singing continues they make fun of Julien. Meanwhile Louise pretends sickness and goes out. She joins Julien in the street and they go off together.

ACT 3

Cottage and Garden on the top of Montmartre. Here Julien and Louise find happiness in love. Below them the great, wonderful city begins to glow in light. The two are enraptured at the sight. *Duet: "Paris, Paris, city of light."* Fireworks light the sky. *Duet: "A woman with heart aflame."* The lovers embrace and retire into the house. As they disappear the Bohemians come with lanterns and streamers to decorate the house. Louise is to be crowned Queen of Montmartre. Girls rush on dancing the *farandole. Chorus: "O joyous day, O day of love."* The King of the Fools appears and the ceremony is ready to begin. Julien and Louise come out and form the center of the throng. With a triumphant chorus, *"Amorous love,"* the maidens crown Louise. In the midst of the gayety Louise's mother appears and the revelers withdraw. She says that since Louise has been gone the Father is ill and now he is about to die. The Mother begs Julien to release her. He does so on condition that she return to him.

ACT 4

Home of Louise. The girl is back with her parents and discovers that she has been trapped into coming home and is held a prisoner. She is sullen and rebellious by turns. The Father tries to reason with her but the lure of Paris and Julien is too strong. She longs to be free. Her passion increases and she tries to depart. But her father stops her. She begins calling for Julien, and the Father, now losing all patience, orders her out of the house. With a scream she runs down the stairs and out into the street. The poor old Father goes to the window and calls, but Louise has gone forever. Paris has claimed another victim.

* * *

LUCIA DI LAMMERMOOR

OPERA IN THREE ACTS BY DONIZETTI
TEXT FROM SCOTT'S "THE BRIDE OF LAMMER-MOOR" BY CAMMERANO

FIRST PRODUCTION—NAPLES, 1835

CAST

LORD HENRY ASHTON.........*Baritone*
LUCIA DI LAMMERMOOR, his sis-ter ....*Soprano*
EDGAR OF RAVENSWOOD, her lover ....*Tenor*
LORD ARTHUR BUCKLAW.......*Tenor*
RAYMOND ....*Basso*
GILBERT ....:..........*Tenor*
ALICE, Lucia's confidante.........*Soprano*
NORMAN, Captain of the guard....*Tenor*

Lucia di Lammermoor

PLACE—Scotland.
TIME—1700.

ACT 1

Grove near Ashton's Castle of Lammermoor. Lord Henry Ashton is very anxious that his sister Lucia marry Lord Arthur Bucklaw, who is wealthy, and has urged her to do so, hoping in this way to avert financial ruin, but she persists in refusing him. He now learns from Norman that she is in love with his most hated enemy, Edgar of Ravenswood, which makes him furious.

SCENE 2

A park near the Castle. Lucia, accompanied by Alice, awaits Edgar. *Aria, Lucia: "In this grove."* Edgar comes with the news that he has been summoned to France, and begs her to let him ask her brother for her hand. *Duet: "Forgive, Lucia, that I in this hour."* Lucia, fearing her brother's hatred, pleads with Edgar not to go to him. They part, promising eternal fidelity.

ACT 2

Lucia's Apartments. Preparations for Lucia's wedding to Lord Arthur are being made, Henry hoping eventually to gain her consent. Through Norman, he has been intercepting Edgar's letters to her, and produces a forged letter to prove that Edgar is untrue to her. *Duet: "Dear sister, come hither."* He now tells her that he has been in a plot against the King, and that the plot has been revealed, urging her to marry Lord Arthur to save him. *Lucia: "Oh, Heaven, they me persuade."* Believing her lover untrue, she consents to the marriage in order to help her brother, and prepares for the ceremony.

SCENE 2

The Hall of the Castle. Just as Lucia has signed the marriage contract, Edgar rushes in, demanding that the ceremony cease. Astonishment at his coming is expressed in the *Sextette: "What restrains me."* When shown the contract signed by Lucia, he believes her false, and after fiercely upbraiding her, departs, cursing her and her family. Ashton rushes after him, and a quarrel ensues, which ends in a challenge for a duel to be fought the following morning.

ACT 3

Hall in Lammermoor Castle. The bride and bridegroom have retired to their rooms, but the merrymaking continues despite the interposition of Edgar. Suddenly word comes that Lucia has gone mad and killed her husband. *Aria: "Oh, dire misfortune."* Lucia now appears, raving, among the guests. The *Mad Scene* follows, in which she sings first of her joy and her lover and then of her miserable marriage. At the conclusion of the song she falls back dying.

SCENE 2

Churchyard. Here Edgar awaits Henry for the fighting of the duel. *Aria: "Graves of my ancestors."* He hears the Castle bell toll, and when informed that it is for Lucia *("Thou hast spread thy wings to Heaven")*, he kills himself.

* * *

MADAME BUTTERFLY

OPERA IN THREE ACTS BY GIACOMO PUCCINI
ADAPTED FROM
JOHN LUTHER LONG'S "MADAME BUTTERFLY"
FIRST PRODUCTION—MILAN, FEB. 17, 1904

CAST

CHO CHO SAN (Madame Butter-
fly) ....*Soprano*
SUZUKI, her servant........*Mezzo-Soprano*
KATE PINKERTON........*Mezzo-Soprano*
LIEUT. PINKERTON, U. S. N.....*Tenor*
U. S. CONSUL SHARPLESS........*Tenor*
GORO, a marriage broker...........*Tenor*
PRINCE YAMADORI.............*Baritone*

[162]

Madame Butterfly

SCENE—Nagasaki, Japan.
TIME—The Present

ACT 1

Lieutenant Pinkerton, finding that he will be stationed in Nagasaki for a few months, desires to contract a marriage and is assured by Goro that it will only be binding as long as he lives with his wife, and that afterwards she can marry again, which is in accordance with the Japanese custom. However, Butterfly, who has agreed to marry the Lieutenant, falls deeply in love with him and believes the contract entirely binding. The American Consul Sharpless, realizing the girl's attitude, begs Pinkerton to forego the plan, but he only laughs at him. To show her trust in Pinkerton, Butterfly renounces her religion, thus severing all connections with her people. *"Hear what I tell you."* After the ceremony Butterfly's uncle, a priest, enters and curses her for forsaking her religion. Pinkerton drives him and the guests away and then attempts to comfort his weeping bride. *Duet, Pinkerton and Butterfly: "Just like a little squirrel." "But now, beloved, you are the world." "O night of rapture!"*

Madame Butterfly

ACT 2

The villa. Three years later. Butterfly is alone with her maid, Pinkerton having returned to America. It is springtime once more, and she awaits him, as he has promised to return when "the robins nest again." Butterfly upbraids her maid for want of faith, as Suzuki does not share her mistress' confidence in Pinkerton. *Butterfly: "Weeping? and why?"* Consul Sharpless appears with a letter in which Pinkerton asks the Consul to break the news of his return with an American wife to Butterfly, but in her great delight at seeing his handwriting and her faith that he will now return, the Consul has not the heart to tell her the truth. She refuses to listen to Goro, who is trying to arrange a marriage with Yamadori, a wealthy noble, even though both Goro and Sharpless try to convince her that Pinkerton's desertion is equal to a divorce, to which she replies: "That may be so in Japan, but I am an American." Finally, as if to settle all doubt, she shows her fair-haired son. The Consul, saddened, leaves as the cannons announce the arrival of the ship. Butterfly and Suzuki decorate the house with blossoms in Pinkerton's honor, and Butterfly awaits his arrival. As the night progresses the child and maid fall asleep, but Butterfly, ever alert, is still waiting.

SCENE 2

At dawn Butterfly is still watching. Suzuki brings the child to her (*Butterfly: "Sweet, thou art sleeping"*) and then persuades Butterfly to rest. Pinkerton and his wife and Sharpless arrive and inform Suzuki of the truth. Pinkerton is overcome at the sight of the flowers and cannot remain. *Pinkerton: "Oh, the bitter fragrance of these flowers!"* Mrs. Pinkerton asks to adopt her husband's son, and Butterfly, expecting Pinkerton, enters while she is speaking. The truth dawns on poor Butterfly, and with wonderful calmness she listens quietly to the request, and replies that Pinkerton shall have the child if he will return for him in half an hour. When they have gone, Butterfly blindfolds her son, giving him an American flag to wave, and then kills herself with her father's sword, which is inscribed: "To die with honor, when one can no longer live with honor." When Pinkerton and Sharpless return she has breathed her last. *Finale, Butterfly: "You, O beloved idol!"*

* * *

THE MAGIC FLUTE

FANTASTIC OPERA IN FOUR ACTS
MUSIC BY WOLFGANG AMADEUS MOZART
LIBRETTO BY SCHICKANEDER
FIRST PRODUCTION—VIENNA, 1791

The Magic Flute

CAST

SARASTRO, Priest of Isis............*Basso*
QUEEN OF NIGHT, a sorceress....*Soprano*
PAMINA, her daughter............*Soprano*
TAMINO, a Prince.................*Tenor*
PAPAGENO, his attendant..........*Basso*
PAPAGENA, Papageno's sweetheart..*Soprano*
MONASTATOS, a Moor............*Tenor*

PLACE—Egypt.
TIME—Ancient Days.

ACT 1

A Wood. Tamino, the Prince, is lost, and is pursued by a huge serpent. As he swoons from fatigue three attendants of the Queen of Night slay the serpent. Each loves the Prince and plans to win him. Recovering, the Prince sees his attendant, Papageno, dressed as a bird. He says it is the way to catch birds. *Aria:* "*I am the bird catcher.*" He also boasts that it was he who killed the serpent. But the Queen's attendants punish him by placing a lock on his lips. The Queen of Night appears to the Prince and urges him to free her daughter who has fallen under the influence of Sarastro, Priest of Isis. Having looked on the picture of the beautiful girl the Prince is willing. *Aria:* "*This is wondrously beautiful.*" The Queen's attendants give the Prince

[166]

a magic flute, remove the lock from Papageno and present him with chimes. The magic instruments are to aid them in all distress.

ACT 2

Room in Sarastro's Palace. The Moor Monastatos has dragged the beautiful Pamina into the apartment. But the timely arrival of Papageno in his outlandish garb saves the maiden and frightens off the Moor. Papageno says that the Prince is coming to rescue the girl. *Duet: "Men feel who love."* The next scene is a grove and the entrance to the temple. The Prince, denied admission at two doors, tries the third. He is met by a priest who informs him what a noble character Sarastro is. *"Whither goest thou, rash stranger?"* Pamina is really being protected in the temple from the sorceries of her mother. But Papageno and Pamina are about to escape when they are caught by the Moor. *The Moor: "I have caught you."* Sarastro appears. *Chorus: "Long live Sarastro."* Pamina humbly tells him that she tried to escape because the Moor desired to possess her. Sarastro punishes the Moor, and decrees that the Prince and Papageno show their worthiness by passing through the ordeals of the temple.

The Magic Flute

ACT 3

A Palm Grove. The priests consider the case of the two lovers, The Prince who loves Pamina, and Papageno who loves Papagena. They are to undergo the ordeals. *Chorus: "O Isis and Osiris."* A courtyard is the next scene. The first ordeal is that of silence under temptation. The three attendants of the Queen of Night tempt the men. *"You at this place?"* Both the Prince and Papageno resist the temptation. The third scene is a garden. Here Pamina lies sleeping. The Moor rapturously looks at her. *Aria: "All feel the joys of love."* The Queen of Night appears and the Moor hides. She gives Pamina a dagger with which to stab Sarastro. *Queen: "Vengeance is in my heart."* When the Queen goes the Moor appears and tries to use the secret to vanquish the girl. But she is saved by the arrival of Sarastro. *The Priest: "In these holy walls."* Back in the hall of ordeals the Prince and Papageno still suffer silence. The latter finally succumbs to temptation. But the Prince remains silent even when Pamina addresses loving words to him. The girl thinks that his love is cold. *Pamina: "All is lost."*

ACT 4

The Pyramids. Pamina is prevented from committing suicide because of the supposed faithlessness of the Prince. Papageno also desires to end his life, but is told to use his magic chimes. He does so and the beautiful Papagena appears before him. *Duet: "Papageno, Papagena."* The shifting scene brings the chief characters to water and a cavern of fire. The Prince appears with his men in armor. *Aria: "He who wanders."* Pamina here finds her loved one, who may speak to her now. With the help of the magic flute both pass harmlessly through fire and water. The final tableau is at the temple. The Prince and Pamina are united by Sarastro, and Papageno and Papagena are likewise happy. The Queen and the Moor are banished.

* * *

MANON

DRAMATIC OPERA IN FIVE ACTS

MUSIC BY JULES MASSANET

BOOK BY MEILHAC AND GILLE

FIRST PRODUCTION—PARIS, 1884

CAST

CHEVALIER DES GRIEUX.........*Tenor*
COMPTE DES GRIEUX, his father...*Basso*

Manon

LESCAUT, a guardsman...........*Baritone*
MANON, his cousin...............*Soprano*
GILLOT MORFONTAIN, minister
   of finance ....*Basso*
POUSETTE, an actress...........*Soprano*
DE BREITIGNY, a nobleman......*Baritone*
ROSETTE, an actress............*Soprano*
JAVOTTE, an actress...........*Contralto*

PLACE—Paris, Amiens Havre. TIME—1721

ACT 1

Tavern at Amiens. *Chorus: "The clock strikes."* Here the minister of finance, Morfontain, entertains his friends. Manon, a gay young girl, who is in charge of her cousin, Lescaut, is on her way to a convent to which she has been sent. At the tavern the old finance minister plans to abduct her in his carriage. But the young Chevalier des Grieux is also attracted by the girl, though he is about to take holy orders. *Des Grieux: "What is your name?"* Manon is charmed by him and in old Morfontain's carriage they elope to Paris.

ACT 2

Des Grieux's Apartments in Paris. Here the flirtatious Manon lives with Des Grieux, who tries to get his father's consent to the

wedding. Lescaut comes with a rich nobleman, De Breitigny. *Quartet: "Dear, Chevalier they frighten me."* Manon flirts with
the nobleman, who tells her that Des Grieux
will be taken away that very night by his
father. Manon, lured by the nobleman's
riches, decides to give up Des Grieux, who
is poverty-stricken and in debt. *Manon:
"What voice is this?"* Des Grieux that night
goes out in answer to a knock on the door
and is seized and carried away.

ACT 3

A Paris Boulevard. Lescaut is surrounded
by actresses with whom he jests. De Breitigny
appears with Manon whom he has given
every luxury. She is very gay. *Manon: "All
roads lead to a throne." "Shall we not follow
young love?"* She overhears Des Grieux'
father tell De Breitigny that the boy is going
to become a monk because of Manon's infidelity. Manon, the flirt, inquires anxiously
about her former lover. In the next scene
Des Grieux' father comes to the Seminary of
St. Sulpice to persuade his son not to become
a monk. He urges him to wed instead.
"Why not marry?" When he leaves, Des
Grieux ponders sadly about Manon. Soon
she herself appears before him. *Duet:*

"Wicked and cruel was I." He tells her love
is dead but she will not believe this. Finally
he is persuaded to go back to Paris with her

ACT 4

Gambling House in Paris. To satisfy
Manon's demands, Des Grieux has become a
gambler: *Chorus: "Imprudent players."* He
goes into the game and wins big sums. *Des
Grieux: "Manon, wonderful siren."* Manon
is joyful and sings, *"The clink of gold and
soft laughter I love."* The stakes go higher
and the old Morfontain accuses Des Grieux
of cheating. The police enter and Des Grieux
and Manon are arrested. *Manon and Des
Grieux: "O, sorrow."*

ACT 5

Road Near Havre. Lescaut and Des
Grieux determine to rescue Manon, who is
to be deported. Soon soldiers appear escort-
ing unfortunate women among whom is
Manon, utterly worn out. But she greets Des
Grieux joyfully. *"Dear Love of mine."* She
asks pardon for her unfaithfulness, and falls
dying into the arms of her lover.

MANON LESCAUT

OPERA IN FOUR ACTS BY GIACOMO PUCCINI
TEXT FOUNDED ON PREVOST'S NOVEL
FIRST PRODUCTION—MILAN, 1893

CAST

MANON LESCAUT..............*Soprano*
LESCAUT, sergeant of the guards..*Baritone*
CHEVALIER DES GRIEUX.........*Tenor*
GERONTE DE RAVOIR, Treasurer-
General ....*Basso*
EDMOND, a student...............*Tenor*

PLACE—Amiens, Paris, Havre, Louisiana.
TIME—Eighteenth Century.

ACT 1

Street in Front of an Inn at Amiens. Students are making merry and flirting with the girls. Des Grieux is among them. Edmond, his friend, sings, *"Youth is ours."* The girls jest with Des Grieux, who is not attracted by them. Soon a coach arrives and Manon and Lescaut step out. Des Grieux is immediately fascinated by the girl. *"Never did I behold."* The girl, who is going to a convent, promises to meet him later. But Geronte, the Treasurer-General, also fascinated, plans to carry the girl off in his carriage. This news Edmond brings to Des Grieux. When the

[173]

charming Manon comes out of the inn Des
Grieux meets her and they elope in the carriage of Geronte.

ACT 2

An Apartment in Geronte's Home. Manon,
after living with Des Grieux awhile, has deserted him for the wealthy Geronte. Lescaut
congratulates her on her elegant surroundings, but the girl is sad and longs for Des
Grieux. *"In those silken curtains."* Soon
singers arrive, having been sent by Geronte
to amuse Manon. They sing the beautiful
Madrigal, *"Speed o'er the mountains."* After
they have gone the dancing master appears
and Manon dances and sings. *"Joyful hours."*
When left alone, Des Grieux suddenly appears to learn if Manon still loves him.
"Manon, kind and gentle." The lovers again
declare their devotion for each other. But
Geronte surprises them and sends for the
police. Des Grieux begs the girl to flee at
once, but she gathers up her jewelry first.
This delay causes her to be captured. She
is dragged off by the gendarmes. Intermezzo.

ACT 3

Harbor of Havre. Manon is in prison waiting to be deported to America as an undesir-
able woman. Lescaut and Des Grieux try

in vain to rescue her. Manon is put among the other women, who are to be deported also. *Chorus: "How lovely she is."* Des Grieux is almost overcome with grief. The captain of the ship, taking pity on him, says that he may go aboard with Manon. Des Grieux is beside himself with joy. *"Joyous madness seizes me."*

ACT 4

A Plain in Louisiana. Manon and Des Grieux are wandering, overcome with fatigue. *Des Grieux: "Fear not to lean on me."* They do not know where to find rest and food. *Duet: "Most cruel fate."* Des Grieux, alarmed over Manon's weakness, goes to find water. Manon thinks he has deserted her. *Manon: "Alone, forsaken."* When he returns she is dying, and in his arms she passes away.

* * *

MANRU

OPERA IN THREE ACTS

MUSIC BY IGNACE PADEREWSKI

LIBRETTO BY NOSSIG

FIRST PRODUCTION—DRESDEN, 1901

CAST

MANRU, a gypsy..................*Tenor*
ULANA, maiden of Galicia........*Soprano*
HEDWIG, her mother.......*Mezzo-Soprano*

[175]

Manru

ASA, a gypsy girl..................*Soprano*
UROK, a dwarf..................*Baritone*
OROS, gypsy chief..................*Basso*
JAGU, gypsy fiddler..................*Basso*

PLACE—Tatra Mountains, Hungary
TIME—Nineteenth Century.

ACT 1

Village in the Mountains. The maidens are gathered around Hedwig. *Chorus: "From on high darts a hawk."* Hedwig tells the maidens that her daughter Ulana has married a gypsy, Manru, and therefore defied a mother's mandate and disregarded a mother's love. Urok, the dwarf, pleads for Ulana's forgiveness, for he loves the girl dearly. The maidens jest and sport with Urok. Ulana arrives very downcast and tells Urok that she thinks Manru does not love her any more. *Duet: "Alas, alas, what suffering."* When the girl comes to the mother's house she is driven back because she still refuses to leave Manru. Now Urok, thinking to win the girl for himself, tells her that gypsies are always inconstant under the full moon, and that Manru will not remain with her. But Ulana still refuses to give up her husband. *"He alone is my joy."* She knows that Urok is a sorcerer and makes him brew for her a potion that will hold the love of

Manru. The gypsy arrives and carries Ulana
off, followed by the curses of Hedwig.

ACT 2

Manru's Hut. Inside, Ulana croons to her
child. Manru, the gypsy blood beginning to
stir, is restless. *Manru: "She sits within."*
But the mother continues singing. *"Sleep,
precious one."* Manru grows still more restless for the old life. *"Who can be joyous in
such a life?"* Urok comes on the scene and
jokes with Manru. Suddenly gypsy music is
heard—the old fiddler Jagu is coming.
Manru greets him joyously and learns the
news that he can come back to the tribe that
he deserted, and become its chief. Asa, the
tribal queen, loves him and wants him to
return. Ulana begs her husband not to leave
her and Jagu departs without him. But
Manru is in a restless mood and Urok urges
him on by picturing the gypsy scenes he
loves so well. Ulana now gives Manru the
potion that Urok brewed for her. *Duet,
Manru and Ulana: "A torrent through my
veins is coursing."* The potion changes his
feelings and he loves his wife as of old.
Duet: "As the balmy breezes."

ACT 3

A Lake. Manru longs so for gypsy life
that his wife's potions and entreaties no

longer affect him. *Manru: "Air, air."* He
tries to resist the call of the wild and the
struggle fatigues him so that he falls asleep.
The gypsy chorus is heard in the distance.
"Like the restless billows." The gypsies come
upon Manru sleeping and recognize him.
Asa, the queen, wants to take him with them.
But Oros, the chief, is not willing, for Manru
has been a traitor. *Oros and chorus: "No, he
is a traitor to his tribe."* But Asa places her
arms around him and tries to bring him back
to the old life. *Asa and Manru: "No, my
wound you ne'er can heal."* Oros departs in
anger, leaving Asa with Manru. Urok comes
on the scene to remind Manru that he has a
wife. In the distance Ulana is heard calling.
But the blood of the gypsy is stirred now and
he turns back to Asa. Ulana, in her misery,
plunges into the lake. Oros returns and
hurls Manru into the waters after his wife,
while Urok gloats over his fate.

* * *

THE MARRIAGE OF FIGARO

COMIC OPERA IN FOUR ACTS
MUSIC BY WOLFGANG AMADEUS MOZART
BOOK BY LORENZO DA PONTE
FOUNDED ON THE BEAUMARCHAIS COMEDY
FIRST PRODUCTION—VIENNA, 1786

The Marriage of Figaro

CAST

COUNT ALMAVIVA, nobleman of
Seville ....*Baritone*
COUNTESS ROSINA, his wife......*Soprano*
FIGARO, the count's valet...........*Basso*
SUSANNA, his betrothed...........*Soprano*
DOCTOR BARTOLO, a physician....*Basso*
BASILIO, music-master...............*Tenor*
CHERUBINO, a page.............*Soprano*
MARCELLINA, housekeeper:.....*Contralto*
ANTONIO, gardener................*Basso*
BARBARINA, his daughter.........*Soprano*
DON GUZMAN, a judge...........*Tenor*

PLACE—Seville.
TIME—Seventeenth Century

ACT 1

Room in the Count's Palace. Figaro and
Susanna are planning for their wedding and
are discussing the future. *Duet: "Should the
Countess ring for you at night."* Figaro assures her that now the Count, who has been
trying to love other women besides his wife,
will cease annoying her. *Figaro: "Should the
little Count dare."* Marcellina, the housekeeper, now declares that Figaro promised
to marry her, and she engages Dr. Bartolo as
counsel. Bartolo, for revenge, is anxious to
take the case. *Bartolo: "Sweet revenge."*

[179]

The Marriage of Figaro

Susanna and Marcellina have some words
and Cherubino comes in. He loves Barbarina,
to whom the Count has also been paying attention, and he wants Susanna's help. They
are interrupted by the arrival of the Count.
Cherubino slips behind a chair. Another arrival makes it necessary for the Count to hide
behind the chair. Cherubino, still saving
himself, slips into the chair itself and Susanna
throws a dress over him. But both Count
and page are discovered, and the latter is
ordered to depart forthwith.

ACT 2

The Countess' Apartments. The Countess
regrets the way of her husband. *"Love, thou
holy impulse."* She determines to catch him.
Susanna admits Cherubino and he is dressed
in woman's clothes to aid in turning the trick.
Cherubino is glad, for he will still be near
Barbarina. *Cherubino: "What is this feeling?"* The Count suddenly demands entrance.
All is confusion and in the subsequent move-
ments Cherubino is forced to jump out of
the window. The Count is mystified. Another angle is added to the mystery when
the gardener brings in a letter that he found
on his mussed-up flower beds. Figaro, by
a vigorous lot of explaining, still protects
the Countess and fools the Count. But at

this moment Marcellina appears to press her breach-of-promise case, and the Count postpones Figaro's wedding.

ACT 3

Apartment in the Count's Palace. The Count plans to make Susanna accept his attentions by threatening to make Figaro marry Marcellina. *Duet, Count and Susanna: "Too long you have deceived me."* Susanna, pretending to yield, says she will meet him in the garden at night. It is suddenly discovered that Marcellina is Figaro's mother, so there is no possibility of his being forced to wed her. The Countess and Susanna determine to punish the Count and Figaro for their flirtatious ways. Each disguising herself as the other, they will go into the garden to meet the lovers.

ACT 4

The Garden. Here Susanna, awaiting the Count, sings a lovely aria, *"O come, my heart's delight."* Cherubino arrives, and, thinking the Countess is his Barbarina, kisses her. The Count, arriving and mistaking the Countess for Susanna, is furious. There is a general mix-up and a bad case of mistaken identity that seems serious while the love-making is on. But soon Susanna and the

Countess reveal their trap, the Count admits that he has been fooled and the three happy couples go back to celebrate the nuptials of Figaro and Susanna and Cherubino and Barbarina.

*   *   *

MARTHA

OPERA IN FOUR ACTS BY VON FLOTOW
LIBRETTO BY ST. GEORGES AND FRIEDRICH
FIRST PRODUCTION—VIENNA, 1847

CAST

LADY, HARRIET DURHAM, maid of
   honor to the Queen..............*Soprano*
NANCY, her confidante......*Mezzo-Soprano*
LORD TRISTAN, Lady Harriet's
   cousin ....*.....Basso*
PLUNKETT, a wealthy farmer......*Tenor*
LIONEL, his foster brother..........*Basso*
SHERIFF OF RICHMOND...........*Basso*
   Three Maids and Three Servants

SCENE—Richmond, England
TIME—Reign of Queen Anne

ACT 1

Lady Harriet's Boudoir. Lady Harriet is bored by her many admirers and the monotony of court life and seeks a new diversion.

[182]

Duet, Nancy and Harriet: "*Of the knights
so brave and charming.*" Her cousin Tristan,
one of her devoted admirers, is now announced (*Terzett, Nancy, Harriet and Tristan:* "*Dear Lady and Cousin*") , and, hearing
the servants singing on their way to the Fair
("*Well, then, young blood over sticks and
stones*"), she decides to go to the Fair as
one of them. She and Nancy attire themselves as servants, and Tristan, much against
his will, accompanies them, dressed as a
farmer.

SCENE 2

The Fair. Here are two young farmers,
Plunkett and Lionel, looking for servants.
Lionel is Plunkett's foster brother, he having
been adopted by Plunkett's father, knowing
nothing of his parentage. He wears a ring,
however, which he remembers having been
given him by his father, with instructions to
present it to the Queen if ever in trouble.
Lionel: "*Lost Proscribed.*" *Duet, Plunkett
and Lionel:* "*The market begins, the bell
rings.*" The sheriff announces that contracts
for servants shall be binding for a year if
money is advanced. Just after this announcement has been made Tristan and the ladies
arrive, and Lionel and Plunkett immediately
engage them, giving them the advance pay-

ment, which they accept. Without knowing
it, they have legally bound themselves for
the year, and when they object, the sheriff
declares they must go with the farmers, which
they do, leaving Tristan in despair.

ACT 2

Farmhouse. The farmers are showing their
servants, who are known to them as Martha
(Harriet) and Julia (Nancy) their duties
and are astonished that they know so little.
*Lionel, Plunkett, Harriet and Nancy: "Come
nearer, bashful maidens."* They attempt to
teach them to spin. *Quartet: "When the
foot and wheel turns lightly."* Lionel falls
desperately in love with Martha. He steals a
rose which she has been wearing and refuses
to return it unless she sings for him. *Martha:
"The Last Rose of Summer."* He declares his
love, but, although his words do make an
impression upon her, she only laughs at him.
Meanwhile Plunkett has been trying to teach
Nancy the household duties, but she is so
saucy that he gives up the task and enjoys
himself with her remarks, regarding her with
great affection. Plunkett and Lionel now bid
their servants good night. *Quartet: "Midnight sounds."* After the men have retired,
the girls escape with the aid of Tristan, who
has learned their whereabouts.

ACT 3

Hunting Park in Richmond Forest. While drinking at a tavern with some other farmers (*Plunkett: "Porter Song"*), Plunkett is astonished at seeing Julia with a hunting party. The heart-broken Lionel is also there. *Lionel: "Like a dream." Chorus of huntresses and song of Nancy: "Huntress, thou sly one."* Lionel also encounters Lady Harriet, whom he knows only as "Martha." and pleads his love, but she declares him to be insane. Plunkett tries to console him. *Finale: "The mistress takes her rest." "May Heaven forgive you."*

ACT 4

The Farmhouse again. Lionel has given his ring to Plunkett to present to the Queen. and it is recognized by her as having belonged to one of her nobles who had been deprived of his estates for some suspected offense, but whose innocence was afterwards proven. Lionel is declared Earl of Derby, but he pays no heed to this, as his mind has become unbalanced through grief. Harriet is persuaded to visit him—for she truly loves him—but he does not recognize her. *Harriet: "To reconcile the dear one." Duet, Harriet and Lionel: "Spring has come, the roses bloom.*" Nancy and Plunkett come to an understanding and plan to restore Lionel's reason.

SCENE 2

Fair at Richmond. A reproduction of the Richmond Fair is arranged, and the girls dress in the costumes they wore at the Fair, and when Lionel sees them the mist seems to clear away from his mind, and his reason is restored. He and Harriet are then betrothed, as are also Nancy and Plunkett. *Finale: "Spring is here."*

* * *

THE MASKED BALL

OPERA IN THREE ACTS

MUSIC BY VERDI

LIBRETTO BY PIAVE

FIRST PRODUCTION—ROME, 1859

CAST

RICHARD, Count of Warwick, Governor of Boston..................*Tenor*
REINHART, his secretary.........*Baritone*
AMELIA, Reinhart's wife.........*Soprano*
ULRICA, negress astrologer:......*Contralto*
OSCAR, a page.....................*Soprano*
SAMUEL, a conspirator.............*Basso*
TOM, a conspirator.................*Basso*

The Masked Ball

PLACE—In and Near Boston.
TIME—End of 17th Century

ACT 1

Hall in the Governor's Mansion. The Governor is receiving and inspects a list of guests invited to the masked ball. At Amelia's name he becomes sentimental. *"I shall behold her."* Reinhart comes to tell the Governor of a plot against his life. *Reinhart: "On the life thou now dost cherish."* The negress Ulrica is brought in charged with being a witch. The Governor makes a jest of the charges and dismisses her. He declares that it will be a lark to go disguised to this witch's hut and consult her. The two conspirators against the Governor's life—Samuel and Tom—also go, thinking that they will now carry out their ends. The next scene shows Ulrica's hut. She is brewing magic. *"King of the Shades."* The Governor is disguised as a sailor. A knock comes on the door and all are made to go out but the Governor, who hides. The new visitor is Amelia, who confesses that she loves the Governor and wants a potion that will make her forget him. The negress tells Amelia where she can get the herb that will do this. Ulrica, *"Hard by the western portal."* Amelia departs and the people come in again. Now

[187]

The Masked Ball

the Governor asks the negress to tell his fortune. *"The waves will bear me."* She tells him that he will soon be killed by the first man who shakes his hand. The Governor laughs and holds out his hand for the conspirators to shake. They, thinking they are suspected, decline to shake. Now Reinhart enters in search of his chief. He grasps his hand, and the Governor tells Ulrica she is a poor prophet for Reinhart is his best friend. The people are astonished to find that the disguised sailor is the Governor and they hail him. *"O, son of glorious England."*

ACT 2

Lonely Spot near Boston. It is midnight and Amelia comes seeking the magic herb that will make her forget the Governor. *"Yonder plant enchanted."* The Governor comes; Amelia confesses that she loves him but begs him to leave her. *Duet: "Like dew thy words fall on my heart."* Reinhart arrives to tell the Governor that the conspirators are waiting to kill him. The latter requests Reinhart to escort the veiled lady to the city without asking her identity. This Reinhart agrees to do and the Governor escapes. But on the way back Reinhart is mistaken for the Governor by the conspirators; the veil is torn from the woman and she stands revealed

as Reinhart's wife. *Reinhart and Amelia:
"Ah, here by moonlight."* Amelia declares
her innocence, but she is denounced by her
husband who now plans to join the conspirators.

ACT 3

Room in Reinhart's House. Reinhart decides to kill his wife. She begs for a last
embrace of her child and while she is out
he relents. *"Is it thou?"* He determines instead to center his energies on killing the
Governor. The two conspirators and he
choose lots and Reinhart is selected to kill
the Governor. A page comes with an invi-
tation to the masked ball. *Page: "What
brilliant lights."* Alone the Governor has
a change of heart and decides to give up
Amelia. In a note Amelia warns him of his
danger but he decides to attend the ball and
face his enemies. From a page Reinhart
learns how the Governor is dressed. In the
midst of the maskers Reinhart stabs the
Governor. The latter falls dying. But before
he expires he tells Reinhart that Amelia is
guiltless and that he had planned to send him
to an honored post in England. The secretary is overcome with remorse as the Governor dies.

DIE MEISTERSINGER

OPERA IN THREE ACTS
MUSIC AND LIBRETTO BY RICHARD WAGNER
FIRST PRODUCTION—MUNICH, 1868

CAST

HANS SACHS, cobbler..............*Basso*
POGNER, goldsmith................*Basso*
VOGELGESANG, furrier............*Tenor*
NACHTIGAL, buckle-maker.........*Basso*
BECKMESSER, town clerk..........*Basso*
KOTHNER, baker...................*Basso*
ZORN, pewterer....................*Tenor*
EISSLINGER, grocer...............*Tenor*
MOSER, tailor.....................*Tenor*
ORTEL, soap boiler...............*Basso*
SCHWARTZ, stocking weaver........*Basso*
FOLZ, coppersmith.................*Basso*
        Master-Singers
SIR WALTHER VON STOLZING,
  Franconian Knight................*Tenor*
DAVID, apprentice to Hans Sachs....*Tenor*
EVA, Pogner's daughter............*Soprano*
MAGDALENA, Eva's nurse.........*Soprano*
A NIGHT WATCHMAN..............*Basso*

PLACE—Nuremberg.
TIME—Sixteenth Century

Die Meistersinger

ACT 1

Interior of St. Catherine's Church. Walther, the knight, here sees Eva, the beautiful daughter of Pogner, the goldsmith. The young people love each other at first sight. But Walther finds out that Eva's father has promised the girl to the winner of the song contest. Beckmesser, the town clerk, is a suitor for her hand and hopes to win in the contest. Walther announces his intention to enter, and his preliminary trial takes place before the master-singers. David, the apprentice, who loves Magdalena, Eva's nurse, gives the new-comer some queer instructions. With Beckmesser as "marker," Walther sings. He is given so many bad marks that the master-singers decide his singing is decidedly poor.

ACT 2

A Street, Showing Homes of Hans Sachs and Pogner. The philosophical Sachs cannot forget the beauty of Walther's voice, although he was rejected. *"The elder's scent is waxing."* Eva, who has heard of Walther's rejection, meets him and declares that she will elope with him no matter now who wins in the contest. The arrival of Beckmesser forces the lovers to hide in the shadow of Eva's

home. The town clerk now serenades Eva
with the song he is to sing in the contest.
The lyrical gallant is interrupted by a jolly
song from Sachs. An altercation follows and
the shoe-maker finally agrees to allow Beckmesser to sing if he, Sachs, can note every
mistake by a beat on a shoe with his hammer.
Beckmesser again begins his serenade, but
so frequent is the pounding of Sachs that the
warbler becomes confused and runs into dog-
gerel. The confusion disturbs the neighbor-
hood and heads appear in windows. From
Eva's window Magdalena looks out and tells
Beckmesser to cease his warbling. David
sees his beloved and thinks that Beckmesser
has been serenading her. He promptly be-
labors him with a club. A near-riot takes
place during which Eva and Walther try to
escape. But they are prevented by Sachs
who drags the young man into his shop while
Eva goes into her own home. Quiet finally
ensues and the night watchman awakens to
announce the hour and that all is well.

ACT 3

Sachs' Workroom. Walther has spent the
night with Sachs. He tells the cobbler of a
wonderful melody that came to him in a
dream, and he writes down two verses of it.
Walther leaves the verses on a table and goes

off to improvise the third and prepare for the contest, which is to take place that day. Beckmesser comes in, finds the verses and appropriates them. Sachs allows him to take them hoping to carry out a plan that will force the master-singers to hear Walther. Eva appears with a shoe to be fixed. She now realizes what a friend and philosopher Sachs is and sings in praise of him. *"Through thee life's treasure."* Sachs in his joy summons David and Magdalena and all witness the christening of Walther's master-song. Eva, with heart full of love begins to sing it. *Quintet: Eva, Magdalena, Sachs, Walther, and David: "Brightly as the sun upon my fortune shines."* The final scene is a field on the shores of the river Pegnitz. All are gathered for the great song contest, and to the *March of the Guilds* the master-singers advance to the sod platform. Sachs addresses the people. *"A master, noble, rich and wise."* All are deeply affected by Sachs' masterly address. The contest begins. Beckmesser sings the lovely melody he took from the cobbler's. But he gets it mixed with another melody and makes a fiasco of his attempt. Sachs now calls on Walther to sing. Before the astonished people the young knight gives a beautiful rendition of the lovely number. The master-singers recognize his talent and

give him the prize. Eva crowns him and
the knight wins the lovely girl in addition
to the master-singers' prize.

* * *

MEFISTOFELE

OPERA IN FOUR ACTS AND A PROLOGUE
AND AN EPILOGUE

MUSIC AND LIBRETTO BY ARRIGIO BOITO

FIRST PRODUCTION—MILAN, 1868

CAST

MEFISTOFELE, the Evil One...... *Basso*
FAUST ....*Tenor*
MARGARET ....*Soprano*
MARTHA ....*Contralto*
WAGNER ....*Tenor*
HELEN OF TROY...............*Soprano*
PANTALIS ....*Contralto*
NEREUS ....*Tenor*

PLACE—Frankfort and Greece

The prologue takes place in the regions of
space. Angels and cherubim sing the praises
of the Creator. Mefistofele, half-way between
heaven and hell, addresses a mocking song
to the Omnipotent. *Mefistofele: "Hail Sov-
ereign Lord."* He is on his way to earth to
tempt the philosopher Faust, who is a man
of great wisdom.

[194]

ACT 1

Square in Frankfort. It is a festal day and students and girls are singing. *Chorus: "Ohe, Ohe!"* Faust appears with his pupil Wagner. They notice a friar who keeps near Faust. The latter, noting his sinister appearance, declares that he must be the Devil. Seeking to escape him, they return to Faust's study. Faust sings of the beauty of nature. *"From the meadows, from the valleys."* All at once the friar appears again. He drops his gray cloak and now stands revealed as the Evil One. *Mefistofele: "I am the spirit that denieth all things."* This number is sometimes called "the whistling ballad." Mefistofele bargains with Faust, the latter being careless as to the future. For Faust's soul it is agreed that he is to be given youth and one hour of genuine happiness.

ACT 2

Margaret's Garden. Here Faust walks with Margaret while Mefistofele entertains Martha, the girl's mother. Faust wants to meet Margaret alone, and in order to prevent discovery the mother is given a sleeping powder. Faust ardently woos and wins the girl. Mefistofele finally warns the lovers that it is time to depart. *Quartet: "Farewell, I must de-*

part." Mefistofele now takes Faust to the
top of the Brocken where the philosopher
sees all the revelry of hades. *Duet: "Ah, wild-
fire!"* The demons dance in wild acclaim
while the fire bursts from the awful depths.
All Hell proclaims Mefistofele its master and
he is given a crystal ball that represents the
Earth. Faust is terrified at seeing Margaret
down in the rocks bound by red-hot chains.

ACT 3

A Prison. Here Margaret lies on a bed
of straw. She has been convicted of murder-
ing her babe. Insane, she prays for pardon,
and sings a sad melody. *"To the sea, O night
of sadness."* Faust arrives with Mefistofele.
The latter gives Faust the key to the prison
and tells Faust that he can escape with the
girl. But Margaret does not recognize Faust.
Duet, Margaret and Faust: "Far, far away."
Mefistofele returns and his presence fills Margaret with terror. She sinks into Faust's arms
and dies while an angel chorus sounds her
final victory over death. Faust and Mefistofele depart as the headsman enters.

ACT 4

The Banks of a River in Greece. Here
Mefistofele tempts Faust still further by giving him the beautiful Helen of Troy. Helen

sings an ode to the moon. *"Moon Immovable."* Faust loves her ardently, and Mefistofele goes back to the Brocken leaving the fair Helen in Faust's arms.

The scene of the Epilogue is Faust's study. Old again, he regrets the way he has lived. *"Nearing the utmost limit."* He is now reading his Bible, and when Mefistofele comes he is not tempted. The Evil One, however, still hoping to gain his soul, surrounds Faust with lovely sirens. Praying for strength, the philosopher dies. Mefistofele, defeated, disappears into the ground. Roses cover the body of Faust and the angel's chorus is heard. Faust, too, has been triumphant in death.

* * *

MIGNON

OPERA IN THREE ACTS
MUSIC BY AMBROISE THOMAS
LIBRETTO BY BARBIER AND CARRE
FOUNDED ON GOETHE'S STORY, "WILHELM MEISTER"
FIRST PRODUCTION—PARIS, 1886

CAST

MIGNON ....*Soprano*
LOTHARIO, her father.............*Basso*
WILHELM MEISTER, a student.....*Tenor*
FILINA, an actress...............*Soprano*

[197]

Mignon

FREDERICK, a young nobleman.. *Contralto*
LAERTES, an actor.................*Tenor*
GIARNO, gypsy chief..............*Basso*

PLACE—Germany and Italy

ACT 1

Courtyard of a German Inn. When a child, Mignon was stolen by gypsies from her father, Lothario, a noble. The latter in his bereavement, has partly lost his mind and wanders as a minstrel in search of the girl. Now he comes upon the merry throng in the courtyard and sings, accompanying himself on his harp. *"A lonely wanderer."* Mignon, now a young woman, is ordered by Giarno to dance. When she refuses he threatens her. Lothario tries to protect her and incurs the anger of the gypsy. Both are saved from violence by a young student, Wilhelm Meister, who is struck by Mignon's beauty. He asks her about her origin of which she remembers little. But she tells him what she does remember of the lovely Italian country in *"Knowest thou the land where the orange grows?"* Wilhelm bargains for her release, and she is to be dressed in boy's clothes and be his page. Lothario and Mignon now bid each other farewell in the Song of the Swallows, *"O swallows gay and blithe."* Meantime the players, who are in the town, have

[198]

been invited to the castle. Wilhelm is enamored of Filina, the principal actress in the
cast, and decides to follow her.

ACT 2

A Boudoir in the Castle. Here Filina is
preparing to play Titania in "A Midsummer
Night's Dream." She is much attracted to
the handsome Wilhelm who comes with
Mignon, now in boy's clothes. To Mignon
she is very cool. Mignon sees Wilhelm make
violent love to the actress. Then, loving him
and hoping to win his affection, she too uses
rouge and the arts of make-up. *Mignon: "I
know a poor maiden."* Then she dons one of
Filina's gowns. But Wilhelm infatuated by
the actress, bids Mignon farewell. *"Farewell
Mignon."* Filina returns to find Mignon arrayed in her finery and she is amused. Maddened by her sarcasm, Mignon tears off
Filina's gown and leaves humiliated and desperate. The next scene shows the castle park.
Here Mignon, jealous of Filina's success in
winning the love of Wilhelm, attempts to
drown herself. But she is prevented by Lothario. Now she wishes that fire would con-
sume the castle. From the great building
come the actors who praise the loveliness and
talent of Filina. The actress herself now
appears and sings the celebrated Polonaise.

Mignon

"*I'm fair Titania.*" Mignon, to escape meeting Wilhelm, goes into the castle. But the
building has been set on fire by Lothario and
soon it is enveloped in flames. Mignon is
rescued by Wilhelm.

ACT 3

Castle of Count Lothario in Italy. Here
the faithful Lothario instinctively comes with
Mignon. Wilhelm, who has now broken
away from the actress, realizes that he loves
Mignon, and follows her. Wilhelm tells Lothario of his love for the girl. "*Pure as a
flower.*" Coming back to his old home restores Lothario to his right mind. Now by
the aid of a girdle, a portrait and a prayer
by Mignon he knows that the girl is his
daughter. He makes her and Wilhelm and
himself happy by giving a father's blessing to
their union.

MONNA VANNA

LYRIC DRAMA IN FOUR ACTS
BOOK BY MAURICE MAETERLINCK
MUSIC BY HENRI FEVRIER
FIRST PRODUCTION—PARIS, 1909

CAST

MONNA VANNA ....*Soprano*
PRINZIVALLE ....*Tenor*
GUIDO ....*Baritone*
MARCO ....*Basso*
BORSO ....*Tenor*
TORELLO ....*Basso*
TRIVULZIO ....*Basso*

PLACE—Pisa. TIME—The Middle Ages.

ACT 1

Palace of Guido Colonna. Pisa is besieged by the Florentine army under Prinzivalle and the food supply is cut off. Guido Colonna, at the head of the Pisa forces, sends his aged father, Marco Colonna, to ask mercy of Prinzivalle. Marco returns with a message from the Florentine general. If Monna Vanna, the lovely wife of Guido, will come to Prinzivalle's tent at night, clad only in her mantle, he will lift the siege and send provisions into the city. Monna Vanna is eager to sacrifice herself to the Florentine when, by doing so, she can save the people of Pisa from starvation.

[201]

But Guido, her husband, determines that she
shall not go. In his selfishness he declares
that her honor is worth more than the lives
of the people. Old Marco urges him to let
Monna Vanna go. Finally, leaving Guido
half mad with jealousy and rage, Monna
Vanna, clad only in her mantle departs for
the tent of the Florentine general.

ACT 2

Tent of Prinzivalle. Monna Vanna comes
to the general's tent. Instead of finding a
barbarian, as she had expected, she discovers
that Prinzivalle is a man of learning. She
also discovers that she knew him when he and
she were boy and girl in Florence. She tells
him that her heart is Guido's. Prinzivalle,
instead of taking advantage of her sacrifice,
treats her with courtesy. He at once starts
his wagon trains, loaded with food, into starv-
ing Pisa. Suddenly messengers come. The
army believes Prinzivalle guilty of treason and
his own soldiers are marching on his tent.
Monna Vanna will not leave him to the
mercy of his own maddened troops, and urges
him to go with her into Pisa. This he consents to do.

ACT 3

Room in the Palace of Guido. Monna Vanna is certain that Guido, learning of Prinzivalle's noble conduct, will greatly honor him. But Guido has spent a night of agony. Now in his jealous rage, he refuses to believe that Prinzivalle did not take advantage of Monna Vanna in his tent at midnight. Guido orders Prinzivalle cast into a dark dungeon. Monna Vanna is astounded at this act, and her love for Guido flickers out in the darkness of her soul.

ACT 4

A Dungeon. Monna Vanna's soul is now illuminated by her love for Prinzivalle, the noble Florentine. She secures the key to his prison and comes to liberate him. She brings him forth to light and love. Then she and Prinzivalle depart from the city, leaving Guido to his fate—misery and desolation, caused by his utter selfishness and lack of faith.

NATOMA

AMERICAN OPERA IN THREE ACTS
MUSIC BY VICTOR HERBERT
LIBRETTO BY JOSEPH REDDING
FIRST PRODUCTION, PHILADELPHIA, 1911

CAST

DON FRANCISCO, a Spanish grandee.*Basso*
PARBARA, his daughter..........*Soprano*
NATOMA, an Indian Girl........*Soprano*
PAUL MERRILL, American Lieu-
    tenant ....*Tenor*
JUAN BAUTISTA ALVARDO, a
    young Spaniard ....*Baritone*
JOSE CASTRO, a half-breed.......*Baritone*
PICO, companion of Castro..........*Tenor*
KAGAMA, companion of Castro.......*Basso*
FATHER PERALTA, Padre of the
    Mission Church ....*Baritone*
CHIQUITA, a dancing girl.... (*Silent Part*)
    PLACE—Coast of California.
    TIME—1820

ACT 1

Hacienda of Don Francisco on Island of
Santa Cruz. Don Francisco awaits the com-
ing of his daughter from the convent-school.
"*Impatient father that I am.*" Alvarado,
Castro, Pico and Kagama come hunting, and
Don Francisco gives them the run of his
estate. Natoma, the Indian maid, appears

[204]

with Lieutenant Paul Merrill who has come off the American ship in the harbor. The Lieutenant begs her to tell him of her people, *"Gentle maiden, tell me."* She relates a remarkable story. *Natoma: "From the clouds came my first father."* The last princess of her race, she wears on her neck the abalone, a token of succor and plenty from the Great Spirit. The Lieutenant is deeply touched. Natoma, stifling her passion for the "Stranger," runs to greet Barbara and her school companions. *Chorus: "Afloat in our open boat."* There is a joyful greeting and the hunters return to the house. The Spaniard, Alvarado, serenades the lovely Barbara whom he loves. *Alvarado: "When the sunlight dies."* But Barbara has eyes only for the American Lieutenant, and in the moonlight she sings of her love. *"My confidant, Oh, yon silver moon."* He too, declares that he loves only her. *Duet, Lieutenant and Barbara: "I love him."* Meanwhile Natoma has overheard a plot by Alvarado to kidnap Barbara the following day during a festival on the mainland.

ACT 2

Plaza in Front of the Mission Church. Natoma appears, sad and despairing. *"Great Manitou, spirit of the hills."* Girls gather

and sell their finery. *Chorus: "Come, buy."*
The dashing vaqueros arrive. *"Vaqueros,
devils to dare."* All hail Barbara, her father
and the citizens. Natoma comes with Barbara, whom she loves despite the hopelessness
of her own passion for the Lieutenant. Barbara is joyous. *"I list to the thrill in golden
throat."* Booming of a cannon announces
the Lieutenant's arrival. He sings a patriotic song: *"No country can my own outvie."*
Alvarado successfully pleads with Barbara to
be his partner in the dance. The number
breaks into the Panuelo, and Barbara rejects
Alvarado's suit. He is furious. But Castro
steps into the throng and challenges anybody
to dance with him the ancient Dagger Dance.
Natoma accepts his challenge. At the close
of this thrilling number Natoma seizes her
dagger and stabs Alvarado, who is about to
kidnap Barbara. The tumult is quelled by
Father Peralta appearing at the door of the
mission. Natoma, dropping her dagger, falls
penitent at the feet of the priest.

ACT 3

Interior of Mission Church. Natoma, remorseful and penitent, sings: *"Beware of the
hawk."* Father Peralta convinces her of the
blackness of her sin and that the Madonna
will receive her with welcome arms. Natoma

finally accepts this mercy and is to become one of the Ursaline nuns. As the Lieutenant, Barbara and the others enter the church, Natoma is ready. The large doors open to receive her into the gardens beyond. She takes the amulet from her neck and places it over Barbara's head. Then the doors close behind her and she is shut out from the world forever.

* * *

"LA NAVARRAISE"

OPERA IN TWO ACTS
MUSIC BY JULES MASSENET
LIBRETTO BY CLARETIE AND CAIN
FIRST PRODUCTION—LONDON, 1894

CAST

GARRIDO, General of Royalist Army.. *Basso*
REMIGIO, a citizen............... *Baritone*
ARAQUIL, his son................. *Tenor*
RAMON, a lieutenant.............. *Basso*
BUSTAMENTE, sergeant......... *Baritone*
ANITA, a girl from Navarre....... *Soprano*

PLACE—Near Bilbao, Basque Provinces

ACT 1

A small square in the village. Garrido, the Royalist general, has fought in vain to re-capture a Basque town from his enemy, the

"La Navarraise"

Carlist general Zuccaraga. The soldiers are returning and Anita—"La Navarraise"—asks about Sergeant Araquil, her betrothed. They know nothing of him, but soon the young man appears. Anita is overjoyed at beholding him again and he is just as happy over coming back to her. *Duet, Araquil and Anita: "I thought of thee."* While they are declaring their love for each other Araquil's father, Remigio, surprises them. He is not pleased that his son loves the girl from Navarre. She is "nobody," while his son is of a proud family. The lovers plead with him, but he is obdurate. Finally, in a spirit of mocking irony, he tells Anita that Araquil shall marry her when she brings a dowry of two thousand duros. The girl, realizing the impossibility of ever getting such a sum, is in despair. Then in the dusk Garrido, the general, appears with his officers. He learns that the commander of Araquil's company has been killed, and he appoints Araquil a lieutenant, and commends him for his bravery. Anita feels that Araquil is lost to her as his father proudly leads him away. But the girl overhears Garrido declare that he would give a fortune if his enemy Zuccaraga were slain. Hope is suddenly revived in her heart, and she boldly tells the general that she will kill Zuccaraga for two thousand

duros. Garrido thinks that she is speaking
only wild imaginings. But she tells him that
none shall know what she has agreed to do,
and she rushes off in the darkness. Araquil
enters wearing the uniform of a lieutenant.
He is miserable without Anita. *"O, my beloved."* But Ramon, his friend, is skeptical
about the girl. He tells Araquil that she was
seen making her way toward the Carlist line,
and that Zuccaraga loves beautiful women.
Araquil is astounded at this and rushes out
of camp, determined to penetrate into the
Carlists' line and find Anita. The soldiers
sing around the fire. *Chorus: "Oh, you poor
soldier."*

ACT 2

Same scene at daybreak. Anita, distraught
as though in a dream, meets Garrido. She
tells the astonished general that she has killed
Zuccaraga. She went to his tent at night;
listened to his proposal, then stabbed him to
the heart and escaped. The general pays her
the two thousand duros and pledges her to
secrecy. The girl is joyous for now she can
bring her dowry to Araquil. *Anita: "My,
gold, so bright and glowing."* Suddenly Araquil appears, supported by soldiers. He has
been wounded trying to force his way into
the Carlist camp. He hopes that he will

die for Anita's guilt is plain to him. He
derides her for her infidelity, but she does
not understand him and shows him the gold
—her dowry. Pledged to secrecy, she cannot
tell him how she got it and he is certain that
it was a present from Zuccaraga—her lover.
Only at the last moment, hearing that the
Carlist general has been assassinated, does the
truth dawn on him. He dies unable to ask
Anita's forgiveness. Anita is beside herself
with grief and her mind gives way. She
laughs and cries by turns, and the curtain
falls on the sad scene.

* * *

NORMA

OPERA IN TWO ACTS BY BELLINI
TEXT BY ROMANI
FIRST PRODUCTION—MILAN, 1832

CAST

POLLIONE, Roman Proconsul.......*Tenor*
OROVIST, Chief of Druids...........*Basso*
NORMA, his daughter.............*Soprano*
ADALGISA, a priestess................*Alto*
CLOTILDA, Norma's friend........*Soprano*
Children of Norma and Pollione

PLACE—Gaul.
TIME—After Roman Invasion.

ACT 1

Grove of the Druids. Norma, the High Priestess, alone has the power of declaring war or peace. Orovist announces that she will come and cut the sacred mistletoe and declare war against the invading Romans. *Orovist and Chorus: "Ascend the hill, Druids."* Norma, however, unknown to all, has broken her sacred vows to the temple and married the Roman Proconsul, by whom she has had two children. *Chorus: "Norma appears."* The ceremony proceeds and she rebukes the Druids for desiring war against the Romans, and invokes peace from the moon with her song, *"Queen of Heaven."* After the ceremony, Pollione, who is untrue to Norma. now loving Adalgisa, meets Adalgisa secretly, and entreats her to abandon her religion and fly with him to Rome *(Duet, Pollione and Adalgisa: "Go and sacrifice to false gods")*, which she promises to do. Overcome with remorse, she confesses to Norma, asking pardon and absolution from her vows. Norma, sympathizing with one who has sinned as she herself has, offers a means of escape, but when she learns whom Adalgisa loves, she is filled with anger and despair. She turns upon Pollione, who now enters, hurling her wrath at him. *Duet and Terzett, Norma, Adalgisa,*

Norma

Clotilda and Pollione: "Go and conceal them both," "Here he robbed me of peace." "Norma, not in this hour."

ACT 2

Norma's Dwelling. Norma enters, determined to kill her two children, who are asleep (Norma: "Both asleep, they see not the steel that pierces them"), but her maternal love overcomes her determination, and she decides to yield her husband and children to Adalgisa, and atone for her sins at the funeral pyre. (Duet, Norma and Adalgisa: "O Adalgisa, hear my prayers." "See, O Norma, oh, have pity." Adalgisa, greatly touched by this sacrifice, promises to beg Pollione to return to Norma, but her efforts are in vain.

SCENE 2

Temple. Pollione refuses to return to Norma, and while Adalgisa is at the temple attempts to seize her against her will. Norma, coming in at this moment, strikes her shield, which is the declaration for war. Her warriors rush in (Battle Song: "Fight! Fight!") and seize Pollione and he is brought before her. Duet, Norma and Pollione: "Now are you in my hands." She informs him she will set him free if he leaves Adalgisa and returns to Rome, which he refuses to do. Her love then overcomes justice and she declares herself to be the erring one and ascends the funeral pyre. Pollione, his love for her returning at her noble sacrifice, follows her (*Duet: "A new sacrifice"*), and they perish together in the flames.

* * *

OBERON

ROMANTIC OPERA IN THREE ACTS
MUSIC BY KARL MARIA VON WEBER
LIBRETTO BY PLANCHE FROM WIELAND'S POEMS
FIRST PRODUCTION—LONDON, 1826

CAST

OBERON, King of the fairies........*Tenor*
TITANIA, Queen of the fairies.....(*Silent*)
PUCK ....*Contralto*
HUON, a knight....................*Tenor*
SCHERASMIN, his shield-bearer...*Baritone*
HARUN AL RASCHID...........*Baritone*
REZIA, his daughter..............*Soprano*
FATIMA, her maid................*Soprano*
PRINCE BARBEKAN ....*Tenor*
EMIR OF TUNIS...............*Baritone*
ROSCHANA, his favorite.........*Contralto*
EMPEROR CHARLEMAGNE........*Basso*
ABDALLA, a pirate.................*Basso*
DROLL ....*Contralto*

Oberon

ACT 1

Oberon's Palace. *Elves' chorus: "Light as fairy feet."* The King Oberon and the Queen Titania have had a quarrel. They cannot agree again until they have found a couple that will love each other through all hardships. Puck comes with a story of Huon, a knight, who has slain in combat the son of Charlemagne. For this the Emperor has commanded him to go to Bagdad, slay the man sitting on the Caliph's left and take the Caliph's daughter Rezia for a wife. Oberon shows Huon and Rezia to each other in vision, and mutual love is the immediate result. He gives to Huon a magic horn that will summon Oberon whenever there is serious trouble. To Scherasmin, Huon's shield-bearer, he gives a cup that will fill with fire for the lips of enemies. The two are quickly transported to Bagdad. *Huon: "Bred to the camp."* In the harem Rezia deplores her forthcoming marriage to Prince Barbekan, whom she does not love. *Rezia: "My lord, my life."* Fatima, her slave, reports the arrival of the knight Huon.

ACT 2

Hall in the Caliph's Palace. Huon, putting the magic cup to the test, gives it to Prince Barbekan who is sitting at the Caliph's left.

Flames leap from it. Huon promptly challenges Barbekan and slays him. The Caliph's soldiers attack Huon but Scherasmin blows on the magic horn and all his enemies are so delighted that they cannot help from dancing. Huon and Rezia escape, and so do Scherasmin and Fatima who have become attached to each other. The next scene takes place in the palace gardens. Scherasmin woos Fatima and the girl declares that she loves him. *Fatima: "Arabia's desolate child."* Huon and Rezia arrive accompanied by Oberon. The King of the fairies warns them against unfaithfulness and transports them to the harbor of Askalon. *Quartet: "On the blue sea."* Testing their love, Puck makes the winds to shipwreck them. *Puck: "Spirits of the air, the earth, the sea."* Huon carries Rezia to a desolate island and leaves her to seek aid. The girl signals to a vessel for help. *Rezia: "Ocean, thou mighty monster."* The vessel answers. It is manned by pirates who carry off the girl. *The mermaids sing: "How beautiful the waves,"* and Oberon and Puck summon the spirits for a dance in the moon light.

ACT 3

Garden of the Emir in Tunis. Here Fatima and Scherasmin work as slaves, having been sold by the pirates to the Emir. *Fatima:*

Oberon

"Arabia, my beloved country." Duet, Fatima and Scherasmin: *"On the banks of the Garonne."* Huon is brought to them by fairy magic. He is advised to disguise himself as a gardener and rescue Rezia who is held in the Emir's harem. In the palace Rezia bewails her fate. *"Grieve, my heart."* The Emir is repulsed when he tries to win her. Roschana, wife of the Emir, in her jealous scheming, sends for Huon. The latter thinks he is to meet Rezia. When he finds himself before Roschana, she uses all her wiles on him. But he does not give way to temptation. He is surprised by the Emir, who condemns both him and Rezia to death. Before the palace the lovers are to be burned alive. But Scherasmin finds the magic horn that has been lost and blows on it. Oberon appears and rescues the sweethearts. They have been true to each other and so Oberon and Titania are united. All go to Aix la Chapelle, where Huon is forgiven and honored by the Emperor.

L'ORACOLO
(THE ORACLE)

A MUSIC DRAMA IN ONE ACT BASED ON "THE CAT
AND THE CHERUB" OF C. B. FERNALD
BY COMILLO ZANONI
MUSIC BY FRANCO LEONI

CAST

WIN-SHEE, a learned doctor.........*Basso*

CHIM-FEN, proprietor of an
   opium den ....*Baritone*

HOO-TSIN, a wealthy merchant......*Basso*

WIN-SAN-LUY, Win-Shee's son......*Tenor*

HOO-CHEE, Hoo-Tsin's little son.*Contralto*

AH-YOE, Hoo-Tsin's niece.........*Soprano*

HUA-QUEE, Hoo-Chee's nurse.....*Soprano*

A policeman, an opium maniac, a fortune-
teller, Chinese men, women and children.

The opening of the play takes place in the
fifth hour of the Chinese New Year's day.
As the dawn approaches, the few remaining
merry makers depart from the opium den,
the more devout members of the populace
wending their way to "the house of prayer.'
Chim-Fen, a proprietor of an opium den,
professes love for Hua-Quee, nurse to Hoo-
Chee, the son of Hoo-Tsin, a rich merchant,
and pretends that he is desirous of marrying her. His purpose, however, is to induce

the nurse to steal a fan from the house of
Hoo-Tsin and to be able to gain admittance
to the house in order to further his nefari-
ous plans. Win-Shee, a learned doctor, has
a son, Win-San-Luy, who is in love with
Ah-Yoe, the niece of Hoo-Tsin. As the day
breaks, they meet and confess to each other
their love. The echo of a hymn comes from
the Temple and joyful songs float in upon
them from the street.

Win-Shee, the learned doctor, is consulted
by Hoo-Tsin as to the future of his little
son. From the books Win-Shee reads that
tragic events are in store for him. Their
conversation is overheard by Chim-Fen, and
when, but for the presence of the little child
and his nurse, the street is utterly deserted,
Chim-Fen when the nurse's back is turned
for a moment finds his opportunity to steal
the child. He does so and hides him in his
opium den. Cunningly he then approaches
Hoo-Tsin, the child's father, asking him for
the hand of the beautiful Ah-Yoe in marriage, on the provision that he find and restore him his child. His proposal is accepted by Hoo-Tsin. San-Luy tells the father
that he will find the child, asking only
that he shall be rewarded in the same manner as Chim-Fen, viz., that he be given Ah-
Yoe as his wife. Chim-Fen is suspected by
San-Luy, who watches him, and after a fierce

struggle succeeds in entering his opium den. He gets the little boy, but is followed by Chim-Fen who kills San-Luy with a hatchet. He then opens a trap door into which he pushes the child.

At the sight of her lover's dead body, Ah-Yoe goes mad. Win-Shee, the learned doctor, overcome by sorrow at the death of his child, determines to discover the murderer.

SCENE 2

Second Night Later. Win-Shee burns several sacred papers and asks aid from the gods. The sound of wailing from little Hoo-Chee reaches his ears. He discovers him beneath the trap door and Hoo-Chee is restored to his father. Win-Shee now lays in wait for Chim-Fen, and the latter in a state of drunkenness approaches him. With tragic calmness, Win-Shee beckons Chim-Fen toward him and makes him sit on a wooden bench beside him. Convinced of the guilt of Chim-Fen, with an inspiration of frenzy, he makes a sudden attack upon him and strangles him. The footsteps of a policeman are heard. As he comes nearer Win-Shee props the dead body of Chim-Fen upon the bench beside him and appears to be discoursing quietly to the dead man as the policeman is passing. As soon as the policeman is out of sight the dead body of Chim-Fen falls to the ground with a thud.

ORPHEUS AND EURYDICE

LEGENDARY OPERA IN FOUR ACTS
MUSIC BY CHRISTOPHER GLUCK
LIBRETTO BY RAMIERI DE CALZABIGI
FIRST PRODUCTION—VIENNA, 1762

CAST

ORPHEUS, the singer............*Contralto*
EURYDICE, his bride............*Soprano*
AMOR, god of love...............*Soprano*
A HAPPY SHADE...............*Soprano*

PLACE—Greece and the Lower World
TIME—Antiquity

ACT 1

Tomb of Eurydice. The beautiful Eurydice, bride of Orpheus, has died, and her husband and friends mourn at her tomb. *Aria and chorus: "Thou whom I loved."* Orpheus is ready to make any sacrifice or brave any dangers to have his wife back again and he prays to the gods for her restoration to him. *Recitation: "Gods, cruel gods."* In answer to his prayer the god Amor appears. He tells the bereaved husband that Zeus has had pity on him. He can go down into Hades and try to win Pluto and his minions solely by his powers of song. Should he rescue Eurydice on no account must he look back at her until he has passed the Styx.

Orpheus and Eurydice

If he does, she will die immediately. *Amor:*
"Fulfil with joy the will of the gods." Orpheus hears this message with great joy and
he implores the gods for aid.

ACT 2

Entrance to Hades. Orpheus appears and
is threateningly greeted by the Furies. *Chorus: "Who is this mortal?"* They revile him
for trying to enter Hades. But the sweet
singer, having recourse to his song, tells of
his love for Eurydice and his grief over
her death. *"A thousand griefs, threatening
shades."* The sweetness of his music wins
the sympathy of the Furies and shades, and
they allow him to enter their terrible realms.

ACT 3

Valley of the Blest. This is a beautiful
spot where the good spirits in Hades find
rest and contentment. Here Orpheus comes
seeking Eurydice. *Recitative: "What pure
light."* A chorus of happy shades greets him.
"Sweet singer, you are welcome." They bring
the lovely Eurydice to him. Orpheus, remembering the warning of Amor, takes his
bride by the hand and averts his gaze as he
leads her from the valley. She does not understand his action. *Duet: "On my faith
relying."*

Orpheus and Eurydice

ACT 4

A Wood. Orpheus has now released the hand of his bride, and hurrying on ahead, calls for her to follow. *"Follow my footsteps."* But Eurydice, still not understanding him, begs him for even one glance, saying that without his love she prefers to die. Orpheus, no longer able to resist her appeals, and not heeding the warning of Amor, turns and clasps Eurydice in his arms. Immediately she dies. *Orpheus: "I lost my Eurydice."* But the god Amor, affected by the grief of Orpheus, now appears to him. The god touches Eurydice and she is restored to life and to her husband's arms again.

* * *

OTHELLO

OPERA IN FOUR ACTS BY VERDI
TEXT BY BOITO
FIRST PRODUCTION—MILAN, 1887

CAST

OTHELLO .... *Tenor*
DESDEMONA, his wife........... *Soprano*
IAGO .... *Baritone*
EMILIA, his wife.......... *Mezzo-Soprano*
CASSIO .... *Tenor*
RODERIGO .... *Tenor*
MONTANO .... *Basso*

PLACE—Cyprus.
TIME—The Fifteenth Century

ACT 1

Before the Palace. Othello has returned victorious from fighting the Turks and is warmly welcomed by the people, but is despised by Iago because he has made Cassio his first lieutenant. Iago also detests Cassio, being jealous of him, and schemes for revenge. He plans to help Roderigo in getting the love of Desdemona, Othello's wife, and then induces Cassio to drink. Cassio becomes intoxicated and they pick a quarrel with him, at which he draws his sword against Montano. Othello enters at this moment and punishes Cassio by depriving him of his rank. He orders them all to disperse. A love scene between him and Desdemona ensues (*"When thou speakest"*), and they go slowly into the Castle.

ACT 2

A Room in the Castle. Iago urges Cassio to ask Desdemona to plead with her husband to restore his rank, and watches him go in search of Desdemona. He then sings the "Credo," in which he declares he has been fashioned only for evil, and, meeting Othello, arouses his jealousy by falsely hinting of Desdemona's affection for Cassio. To strengthen this insinuation he tells Othello that Cassio has in his possession a handkerchief given him by Desdemona. Othello, in despair, sings a farewell to peace of mind, glory and ambition (*"And Now, Forever, Farewell."*) Iago now offers to help Othello punish the guilty.

ACT 3

Hall of the Palace. Desdemona has been interceding for Cassio and Othello's suspicions are confirmed. He denounces her and she goes to her room, unable to understand his change in manner. He, too, is heartbroken. *Othello: "Had it pleased Heaven."* Iago now enters, telling him he has heard Cassio utter Desdemona's name in his dreams. *Cassio's Dream.* He bids him hide and listen to his conversation with Cassio, who is just entering. Iago then arranges the conversation with Cassio in such a manner that to Othello it appears that he is talking of Desdemona, while in reality he is speaking of his sweetheart. Iago cleverly manages to make it appear to Othello that he is getting the handkerchief from Cassio. When Cassio leaves, Othello, convinced of his wife's guilt, swears to kill her, and Iago promises to slay Cassio. A message from the Venetian Embassy is now brought to Othello, in which he is advised that he has been deposed and Cassio appointed his successor. Enraged with jealousy, he publicly denounces Desdemona (who has just come in), and flings her to the ground. While she is taken away, fainting, by her maids, he falls in a swoon, at which Iago sneers and laughs.

ACT 4

Desdemona's Bedroom. Here the heartbroken Desdemona is preparing to retire, assisted by her faithful maid, Emilia. *Desdemona:* "*Willow Song.*" Emilia leaves her and she kneels before the image of the Madonna, singing the beautiful "*Ave Maria.*" Othello enters after she has fallen asleep and awakens her with a kiss. He again accuses her, but she in vain protests her innocence. Overcome with jealous rage, he smothers her. Emilia coming in, sees Desdemona lifeless and shrieks for help. All rush in, including Iago, and Emilia, realizing the treachery of her husband, denounces him, declaring to Othello that Desdemona was innocent. The handkerchief episode is explained and Emilia declares her husband procured it from her. At this Iago slays his wife, and the broken-hearted Othello, who, too late, realizes the truth about the woman he loved so much, stabs himself. *Othello's Death.*

I PAGLIACCI

OPERA IN TWO ACTS AND A PROLOGUE
WORDS AND MUSIC BY R. LEONCAVALLO
FIRST PRODUCED IN MILAN, MAY 21, 1892

CAST

CANIO, Chief of a Village Comedy
Troupe (Clown) ....*Tenor*
NEDDA, his wife (Columbine) .....*Soprano*
TONIO (Taddeo) ....*Baritone*
BEPPO (Harlequin) ....*Tenor*
SILVIO, a Young Peasant...........*Tenor*

ACT 1

In a Calabrian Village. During the over-
ture the curtain ascends and Tonio appears
from behind a second curtain. *Tonio: "A
word allow me."* This explains the nature of the performance as an actual occur-
rence and the play begins. The players led
by Canio and Nedda parade amongst the
villagers in a donkey cart. *Chorus: "This
way they come with fife and drum."* Canio
invites them to attend the performance that
evening. He goes with Beppo to the village
tavern, leaving his wife Nedda, alone. The
Angelus is heard. *"Ding dong, the shadows
fall."* Tonio, a hunchback, approaches
Nedda, declaring that despite his deformity
he loves her madly, she laughs at him and

when he attempts to kiss her she strikes him with a whip. He leaves in a rage vowing vengeance. Silvio, a rich young peasant who loves Nedda and is beloved by her, appears and urges her to fly with him that night. Tonio, who has spied upon them, rushes to fetch Canio. Silvio presses his suit and as he kisses her Canio arrives, led by Tonio and attempts to stab Silvio, who is warned by a cry from Nedda. Tonio laughs with delight at Nedda's predicament. Canio who has failed to catch Silvio returns, and in a frenzy tries to stab Nedda, but is prevented by Beppo, who snatches the dagger from him. Beppo persuades Nedda to dress for the performance and Canio breaks down in agony of grief. *Canio: "To jest with my heart maddened with sorrow."*

ACT 2

The scene the same as Act 1. The villagers arrive and are seated. Silvio enters and when Nedda is collecting the money she cautions him to beware of Canio. The play begins. Nedda as Columbine in the absence of her husband, The Clown (Canio), hopes to receive the Harlequin (Beppo) alone, but the Pantaloon, (Tonio) arrives instead and declares in his idiotic way his love for Columbine. She repulses him as she hears the voice of Harlequin who comes in through a window. They are supping together when Pantaloon rushes in to say that the Clown is returning, unexpectedly. Harlequin escapes through a window after a fond farewell from Columbine. At this moment the Clown arrives and demands to know who the lover is. Columbine feigns ignorance. Canio, maddened by jealousy, demands again and again the name of her lover. The audience up to now have believed this a piece of splendid acting. Suddenly they realize it is no play, but a real tragedy being enacted before them. Canio, driven to frenzy, seizes a knife from the table and stabs her to the heart. Silvio drawing his dagger rushes forward just as the dying Nedda calls out his name for help. Canio suddenly enlightened plunges his dagger in Silvio's breast. *Canio: "No Punchinello am I—but a man."* The villagers surround and disarm him. He stands in a stupor and exclaims, "The Comedy Is Ended."

PARSIFAL

MUSIC DRAMA IN THREE ACTS
MUSIC AND DRAMA BY RICHARD WAGNER
AFTER THE EPIC OF WOLFRAM VON ESCHENBACH
FIRST PRODUCTION—BAIREUTH, 1882

CAST

AMFORTAS, keeper of the Holy Grail
.... *Baritone*
TITUREL, his father................*Basso*
GURNEMANZ, keeper of the gate....*Basso*
PARSIFAL, the "guileless fool"......*Tenor*
KLINGSOR, a magician..........*Baritone*
KUNDRY, the enchantress...*Mezzo-Soprano*

PLACE—Montsalvat in the Mountains of
Spain.
TIME—Middle Ages.

"Parsifal" is the legend of the Holy Grail,
the cup which caught the blood from the
side of Christ on the cross and which He
blessed. This cup and the sacred spear that
pierced the side of Christ were found by
Titurel and the Knights of the Holy Grail
who guard it in their temple at Montsalvat.
Becoming old, Titurel appointed his son,
Amfortas, keeper of the Grail. Angry at
not being made a Knight, Klingsor, a magician, built an enchanted garden and castle
near the castle of the Grail. In this he was

aided by Kundry, a woman who laughed at Christ on the cross, and who is by turns remorseful and defiant, hideous and lovely. Kundry was surrounded with beautiful maidens. In these gardens the enchantress tempted Amfortas and he was wounded by Klingsor with the sacred spear. He cannot die nor can the wound heal until it is touched by the sacred spear in the hands of a "Guileless Fool."

ACT 1

Gurnemanz, keeper of the gate, declares that only one man can heal the wound. But Kundry, penitent now, comes with balsam from Arabia to heal Amfortas' wound. Amfortas is borne by on a litter. He takes the balsam but does not hope for a cure until the "guileless one" comes. Gurnemanz here relates the story of the Grail and the wounding of Amfortas. Suddenly a wounded swan falls among them. Soon Parsifal appears. Gurnemanz rebukes him, "Couldst thou murder?" He confesses to having shot the swan, not seeing any wrong in it. Gurnemanz is impressed by his innocence. Kundry tells the young man that his mother is dead. Astounded he seizes her. Gurnemanz prevents him from doing her harm. Again he sees no wrong. Gurnemanz, still more impressed, invites the youth to go with him to the temple of the Grail. The next scene finds them in a great hall. The Knights are about to celebrate the feast of communion. *Chorus: "The Holy Supper."* Amfortas is borne in on a litter. The aged Titurel commands him to unveil the Grail which gives spiritual strength to all who look on it. Amfortas feels that he is unworthy. *"No. Leave it unrevealed."* But he finally obeys. The Grail glows in a shaft of light. The Knights drink from their goblets and eat bread. Parsifal does not join in the communion. When the Grail is covered again all withdraw except Gurnemanz and Parsifal. The former now believes that Parsifal is nothing but a stupid fool and warns him against further shooting of swans.

ACT 2

Apartment in the Castle of Klingsor. The magician Klingsor knows that his power is threatened by the "guileless fool." He awakes Kundry from her sleep. *"Arise, draw near to me."* The half-obedient, half-rebellious woman is mocked by Klingsor because of her remorse. He orders her to exert all her charms to lure Parsifal. Darkness falls, and the castle sinks. In its place appear the enchanted gardens peopled by lovely maidens

They bewail the slaughter of their lovers.
Maidens: "Here was the tumult." Soon
Parsifal scales the wall and they become
amorous. Arraying themselves as flowers
they beguile him. Yet he does not succumb
to temptation. But Kundry, bewitchingly
beautiful, lies in wait for him. *"Parsifal,
thou foolish pure one."* She tells him of his
father and mother and he sinks down at her
feet. Her arms around him, she presses her
kiss on his lips. Now, for the first time, he
knows passion and he feels what he thinks
is the wound of Amfortas in his own breast.
"The spear wound, the spear wound!" He
knows now how Amfortas was lured to sin
in love's gardens. *"Thus it called him."*
He stands erect, his eyes opened at last, and
denounces Kundry. She suffers intense grief.
Kundry: "Cruel one." Parsifal tells her if
he sinned with her he would be damned
also. *"Eternally should I be damned with
thee."* Klingsor appears and hurls his spear
at Parsifal. But it hangs in mid-air and
Parsifal seizes it. Klingsor is annihilated
together with his garden. Kundry falls in-
sensible. Parsifal disappears.

ACT 3

Montsalvat. Years have passed. Parsifal,
wandering, ever holds to the sacred spear.

The aged Gurnemanz finds Kundry in a thicket almost lifeless. He revives her. She has repented and has consecrated herself to the service of the Grail. Parsifal comes with the spear. Gurnemanz now recognizes him as the "guileless one" and is overjoyed. *"Glory, bounteous bliss."* Kundry humbly washes the feet of Parsifal and dries them with her hair. Gurnemanz annoints him. Parsifal baptizes Kundry, exhorting her to trust in God. He sings of the country's beauty: *"How fair the fields and meadows."* It is Good Friday and the bells call the Knights to prayer. Parsifal is arrayed in a robe of the Grail Knights. The scene changes to the interior of the temple. Titurel is dead and his body is brought in with the Grail. Once more the cup is to be unveiled. Amfortas shrinks in agony from again looking on the Grail. He pleads with the Knights to slay him and rid him of his terrible pain. But now Parsifal enters, and touches the wound of Amfortas with the spear. Instantly it heals. Titurel, coming back to life for a moment, sees Parsifal kneeling before the Grail. Kundry dies forgiven, and a dove descends and hovers over the head of Parsifal —the new keeper of the Grail.

PELLEAS AND MELISANDE

LYRIC DRAMA IN FIVE ACTS
MUSIC BY CLAUDE DEBUSSY
TEXT BY MAURICE MAETERLINCK
FIRST PRODUCTION—PARIS, 1902

ARKEL, King of Allemonde..........*Basso*
GENEVIEVE, his daughter-in-law..*Soprano*
GOLAUD, her elder son..........*Baritone*
PELLEAS, her younger son..........*Tenor*
MELISANDE, wife of Golaud......*Soprano*
YNIOLD, son of Golaud............*Soprano*
A PHYSICIAN....................*Baritone*

PLACE—Allemonde.
TIME—Antiquity

ACT 1

Fountain in a Forest. Melisande, a mystic maiden with long, yellow hair sits brooding over the fountain. She is discovered by Golaud, a mighty hunter. She is frightened but Golaud reassures her. She says she has been cruelly treated but does not tell by whom. She has lost her crown in the fountain but will not let Golaud recover it. Golaud is fascinated and takes Melisande away with him. The scene now changes to a hall in Arkel's castle. Genevieve reads a letter from her son, Golaud, saying that he has wed a strange maiden, Melisande. If a

light is placed in the castle he will know
whether he will be received with his bride.
Pelleas, a youth of wild, passionate nature
prepares the light for his brother Golaud.
There is another change of scene, showing
the gardens of the castle. Melisande is impressed by the gloominess of the great castle.
Pelleas is sad too and says he will depart the
next day. Melisande regrets that the handsome, mystically inclined youth must leave
the dreary old mansion.

ACT 2

A Pool in the Park. Pelleas, who loves
Melisande, is here with her. She in her
playfulness drops her wedding ring into the
pool. Pelleas says that it cannot be recovered.
When she wishes to know what to tell Golaud,
Pelleas urges her to tell him the truth. In
the next scene Golaud lies wounded in the
castle. Strangely, his horse threw him just
when Melisande lost the ring in the pool.
Melisande ministers to him and nurses him
back to health. She is sad, and in comforting
her Golaud notices that the ring is missing.
Instead of telling the truth she says she lost
it in a cave while escaping from the tide.
He commands her to go and find it even
though it is night. Pelleas is to go with her.
Melisande and Pelleas reach the cavern. A

beam of the moon reveals three blind beggars and Melisande is terrified. Pelleas leads her out.

ACT 3

Balcony of Melisande in the the castle. Melisande is combing her wonderful tresses. *Melisande: "To the foot of the tower my tresses flow."* Pelleas, standing below, lets her hair fall about him and passionately kisses it. Golaud surprises them and upbraids them, declaring that they are but children. Pelleas and his brother depart. Golaud takes Pelleas down into the castle vaults and, as a warning, shows him the dark, terrible pits. The two come up out onto a terrace and here Golaud warns Pelleas to be less ardent in his attention to Melisande, who is about to become a mother. Later, outside of Melisande's chamber, Golaud questions his little son about Pelleas and Melisande. The child's replies increase Golaud's jealousy. He holds the lad up to the window to observe Pelleas and Melisande. They are regarding each other sadly.

ACT 4

Apartment in the Castle. Here Melisande and Pelleas agree to have a farewell meeting by the fountain. The aged King Arkel has a

premonition that Melisande will not live
long. He sees only innocence in her eyes.
But the jealous Golaud, entering, believes
her guilty and mistreats her. He handles
her roughly and desists only when the aged
Arkel interferes. In the next scene Pelleas
and Melisande meet at the fountain. Melisande now declares that she loves only Pelleas.
Pelleas is enraptured. *Pelleas: "Your voice
sounds like the sea in springtime."* The
lovers embrace passionately. But Golaud is
watching them and he rushes upon them.
With his sword he slays Pelleas while Melisande flees.

ACT 5

Melisande's Bedchamber. Melisande is now
the mother of a child and her life hangs
by a thread. Golaud, remorseful now, knows
that Melisande was innocent and begs her
forgiveness. Listlessly she forgives him. The
serving women enter and Melisande quietly
passes away. Old King Arkel takes his great-
grandchild in his arms declaring: "A life
is ended, a life begins."

In the popular sense this work has no arias,
choruses, or duets. The music, designed to
express various moods and shades of feeling,
largely created "the Debussy school."

PHILEMON ET BAUCIS

OPERA IN TWO ACTS BY GOUNOD
TEXT BY BARBIER AND CARRE
FIRST PRODUCTION—PARIS, 1860

CAST

PHILEMON, an old peasant........*Tenor*
BAUCIS, his wife.................*Soprano*
JUPITER ....*Baritone*
VULCAN ....*Basso*

PLACE—Phrygia.
TIME—Mythical Period.

ACT 1

Philemon and Baucis, who, though old, still love one another dearly, are seated in front of their cottage at dusk. *Duet: "It is the hour of rest."* A terrific storm suddenly arises (*Bacchanalian Chorus: "Daughters of Athor, mad bacchantes"*), in the midst of which two strangers appear asking for shelter. They are the gods Jupiter and Vulcan, who have come to punish the impious Phrygians, but are disguised as wanderers. *Jupiter: "Strangers are we in this country."* They are welcomed by the aged couple, and Philemon lights a fire to dry their wet clothing. *Philemon: "Look! the flame has caught; the wood is smoking."* They now offer the strangers food (*Quar-*

tet: "Be seated at our table. Accept our humble cheer") , and the gods are so pleased with the hospitality tendered them that Jupiter changes the water in the pitcher to wine. Baucis recognizes Jupiter by this act and is consequently awed, but he reassures her, and promises fulfillment of any wish she may make. Her wish is that she and Philemon are made young again. *Baucis: "Ah, were I beautiful once more."* Jupiter promises to grant this wish, in addition to sparing them the fate of their neighbors. *Quartet: "A sombre veil extends its shade."* They fall asleep and Jupiter casts a spell over them.

ACT 2

Intermezzo, during which the Phrygians are punished in a bad storm. When Baucis wakens, her thoughts turn to her youth. *"Philemon would love me ever."* She sees beside her a handsome youth asleep (*Baucis: "Memories steal o'er me"*) and realizes that their youth has been restored. Philemon awakens, but does not know her. *Baucis: "Ungrateful one, my heart all filled with love."* The cottage has been transformed into a palace. The susceptible Jupiter falls in love with Baucis. *Jupiter: "Venus herself is not more fair."* He woos so ardently that Baucis runs off, hiding in the woods (*Baucis: "O laughing Nature! O fragrant gardens"*), but he follows, and when he overtakes her she kneels in supplication. *Jupiter: "Do not kneel, fair mortal."* Although faithful to Philemon, Baucis is flattered at Jupiter's declaration of love. *Duet: "O Philemon! Think not that I forget."* Philemon is furiously jealous and quarrels with his wife. Vulcan, whose grievance is the indiscretion of Venus, scolds Baucis and Philemon for quarreling, but makes himself unpopular by declaring all women false. *Terzett: "Live the gods like us, or no."* When Baucis discovers that she has offended Philemon she is grief-stricken (*Baucis: " 'Neath the weight of age our loving hearts"*) and pleads with Jupiter to make her old again. Philemon, hearing this, is convinced of her love for him, and joins her in the request. Jupiter, astonished at their sincere devotion, allows them the joys of their youth, but promises never to interfere with their happiness again. *Quartet: "O happiness enchanting."*

LE PROPHETE

OPERA IN FIVE ACTS BY MEYERBEER

TEXT BY SCRIBE

FIRST PRODUCTION—PARIS, 1849

CAST

JOHN OF LEYDEN.................*Tenor*
FIDES, his mother...................*Alto*
BERTHA, his sweetheart.........*Soprano*
JONAS ....⎫ ...*Tenor*
MATTHIESEN ...⎬ Anabaptists ⎬....*Basso*
ZACHARIAS ......⎭ ....*Basso*
COUNT OBERTHAL............*Baritone*

PLACE—Holland, in and near Munster.
TIME—1536.

ACT 1

Dorchet, Holland. Bertha is to wed John of Leyden, but being a vassal of Count Overthal must first get his consent. She prepares to go with Fides, John's mother, to make the request. At this time the Anabaptists, headed by Matthiesen, Jonas and Zacharias, are inciting the people to revolt. They attack the Castle, but are unsuccessful. Bertha and Fides now appear and make their request. The Count, struck with the girl's beauty, refuses to grant it, claiming her for himself, and keeps the two women at the palace as captives.

Le Prophete

ACT 2

Inn of John of Leyden. The Anabaptist leaders, coming to the Inn, are greatly impressed with his resemblance to David, and urge him to become their leader. When he tells them of a dream he has had (*John: "Under the vast dome a splendid temple"*), they proclaim him sent from Heaven and entreat him to become their Prophet. He refuses, thinking only of Bertha. *John: "There's a sweeter empire."* Bertha, who has escaped from the Castle, rushes in just at this moment and cries to him to save her. He hides her a moment before the entrance of the Count, who demands the girl, threatening to kill Fides, whom he has brought with him, unless Bertha is given up. Torn between love for his mother and sweetheart, in despair, he gives up Bertha to the tyrant. His mother, alone with him, expresses her gratitude in the song *"Ah, my son."* Just after she leaves him, the Anabaptists return and promise him revenge. He hesitates no longer and joins them. He leaves a blood-stained garment to lead Fides to believe he has been killed, and accompanies them. He is made their leader and regarded as a Prophet.

ACT 3

Anabaptists' Camp near Munster. Here provisions are brought to the Anabaptists over a frozen lake by skaters. Oberthal has been taken a prisoner and is about to be executed, but John, learning from him that Bertha is still alive and in the City of Munster, saves his life. He decides to attack the city at once and assembles his followers, praying for victory. *John:* "*King of Heaven.*"

ACT 4

Public Square of Munster. The Anabaptists have captured the city, and John governs it as a Prophet, feared and denounced by the people. Fides is here begging for bread and is met by Bertha, whom she informs of John's death. Bertha, believing the leader of the Anabaptists guilty of killing her lover, swears vengeance.

SCENE 2

Before Munster Cathedral. The Prophet is about to be crowned. *Coronation March.* As John passes into the church his mother sees him and greets him as her son. Realizing that it would be fatal to both for him to acknowledge her, he denounces her, telling his followers to kill him if she persists. Finally, realizing the situation, she declares she has made a mistake, and is taken away as a prisoner, believed to be mad.

ACT 5

Prison Vaults beneath Palace at Munster. Fides, imprisoned, believes her son will come to her. *Fides: "Oh, my cruel destiny."* An officer announces the Prophet. *Fides: "He comes."* He arrives, and she denounces him for his part in the terrible deeds and for representing himself as a Prophet. He repents, asking her forgiveness. Bertha, who has come by a secret passageway, now appears, intending to kill the Prophet. She is amazed when she learns that her lover is the Prophet, and, grief-stricken at the thought of his deeds, stabs herself and dies, cursing him.

SCENE 2

Great Hall of Palace. John has learned that Jonas, Matthiesen and Zacharias, fearing their enemies, intend to betray him in order to save themselves, and he plans accordingly. While the Anabaptists are banqueting with him, the Bishop of Munster, Count Oberthal and Jonas, Matthiesen and Zacharias enter and demand him as their prisoner. He secretly gives a signal and just as he is seized a terrible explosion is heard and the Palace is soon in flames. Fides rushes in, forgiving her son, and both of them, together with all of John's enemies, perish.

* * *

I PURITANI
(THE PURITANS)

OPERA IN THREE ACTS
MUSIC BY VINCENZO BELLINI
LIBRETTO BY COUNT PEPOLI
FIRST PRODUCTION—PARIS, 1835

CAST

LORD GAUTIER WALTON, Puritan
Governor-General ....*Basso*

ELVIRA, his daughter...........*Soprano*

SIR GEORGE, Elvira's uncle........*Basso*

LORD ARTHUR TALBOT, a cavalier
beloved by Elvira.................*Basso*

SIR RICHARD FORTH, a Puritan, who
loves Elvira.....................*Baritone*

SIR BRUNO ROBERTSON, Puritan..*Tenor*

QUEEN HENRIETTA, widow of Charles
I ....*Soprano*

PLACE—Near Plymouth
TIME—Shortly After the Execution of
Charles I

I Puritani

ACT 1

Outside the Fortress at Plymouth. Civil war is being waged between the Puritans, under Cromwell, and the Royalists. Sir Richard Forth, a Puritan, loves Elvira, whose father is favorable to the match. But Lord Walton declines to force his daughter to wed Sir Richard in view of the fact that she does not love him. The Puritan lover is disconsolate. *Sir Richard: "Ah, to me forever lost, flower of love."* The next scene occurs in Elvira's apartments. Her uncle, Sir George, has been successful in persuading her father not to force her to wed Sir Richard. *Sir George: "The night was growing dark."* Elvira is joyous at this news. Suddenly trumpets sound the arrival of Lord Arthur, the Royalist Cavalier, whom Elvira loves despite his politics. The Cavalier comes with presents among which is a white bridal veil. But soon after reaching Plymouth the Royalist discovers that Henrietta, widow of Charles I, is in prison and her fate will be the same as the King's. His loyalty to the Royalist party compels him to aid her in escaping. The Queen puts on Elvira's veil and the guards mistake her for the bride. Thus she escapes from prison. Elvira thinks that Sir Arthur has deserted her and she becomes insane. All the Puritans swear that Sir Arthur's supposed infamy will be avenged.

ACT 2

Camp of the Puritans. Announcement is made that Lord Arthur has been condemned to death by Parliament for aiding the Queen to escape. The demented Elvira appears and sings a lovely melody. *Elvira: "It was here in accents sweetest he would call me."* Elvira's uncle, Sir George, pleads with Sir Richard Forth to pardon Lord Arthur. The Cavalier's rival promises to do this providing Lord Arthur comes without arms. If he still is hostile to the Puritans he must die. Sir George assents to these conditions and he and Sir Richard pledge their loyalty to the Puritans in a splendid duet: *"Sound, sound the trumpet."*

ACT 3

Garden near Elvira's Home. Lord Arthur, pursued and fleeing from his enemies, hopes to get out of England. But before fleeing the country, he longs to see Elvira again. Elvira comes out into the garden, and seeing her lover, her reason instantly returns to her. In their happiness the sweethearts sing: *"Come, come to my arms."* Drums are heard and Elvira, fearing for Lord

I Puritani

Arthur, again becomes hysterical. Concern for her causes the Royalist to be captured by the Puritans. He is to be executed. But just in time a message comes from Cromwell telling of the defeat of the Royalists and the pardoning of all prisoners. Elvira again regains her reason and she and Lord Arthur are happily united.

* * *

THE QUEEN OF SHEBA

OPERA IN FOUR ACTS
MUSIC BY KARL VON GOLDMARK
LIBRETTO BY MOSENTHAL
FOUNDED ON THE BIBLICAL STORY
FIRST PRODUCTION—VIENNA, 1875

CAST

KING SOLOMON.................*Baritone*
HIGH PRIEST.....................*Basso*
SULAMITH, his daughter..........*Soprano*
ASSAD, favorite of Solomon.........*Tenor*
QUEEN OF SHEBA.........*Mezzo-Soprano*
ASTAROTH, her slave............*Soprano*

PLACE—Jerusalem.
TIME—Reign of Solomon

ACT 1

Solomon's Palace. Preparations for a splendid wedding are in progress. Assad, favorite courtier of Solomon, is to wed Sulamith, daughter of the High Priest. Assad has been sent to act as escort to the Queen of Sheba who is coming to visit Solomon. When he reaches Jerusalem and the Palace again he is greatly downcast. He tells Solomon that he does not love Sulamith but an eastern woman whom he accidently surprised while she was bathing in a stream. Now the Queen of Sheba appears in gorgeous array before Solomon. When she removes her veil and Assad sees her face he recognizes in her the young woman he saw in the bath. He goes toward her impulsively. But the proud and inconstant Eastern Queen refuses to recognize him and is presented to Solomon. Assad is beside himself with grief and disappointment.

ACT 2

Gardens by Moonlight. Here the Queen plans to lure Assad for she feels that she truly loves him despite her rejection. She has her slave sing a tender Oriental melody. Assad responds with a gradually rising song of passion, *"Magic Tones."* The Queen meets him and successfully uses her wiles to win him body and soul. The guards interrupt the passionate avowals. Now the Queen is beside herself with jealousy for

she learns that Solomon has commanded
Assad to marry Sulamith the next day. The
action of the next scene takes place inside
the Temple. Solomon and the Queen attend.
The latter brings as a bridal gift a golden
cup filled with pearls. Assad, utterly van-
quished by the loveliness of the Queen,
throws away his wedding ring and casts himself at her feet. Again the eastern beauty's
pride conquers her passion, and she denies
any feeling for Assad. The priests, believing the young man is possessed of evil spirits,
now begin a ceremony for the casting out of
the spirits. But suddenly the Queen softly
whispers Assad's name. Again the young
man is beside himself and begins praying
to the Queen as a goddess. The priests
sentence him to death for this blasphemy.
But Solomon, suspecting the true state of
affairs, orders Assad to be led away.

ACT 3

Festival Chamber of the Palace. A great
reception is given for the Queen, and the
dancers dance in her honor. The Queen
demands Assad's release from Solomon.
When he refuses she tries to ensnare even
him by her wiles. But in this she fails and
goes off vowing vengeance on the King. Sulamith pleads to Solomon for her loved one.

He deals with her kindly and promises peace in the end.

ACT 4

The Desert. Here Assad wanders for he has been exiled by Solomon. He is repentent now and longs to see Sulamith again. Here the Queen of Sheba finds him but the inconstant woman's wiles do not affect him now. Sulamith also finds him and forgives him. He dies happy in her arms.

* * *

RIGOLETTO

OPERA IN THREE ACTS
MUSIC BY GIUSEPPE VERDI
LIBRETTO BY PIAVE FROM HUGO'S
"THE KING AMUSES HIMSELF"
FIRST PRODUCTION—VENICE, 1851

CAST

DUKE OF MANTUA.................*Tenor*
RIGOLETTO, his hunchback jester....
..............................*Baritone*
GILDA, Rigoletto's daughter.......*Soprano*
SPARAFUCILE, an assassin..........*Basso*
MADDALENA, his sister..........*Contralto*
COUNT MONTERONE..........*Baritone*
COUNT CEPRANO..................*Basso*
COUNTESS CEPRANO, his wife....*Soprano*

Rigoletto

GIOVANNA, friend of Maddalena....
.... *Contralto*
BORSA, a courtier.................. *Tenor*

PLACE—Mantua.
TIME—Sixteenth Century

ACT 1

Court in the Duke's Palace. The Duke is a young profligate who loves every pretty woman he meets. He has now made a new conquest—a lovely young girl. He knows nothing of her except that she is visited by a man supposed to be her lover. The Duke: *" 'Mid the fair throng that sparkle around me."* The nobles are bitter against the Duke and his hunchback jester, Rigoletto, who mocks them. But they plan to get even with Rigoletto. One of them declares that the Jester, known as a woman hater, really has a sweetheart. They plan to watch him and have some fun. The old Count Monterone enters. The Duke has betrayed his daughter and he denounces him. Rigoletto mocks the old man. In his rage Monterone hurls an awful father's curse at Rigoletto. This curse makes a deep impression on the jester, for he has a daughter, whom he hides from the world. In the next scene the Jester is entering his own home. The assassin Sparafucile meets him and wants work to do,

Rigoletto says he will send for him if he needs him. Rigoletto: *"Yon assassin is my equal."* The Jester affectionately greets his lovely daughter Gilda. The girl assures him she has never been out except to Mass on Sunday. But she does not tell him of the student whom she has fondly observed. Rigoletto urges the maid to closely guard Gilda. *Duet, Rigoletto and Giovanna: "Safely guard this tender blossom."* When Rigoletto goes the student appears. He is none other than the Duke. He allays the girl's fears. *Duke: "Love is the sun by which passion is lighted."* Gilda is won, and when the Duke leaves she is in a romantic mood. *Gilda: "Carved upon my inmost heart."* The nobles now appear masked and Rigoletto comes upon them. In reply to his questions they tell him they are going to kidnap a lady of whom the Duke is very fond. Rigoletto wants to join in the fun and he too masks. The courtiers lead in a circle and stop before his own house. While they abduct his Gilda he holds the ladder for them. When they are gone Rigoletto discovers his horrible act and swoons.

ACT 2

Hall in the Duke's Palace. The courtiers tell the Duke they have captured Rigoletto's mistress, not knowing that she is the Jester's daughter and another conquest of the Duke's. *Chorus: "On mischief bent."* But the Duke learns that the girl is secreted in an adjoining room and he goes to her joyfully. Outside Rigoletto's voice is heard. *"Poor Rigoletto."* He enters, feigning indifference so that he may find Gilda. The courtiers all mock and baffle him and he is furious. *Rigoletto: "Race of Courtiers, vile rabble."* Gilda enters and she and her father embrace. The courtiers are astonished and retire in confusion. Gilda now confesses her guilt. *Gilda: "On every festal morning."* The Count Monterone passes and recalls his curse. Rigoletto cries that vengeance will not long be delayed—on the Duke. *Rigoletto and Gilda: "Yes, my vengeance."*

ACT 3

Home of Sparafucile. Rigoletto and his daughter appear. Gilda is in male attire ready to flee after vengeance has been consummated. The Duke is at the house and while drinking sings the celebrated air, *"Woman is fickle."* Gilda, concealed and watching, is astounded to see the Duke making love to Maddalena, sister of Sparafucile. *Great quartet; Rigoletto, Gilda, Duke, Maddalena: "Fairest daughter of the graces."*

The Duke retires to a room to go to sleep.
Rigoletto tells Gilda to hasten to Verona
and he will join her. The Jester now bargains with Sparafucile to murder the Duke.
It is agreed that Rigoletto will be given his
body in a sack at midnight. Rigoletto departs just as Gilda, who has disobeyed him,
returns. She hears Maddalena pleading with
her brother for the Duke's life as she herself loves him. Sparafucile says if a substitute can be had the Duke can escape.
Gilda now resolves to sacrifice herself to
save the Duke. When Rigoletto returns at
midnight a sack containing a human body is
handed to him to be thrown into the river.
As he drags it with him he suddenly hears
the sound of the Duke's voice: *"Woman is
fickle."* He opens the sack and his horrified
gaze rests on the dying Gilda. *Duet: "Rigoletto and Gilda: "In heaven above."* The
girl dies in his arms. The old Monterone's
curse is complete.

DAS RHEINGOLD

MUSIC-DRAMA IN FOUR SCENES
MUSIC AND DRAMA BY RICHARD WAGNER

CAST

WOTAN.........	⎫	........Baritone
DONNER........	Gods	..........Basso
FROH...........		..........Tenor
LOGE...........	⎭	..........Tenor
FRICKA.........	⎫	.........Soprano
FREIA.........	Goddesses	...Soprano
ERDA.........	⎭	.....Contralto
FASOLT........	Giants	.........Basso
FAFNER........		.........Basso
ALBERICH, a dwarf.	Nibelungs	.Baritone
MIME................		....Tenor
WOGLINDA...	⎫	...Soprano
WELLGUNDE.	Rhine Maidens	..Soprano
FLOSSHILDE..	⎭	..Contralto

"The Rheingold" is the first of the wonderful Ring of the Nibelung, the prelude to the Trilogy—"Die Walkure," "Siegfried," and "Gotterdammerung" ("Twilight of the Gods").

SCENE 1

Bottom of the Rhine. Here the three Rhine Maidens swim about guarding the Rheingold. Their beauty has caught the eye of Alberich, prince of the Nibelungs, a dwarf

[256]

race that lives down in the earth. He is
amorous but the Rhein Maidens make sport
of him. With the rising of the sun the Rheingold is revealed. The Rhine Maidens fool-
ishly tell Alberich that he who fashions a
ring from this treasure will possess power to
rule the world. Only one thing he cannot
have—Love. They do not think that Alberich
has high ambitions. But he snatches the
Rheingold from the rocks and disappears,
leaving the Maidens to mourn bitterly their
loss.

SCENE 2

Near the Castle of Walhalla on the Mountain Top. The Abode of the Gods. Wotan
and his wife Fricka awaken from a long sleep
to find that the giants have built for them
the wonderful castle of Walhalla. Wotan is
joyful, but Fricka reminds him of the price
he must pay. He has promised the giants
to give them Freia, the goddess of youth and
beauty. But Wotan says he only made the
bargain in jest. But the giants Fasolt and
Fafner eagerly pursue the goddess Freia.
Wotan now realizes that he must let the giants
have the goddess and they take her away.
The gods, without Freia, age rapidly. But
the god Loge has a plan to win her back. If
they can get the Rheingold from Alberich

they can give that to the giants in return for Freia. The giants tell them that if the Rheingold is not forthcoming without delay they will never have Freia again.

SCENE 3

Alberich's Cave. With the Rheingold, Alberich has become all-powerful and arrogant. The ring he has fashioned gives him power over everything. He makes Mime fashion a magic helmet that will transform the wearer or make him invisible. The gods Wotan and Loge come to secure from Alberich his wonderful treasures. Loge craftily doubts the power of the magic helmet. Alberich quickly transforms himself into a dragon. Then he becomes a toad. Wotan steps on the toad and Loge takes the helmet. Alberich resumes his natural shape and the gods bind him and take him away with them.

SCENE 4

Near Walhalla. Wotan and Loge drag the infuriated Alberich with them. They demand from him the Rheingold. He is forced to order the Nibelungs to bring the precious treasure up to the gods. Then the gods demand the ring. He is beside himself with rage at this but is forced to part with the ring also. But he curses it. *Alberich:* "Am I now free?" He declares it will bring misfortune to whoever holds it. But Wotan, paying very little attention to this curse, greatly admires the ring. The giants now come and demand that enough gold be placed around Freia to hide her. This the gods do, but there is a small opening still and into this the giants demand that the gods place the ring. The gods refuse and the giants are about to carry Freia off again when Erda rises from the earth. She warns Wotan that the curse of Alberich will stick to the ring and urges him to part with it. *Erda: "Waver, Wotan, waver. Quit the ring accursed."* Wotan gives up the ring. Immediately the power of the curse is shown for the giants quarrel as to who shall have it. A struggle ensues and Fafner kills Fasolt, and then departs with the treasure. Wotan now leads the gods back to Walhalla on a rainbow constructed by Donner, the god of thunder. As the gods cross the bridge the song of the Rhein Maidens is heard bewailing their loss. *"Rheingold, rarest gold."*

ROBERT LE DIABLE
(ROBERT THE DEVIL)

OPERA IN FIVE ACTS
MUSIC BY GIACOMO MEYERBEER
BOOK BY SCRIBE AND DELAVIGNE
FIRST PRODUCTION--PARIS, 1831

CAST

ROBERT, Duke of Normandy........*Tenor*
BERTRAM, his friend, the Evil One...*Basso*
RAMBALDO, a minstrel............*Tenor*
ISABELLA, Princess of Sicily........*Soprano*
ALICE, foster sister of Robert......*Soprano*
KING OF SICILY....................*Basso*

PLACE—Palermo.
TIME—Thirteenth Century.

Robert of Normandy is the son of an off-
spring of Satan and the Duchess of Normandy, such unions being not altogether im-
possible in the popular mind in those be-
nighted days. For his recklessness, daring
and evil powers Robert has been banished.
He is wandering in Sicily where he loves the
Princess Isabella.

Act 1

Camp near Palermo. Robert, his mysteri-
ous friend Bertram and the knights are feasting. A minstrel, Rambaldo, comes from

[260]

Normandy. He sings, *"Once there ruled in Normandy,"* and tells the story of the union of Robert's mother with the Evil One. Robert has him held a prisoner. But he is released when his, Rambaldo's, sister Alice, arrives. She proves also to be Robert's foster sister. She carries the will of Robert's mother. *"Go, she said, do not tarry."* Robert is not to read the will until he has proved himself. But Bertram induces Robert to gamble. *"Now fortune, smile on."* He loses everything to Bertram, even horse and armor. He fails to attend the tournament and loses his honor.

ACT 2

Chamber in the Palace. *Isabella: "How hateful to me all this splendor."* Alice brings a letter from Robert, and Isabella sends him money for new armor and weapons so that he can ride in the tournament. But Bertram already has lured Robert away.

ACT 3

Entrance to Cavern of Satan. Bertram here meets the demons. *Bertram: "I have well spread my toils."* He plans to gain the soul of Robert. Alice, who has come to seek Rambaldo, overhears the diabolical plan, and determines to save Robert. Bertram, arising from hell, threatens her if she reveals anything. Bertram induces Robert to consent to secure a magic branch from a ruined abbey. This will restore all his possessions, Bertram declares. In the next scene Bertram invokes the aid of the buried nuns in completing Robert's downfall. *Bertram: "Ye slumbering nuns."* The nuns appear as lovely maidens. They lead him to the grave of St. Rosalie. There he secures the magic branch.

ACT 4

Hall in the Palace. With the branch Robert makes knights and ladies fall asleep while he himself is invisible. He intends to carry Isabella off. *Robert: "O, how beautiful."* *Isabella: "Robert, my beloved."* At her pleading, he discards the magic branch and the spell is broken. He is attacked by knights, but Bertram saves him.

ACT 5

Entrance to the Cathedral of Palermo. Here Robert brings Bertram, who trembles on holy ground. The latter tries to get Robert to sign over his soul. But Alice saves him by recalling his mother's words of warning. Bertram is none other than his own evil father. She declares that Isabella has come to the cathedral to be married to him. *Trio:*

Robert le Diable

"What shall 1 do?" Robert still hesitates when the clock strikes the magic hour of twelve. Bertram disappears and Robert enters the church to marry Isabella. Alice weds Rambaldo.

* * *

ROMEO AND JULIET

OPERA IN FIVE ACTS
MUSIC BY CHARLES GOUNOD
LIBRETTO BY BARBIER AND CARRE FROM
SHAKESPEARE'S LOVE TRAGEDY
FIRST PRODUCTION—PARIS, 1867

CAST

CAPULET, a Veronese noble........*Basso*
JULIET, his daughter.............*Soprano*
PARIS, his kinsman...............*Baritone*
GREGORIO, his kinsman..........*Baritone*
TYBALT, his nephew..............*Tenor*
ROMEO, a Montague................*Tenor*
BENVOLIO, friend of Romeo.......*Tenor*
STEPHANO, page to Romeo.......*Soprano*
GERTRUDE, Juliet's nurse...*Mezzo-Soprano*
FRIAR LAWRENCE.................*Basso*
DUKE OF VERONA.................*Basso*

PLACE—Verona.
TIME—Middle Ages

Romeo and Juliet

ACT 1

Ballroom in Capulet's Home. Capulet is giving a great function, introducing his daughter Juliet to society. He presents her to the guests. Juliet sings a lovely waltz song: *"Song, jest, perfume and dances."* Romeo Montague enters the enemy's country masked. He is fascinated by Juliet and the girl by him. *Duet: "Lovely angel."* Tybalt recognizes in Romeo a Montague and threatens to kill him. But he is restrained by Capulet and the merriment continues.

ACT 2

Capulet's Garden, Showing Juliet's Balcony. Romeo, again braving danger, appears below Juliet's window in the night. *Romeo: "Rise, fairest sun in heaven."* Juliet appears speaking to the stars. *"Ah me—and still I love him."* Romeo reveals himself. *Duet: "Ah, go not yet."* They vow eternal constancy.

ACT 3

Cell of Friar Lawrence. Here Romeo and Juliet meet to be married. The Friar consents to wed them hoping that this will end all enmity between two powerful houses. After the marriage Juliet returns home with Gertrude, her nurse. The next scene is a street in Verona. Stephano, the page, sings an air before Capulet's home, thinking his master Romeo is still there. He arouses Gregorio and a fight ensues. The battle is interrupted by the arrival of Mercutio and Tybalt, who also begin to quarrel. Romeo appears, tries to make peace, and is insulted by Tybalt. He fights and slays him. The Duke of Verona hears of the act and banishes Romeo from the kingdom.

ACT 4

Juliet's Room. Here Romeo is secretly taking leave of Juliet before leaving the country. She pleads with him not to depart, but his going is a necessity. As he leaves Capulet and the Friar enter. They tell Juliet it was Tybalt's dying wish that she marry Paris. When alone with the Friar, Juliet tells him she prefers death to separation from Romeo. The good man, deeply touched, reveals a plan whereby she may be reunited to her husband. He gives her a sleeping potion which she is to take just before her proposed wedding to Paris. All will think she is dead. *Friar: "Loud will they praise the sound of lamentation."* When Capulet comes with Paris she drinks the potion and sinks unconscious into her father's arms. All think she is dead.

ACT 5

Tomb of Juliet. The lovely girl, who is mourned as dead, lies on her bier, still in a trance. Romeo has failed to get the Friar's message explaining the ruse. He forces his way into the tomb. Beside himself with grief, he drinks a vial of poison. But soon Juliet regains consciousness. Romeo heedless of the poison, embraces her in wild joy. *Romeo:* " *'Tis I—Romeo, thine own."* Duet: *"Come, the world is all before us."* But Romeo now remembers the poison and tells Juliet that he will soon be dead. Juliet, realizing that life is hopeless without Romeo, remembers her dagger. She draws it out and stabs herself. The lovers die in each other's arms, just as in the tragedy of Shakespeare.

* * *

DER ROSENKAVALIER

COMEDY IN THREE ACTS BY HUGO HOFMANNSTHAL

MUSIC BY RICHARD STRAUSS

FIRST PRODUCTION, DRESDEN, 1911

CAST

PRINCESS VON WERDENBERG, (wife of Field Marshal Prince von Werdenberg) ....*Soprano*

BARON OCHS OF LERCHENAU, her cousin ....*Bass*

Der Rosenkavalier

OCTAVIAN (a young gentleman of noble family) ....*Mezzo-Soprano*
HERR VON FANINAL (rich merchant, newly ennobled) ....*High Baritone*
SOPHIA, his daughter........*High Soprano*
MISTRESS MARIANNE LEITMETZER (duenna) ....*High Soprano*
VALZACCHI (a man of affairs) .....*Tenor*
ANNINA (his partner) ....*Alto*
Commissary of Police; Major-Domo of the Princess; Major-Domo of Faninal; the Princess' Attorney; Landlord; Singer; Scholar; Flute Player; Hairdresser; three orphans of noble family; milliner; footmen; waiters, etc., etc.

TIME—Early years of reign of Maria Theresa.
PLACE—Vienna.

ACT 1

Chamber of the Princess' Residence. Octavian, a young lad, kneeling on a footstool, embraces the princess, who is *en deshabille*. *"Why is it day?"* Footsteps, which they fear are those of the Prince returning unexpectedly from a hunting trip, disturb the love scene. Octavian hides behind a screen and returns shortly in the dress of a ladies' maid. They are much relieved to find when the door opens that it is the Baron Ochs von Lerchenau, a cousin

[267]

of the princess, but an altogether odious
character. He has come to the Princess
to have her recommend a well born gentleman to convey the silver rose—the customary
love-token—to his bride-elect, whom he
is marrying for her wealth, but considers
that he is demeaning himself in marrying
her. Octavian, disguised as the maid, at-
tracts him and he flirts with "her" and invites "her" to sup with him. The Princess,
as was the practice among royal ladies, sees
her hairdresser, milliner, lawyer, etc., during the call, and before the baron departs,
promises to have a young nobleman deliver
the silver rose. A love scene with Octavian
ensues, during which she tells him she will
allow him to be the rose-knight although
she knows what will happen in consequence.

ACT 2

Faninal's House. Octavian delivers the
silver rose, but falls in love with Sophia and
presses his own suit and not the Baron's.
The Baron arrives to have the contract duly
drawn and signed but by this time Sophia
and Octavian are in love, and she repulses
him, despite her father's wishes. The Baron's
remarks disgust Sophia and Octavian resents
them. Sophia's father, who is socially ambitious and anxious for the marriage with

the Baron, sides with the Baron and threatens to force Sophia to marry him. A note, reminding the Baron of his appointment with the Princess' ladies'-maid, is handed him and he departs to meet "her" (Octavian).

ACT 3

Tavern. Here, Octavian, disguised, keeps his appointment with the Baron. It has all been prearranged and many tricks are played on the Baron, even to the extent of an arrest by the police. In his effort to clear himself, he is really disgraced, and denounced by Faninal who has been sent for. The Princess' arrival is the signal for the police to withdraw and for Octavian to reveal himself. The Baron, promising to behave, pays all bills and as soon as he departs the lovers are united by the Princess.

SALOME

MUSIC DRAMA IN ONE ACT
MUSIC BY RICHARD STRAUSS
LIBRETTO BY OSCAR WILDE
FIRST PRODUCTION—DRESDEN, 1905

CAST

HEROD, Tetrach of Judea..........*Tenor*
HERODIAS, his wife.............*Contralto*
SALOME, her degenerate daughter..*Soprano*
JOKANAAN, the prophet..........*Baritone*
NARRABOTH, a young Syrian......*Tenor*
A PAGE........................*Contralto*

PLACE—Tiberias in Galilee.
TIME—30 A. D.

The scene is the magnificent terrace of
Herod's palace. At the back is a cistern in
which Jokanaan, the Prophet, has been im-
prisoned by Herod because of his teachings.
But fearing the Jews, he will not put
Jokanaan to death. Narraboth and his sol-
diers guard the entrance to the banquet hall.
Inside a great banquet is being given by
Herod and Herodias. Narraboth is madly
infatuated with the beautiful, passionate
Salome and expresses his love. A page tries
to dissuade him from such wild passions.
From the cistern now comes the voice of
Jokanaan telling of the coming of a greater
One than he. Salome meanwhile has come

out onto the cool terraces to escape the amorous eyes of Herod, her mother's husband. She hears the wonderful voice of the Prophet and her curiosity is aroused to a high pitch. She orders Narraboth to bring from the cistern the man feared by both Herod and Herodias. For love of Salome, the young Syrian disobeys his orders and has Jokanaan brought up onto the terraces. The stately, godly man begins a terrible denunciation of Herodias, the sinful queen. Salome is infatuated and longs to possess this wonderful man. She gives vent to her feelings in wild, abandoned words the burden of which is, *"I long to kiss thy mouth, Jokanaan."* This wild raving drives Narraboth to suicide. He kills himself at Salome's feet yet she does not notice him even a moment so infatuated is she with the Prophet. But the man of God denounces her and goes back to the cistern. Salome, now wild with passion, seizes hold of him and drags herself along the ground to the cistern. The Prophet finally descends leaving the abandoned girl alone with her unholy love. Now Herod, Herodias and the entire court come out onto the terraces. Herod, wine-drunk and fearful of impending dangers, is again fascinated by the lovely Salome. Again the warning voice of the Prophet comes up from the cistern. Herodias urges Herod to order the execution of the Prophet. But he still fears the Jews and refuses to have the man of God murdered. The Prophet's denunciations and prophesies continue to come from the cistern, driving Herodias to desperation. Now Herod, completely fascinated by Salome, orders her to dance for him, promising her anything to the half of his kingdom. The girl then begins the Dance of the Seven Veils in which she discards one veil after another and finishes almost nude before Herod. Now Salome wants her reward. Urged on by her mother, she demands nothing less than the head of Jokanaan. This horrible demand sobers Herod and he tries to dissuade Salome. But she is obdurate, and Herod shudders in terror. Finally he is forced to consent and a headsman descends into the well. He comes up with the dripping head of the Prophet on a platter. The court is horrified but Herodias is joyful. Salome, still beside herself with passion, demands the head. It is presented to her. She now begins her dances and gyrations with the head. *"I am athirst for thy body, and neither wine nor fruit can appease my desire."* Herod is in terror and orders the torches extinguished. Salome continues her adoration of the head in the semi-darkness. Unable to bear any longer her shameless exhibition of unholy and degenerate love, he orders the soldiers to kill her. With their shields the guards crush out Salome's life.

* * *

SAMSON AND DELILAH

OPERA IN THREE ACTS

MUSIC BY CAMILLE SAINT-SAENS

LIBRETTO BY FERDINAND LAMAIRE FROM

THE BIBLICAL STORY

FIRST PRODUCTION—WEIMAR, 1877

CAST

DELILAH ....*Contralto*
SAMSON ....*Tenor*
HIGH PRIEST OF DAGON.......*Baritone*
ABIMELECH, Satrap of Gaza.........*Basso*
AN OLD HEBREW..................*Basso*
PHILISTINE MESSENGER..........*Tenor*
FIRST PHILISTINE................*Tenor*
SECOND PHILISTINE.....:........*Basso*

PLACE—Gaza in Palestine
TIME—1150 B. C.

ACT 1

Square in Gaza. The Hebrews are lamenting greatly because of their helplessness against the Philistines. But Samson, the mighty, bids them hope and trust in God. *Samson: "Let us pause, O my brothers."*

[273]

These words bring cheer and comfort. But soon the crowd engages with the Philistines. In the struggle Samson slays Abimelech. A messenger comes with a message to the High Priest that everywhere the Hebrews are in revolt. The Philistines flee while the High Priest curses Samson. *High Priest: "Curses on his head."* The old Hebrews are joyous. *"Praise the Lord."* But now from the temple comes the lovely Delilah, attended by the equally lovely Priestesses of Dagon. She fascinates Samson despite his effort to resist. *Delilah's spring song: "Spring voices are singing."* She invites him to her home in the valley of Sorek, and as the curtain falls it is evident that he is in her power.

ACT 2

Home of Delilah. Delilah calls on Love to aid her in completing the downfall of Samson. *"O, Love, in my weakness give power."* The High Priest urges her to be firm in her purpose to deliver her lover to the Philistines. Samson comes and Delilah greets him with seeming devotion. She sings the beautiful aria: *"My heart at thy sweet voice."* She seeks to discover the secret of his marvelous strength. But he resists manfully. Finally he follows her to her bedchamber, telling her that his strength lies in

[274]

his hair. Here he falls asleep. Delilah cuts off his locks and the Philistines surround and overpower him. In revenge they put out his eyes.

ACT 3

The Prison at Gaza. Here the shorn Samson is grinding at the mills. He prays to God to forgive him his sin. *"O, see my pain, Lord."* Outside the Hebrews mournfully reproach him for his weakness against the charms of Delilah. The Philistines take him out of the prison and march him in triumphal procession to their temple. In the great temple Delilah and the maidens rejoice over Samson's downfall. *Chorus: "The sun rises."* They will have sport with Samson and he is ordered to sing in praise of Delilah. The Philistines are delighted and Delilah taunts him. But Samson prays to his God in whom he still has faith. He has a boy lead him between the two main pillars that support the temple. With a final prayer his former strength returns. Grasping the marble pillars and bending forward, he brings down the entire temple on the wicked Philistines and himself.

SECRET OF SUSANNE

OPERA IN ONE ACT
MUSIC BY ERMANNO WOLF-FERRARI
BOOK BY MAX KALBECK FROM A FRENCH STORY
FIRST PRODUCTION—MUNICH, 1909

CAST

COUNT GIL......................*Baritone*
COUNTESS GIL, his wife.........*Soprano*
SANTE, a dumb (speechless) servant

SCENE

Drawing Room of the Count's Home with Windows at Back. The Count comes in considerably worried for he has seen a woman on the street who resembles his wife and he knows that the Countess does not venture out alone. He thinks that his eyes may have deceived him, but he knows that his nose does not. Surely there is cigarette smoke in the air. He does not smoke, Sante does not—so whence the odor? Answer—another man. But when the lovely young Countess comes in the jealous husband forgets his suspicion and is all adoration. *Count: "Sweeter than the sweetest; fairer than the fairest."* They sip chocolate together. *Duet: "Tell me, do you remember?"* But when he embraces her the odor of tobacco smoke on her gown sends Cupid scudding for safety. He immediately

[276]

demands if the Countess has not some secret she is keeping from him. Now the Count is secretly certain that there is another man in the case. He storms about the room and in his fury smashes up the furniture and bric-a-brac in shameful fashion. The Countess leaves the room in tears and the Count in the depths of despair. Now comes the lovely orchestral interlude during which Sante clears up the wreckage. When the Countess returns the Count decides to depart. After trying in vain to allay his suspicions, the dutiful wife gives him his hat and gloves and he hurries off in a beastly temper. Thinking she is now free to enjoy herself the Countess lights a cigarette and begins to enjoy a smoke, showing that she has become somewhat addicted to the habit. She is surprised by the quick return of the Count, and in her confusion tosses the cigarette into the fire. But the odor of its smoke remains, and every sniff of it increases the rage of the Count. He rushes desperately from one part of the room to another looking for his rival whom he expects to annihilate. His wife wants to know what on earth he is looking for. He snaps, *"My umbrella."* The Countess hands him his umbrella. He is in such a rage that he smashes it over his knees and rushes out again, hoping to get on the trail of the man who is breaking up his once happy abode. The Countess, though troubled by this wild jealousy, finds philosophic comfort in another cigarette which she slowly puffs after turning down the light. *Susanne: "What joy to watch with half-closed eyes the gossamer mist rising in azure rings."* Suddenly the Count appears at a window. He leaps into the room, sure now that he has his man. Susanne holds the lighted cigarette behind her. The Count thinks she is hiding her lover and makes a grab for him. His hand encounters the hot end of the cigarette. The terrible secret is revealed—the wife smokes. The Count is happy and he and his wife take puffs from the same cigarette. *Duet: "All life ends in smoke."* Merrily they dance—Sante appears and is astonished at the procedure. But the Count and Countess go off to their apartments where he too lights a cigarette.

SEMIRAMIDE

TRAGIC OPERA IN TWO ACTS
MUSIC BY G. ANTONIO ROSSINI
LIBRETTO BY ROSSI, FOUNDED ON VOLTAIRE'S
TRAGEDY, "SEMIRAMIS"
FIRST PRODUCTION—VENICE, 1823

CAST

SEMIRAMIDE, Queen of Babylon..*Soprano*
ARSACES, commander of Assyrian
  Army ....*Contralto*
GHOST OF NINUS.................*Basso*
OROE, chief of the Magi.........*Basso*
ASSUR, a Prince of Royal Blood....*Baritone*
AZEMA, a Princess...............*Soprano*

PLACE—Babylon.
TIME—Antiquity

ACT 1

Temple of Belus. Ninus (or Agamemnon) King of Babylon, has been murdered by his wife Semiramide. In the murder the Queen was aided by Assur, a prince of whom she was enamored. Now a festival is in progress and Semiramide is to choose a successor to reign over Babylon. Assur expects the Queen to choose him. But Semiramide has already decided in her own mind to select Arsaces, the victorious commander of her armies, of whom she has become violently enamored.

Semiramide

As the religious rites continue strange evidences of the power of the gods are seen and felt. The people regard them as ill omens and eagerly await the coming of Arsaces who has been sent to the Oracle. Finally he arrives. *Arsaces: "Behold me at length in Babylon."* He delivers a scroll which reveals the fact that King Agamemnon was murdered. He now plans to wed Azema, the Princess. But Assur tells him that he has won Azema and also the Queen's favor so that she will name him her successor on the throne. In an ante-room of the palace Azema confesses her love for Arsaces. The next scene is a garden where Semiramide is softly singing. *"At length a brilliant ray lights up my soul."* Arsaces comes and she warmly praises him and tells him to wait but a little while and Assur's plans will be thwarted. *Duet: "To visions most delightful."* Now the court gathers in a magnificent hall in the palace. Here Semiramide declares that Arsaces shall be her successor and that he shall marry her as well. Arsaces is astonished; so is Assur. The former declares it is not the throne he desires but Azema. But all at once all eyes are turned to the tomb of Ninus. From it issues the ghost of the murdered King and it commands Arsaces to come down into the tomb.

[280]

ACT 2

Ante-room of the Palace. Here Semiramide and Assur meet. Each accuses the other of crime in the murder of Ninus. *Duet: "O night of horror."* The second scene is the interior of the sanctuary. Arsaces, returning, comes to be crowned with Ninus' crown. He has learned from the tomb that Ninus' son still lives. The chief of the Magi informs that he is Ninus' lost son and son also of Semiramide. He is astounded, but the Magi chief unfolds still further secrets. Arsaces learns of the murder of Ninus by his mother Semiramide. The deed must be avenged by him. He finds Semiramide and shows her the paper written by Ninus just before he died. In this he tells of his murder by Assur and Semiramide. The Queen is overcome with grief and remorse, and learning now that Arsaces is her son, urges him to slay her. But this he will not do because she is his mother. *Duet: "Dark day of horror."* Arsaces takes his vengeance out on Assur whom he pursues even to the dark tomb. Here in the gloom Semiramide comes between the men and receives the fatal thrust meant for Assur. The opera ends with Arsaces fainting in the arms of the Magi chief and Assur in the grip of the guards.

SIEGFRIED

MUSIC DRAMA IN THREE ACTS
MUSIC AND DRAMA BY RICHARD WAGNER
FIRST PRODUCTION—BAYREUTH, 1876

CAST

SIEGFRIED .... *Tenor*
MIME .... *Tenor*
WOTAN .... *Baritone*
ALBERICH .... *Baritone*
FAFNER .... *Basso*
ERDA .... *Contralto*
BRUNNHILDE .... *Soprano*

Sieglinde, sent into the forest by Brunnhilde before the Valkyrie is placed on the
fire-encircled rocks, has given birth to Siegfried, a son. Sieglinde dies in giving birth
to the child but bequeaths him and the
broken pieces of the sword to Mime, the
Nibelung. The latter hopes to forge for
Siegfried a sword with which he can slay
the giant Fafner, now a mighty dragon, and
regain the Ring.

ACT 1

Mime's Smithy in the Forest. Mime is trying to forge the sword for Siegfried. *"Heart-
breaking bondage."* The hero Siegfried rushes
in on his timid foster father and badly scares

him with a huge bear he has been driving. Then he takes the new sword and easily breaks it. He now questions Mime about his origin. The dwarf tells him about Siegmund and Sieglinde and the broken sword. Siegfried commands Mime to mend the sword and he goes back into the forest. The god Wotan comes in the guise of the Wanderer. He tells Mime that he who does not know fear will be able to forge the sword and that he will also take Mime's head. When Siegfried returns Mime tries to make him understand fear. *"Feltest thou ne'er in forest dark?"* But Siegfried cannot understand. Then Mime tells him of the mighty dragon Fafner in the forest. He is eager to go after him. But Mime refuses to mend the sword. Siegfried forges it himself and is in high glee. Mime plans to murder Siegfried in his sleep if the youth succeeds in killing the dragon and gaining the Ring.

ACT 2

The Dragon's Cave. Alberich waits. The dwarf hopes to slay the slayer of Fafner and thus get the Ring. Wotan announces the coming of the hero to Alberich. The latter awakens the dragon and wants the Ring in return for the warning that may save his life. But the dragon refuses him any reward. Sieg-

fried in the forest listens to the lovely songs
of the birds. Now he blows his horn, arous-
ing the dragon. The beast bears down on
him, and Siegfried joyously enters into the
combat. He quickly slays the monster. Its
blood on his lips makes him understand the
wonderful language of birds. In obedience
to the instruction of the warblers, he enters
the cave to get the Ring. He secures it and
as he comes out he is enabled to read the
treacherous mind of Mime. He kills the
dwarf without further ado. Again in the forest he listens to the magic song of the birds.
*Bird: "Hey, Siegfried has now slain the sinis-
ter dwarf."* Then he learns of Brunnhilde
sleeping on the rocks encircled by fire. The
bird guides him to the sleeping Valkyrie.

ACT 3

Wild Spot in the Mountains. Wotan, fatigued with the struggle, tells Erda, his earth-
goddess wife, that he does not fear the end
of the gods but welcomes it. He is willing
to have Siegfried possess the Ring and with
Brunnhilde rule the world. But to test Siegfried's courage he blocks his path. With a
stroke the hero splinters Wotan's sword and
plunges on. *Siegfried: "Heavenly glow,
brightening glare."* He plunges through the
flames and reaches the sleeping Brunnhilde

on the rocks. He arouses her with a tender
kiss. She is joyous to recognize in him the
hero who can save the world. Feeling passion for the first time, Siegfried ardently
declares himself. Brunnhilde, the goddess,
begs him to spare her. *Brunnhilde: "Deathless was I; deathless am I."* But Siegfried
ignores her plea, and soon Brunnhilde discovers that she is only a woman after all.
Brunnhilde: "O, high-minded boy." She
sinks into Siegfried's arms as the curtain falls.

* * *

SIMON BOCCANEGRA

OPERA IN THREE ACTS AND PROLOGUE BY VERDI
ORIGINAL LIBRETTO BY PIAVE, REVISED BY
ARRIGO BOITO

FIRST VERSION PRESENTED IN VENICE IN 1857. RE-
VISED VERSION PRESENTED IN MILAN, 1880. FIRST
GIVEN AT METROPOLITAN IN 1931. AGAIN IN
1939.

CAST

PAOLO ALBIANI, a gold-spinner of
  Genoa ....*Baritone*
PIETRO, a Genoese commoner........*Bass*
SIMON BOCCANEGRA, a corsair
  (later Doge of Genoa) ....*Baritone*
JACOPO FIESCO, Genoese nobleman..*Bass*
AMELIA GRIMALDI, daughter of
  Boccanegra ....·...*Soprano*

[285]

Simon Boccanegra

GABRIELE ADORNO, her lover.....*Tenor*
Amelia's maidservant..............*Soprano*
A captain of the guard.............*Tenor*

PLACE—Genoa
TIME—14th century

PROLOGUE

The determination of two commoners, Paolo Albiani, goldsmith, and his henchman, Pietro, has torn Genoa into factions. The two conspirators are huddled in the public square outside the dwelling of the hated aristocrat, Fiesco. Boccanegra, a young corsair, enters. To his surprise the plotters offer him the Doge's crown. He is in love with Maria Fiesco, and because she is kept from him by her proud father, Boccanegra joins the plot. The gates of the Fiesco palace open and Jacopo announces, weeping, that his daughter Maria is dead. Seeing Boccanegra, his sorrow turns to rage, for the corsair is the father of Maria's illegitimate child. Simon pleads forgiveness. Fiesco says: "Not until you yield me the daughter Maria bore you!" Then the crowds enter acclaiming Boccanegra for Doge.

ACT I

The scene is the Grimaldi gardens. Twenty-five years have passed. Boccanegra is Doge.

and under Paola's guidance, a tyrant. Meanwhile Fiesco, concealing his identity under the name of Andrea, has organized the Guelphs who meet secretly outside Genoa. Fiesco lives in the Grimaldi palace overlooking the sea. With him lives Amelia, an orphan, whom he has raised as his heiress without knowing that she is his Maria's child by Boccanegra. Now grown to lovely womanhood, Amelia stands singing when Gabriele Adorno, her lover, and one of Fiesco's plotters against the Doge, enters. Just then the Doge appears to claim Amelia's hand for his old favorite Paolo. She confesses that she is not Grimaldi's daughter, and by means of a locket discovers she is the Doge's daughter. They embrace. Scene changes to council chamber where Simon tells Paolo that Amelia is not for him. Paolo, in revenge, has his hirelings abduct her. A riot breaks out headed by Adorno and an elderly nobleman whom the Doge does not recognize. Adorno tells Simon that Amelia has been kidnapped by one of the Doge's powerful clique. He threatens to plunge his sword into Simon's breast, when Amelia appears and pleads for Adorno's life. The Doge demands the name of the abductor. She tells him that the guilty one is in the room. Paolo is forced to repeat after Simon a solemn curse upon the guilty one. Sick with fright and horror he does so, and rushes from the room.

ACT II

Paolo, now an outcast bent upon revenge, pours a phial of poison in the Doge's drinking bowl. He also has tried unsuccessfully to get Fiesco to assassinate Simon. Then he brings Gabriele, whom he has worked up to kill the tyrant, to the Doge's chambers. Amelia enters and pleads for her father's life. Trumpets announce the approach of the Doge. Amelia secretes Adorno in an alcove. The Doge sends her from the room. Wearily he drinks from the poison bowl and falls asleep. Adorno emerges from the alcove to stab the Doge, but Amelia, who has reentered, restrains him. The Doge awakes and tells Adorno to strike since he already has taken that which he loves better than life, his daughter. In humility Adorno joins swords with the Doge against his enemies.

ACT III

The Guelph rebellion has been crushed. Generously, Simon spares the lives of the leaders, including Fiesco. The scene is within the Ducal palace. The wretched Paolo is being led forth to execution. As he passes Fiesco he says: "Boccanegra will follow me in death. I have poisoned him." The Doge

enters, groping for his throne. The palace
is darkened. "For a breath of air," Simon
gasps. Fiesco advances triumphantly. "Your
hour has come, Simon!" he shouts. Simon,
knowing death is near, summons Amelia and
Gabriele whose marriage has just been sol-
emnized. In his last breath he tells his beloved Amelia that Andrea, the Guelph, really
is Fiesco, her own grandsire. The ancient
feud is at an end. The dying Simon bequeaths his ducal crown to Gabriele Adorno.

* * *

LA SONNAMBULA

OPERA IN THREE ACTS

MUSIC BY VINCENZO BELLINI

LIBRETTO BY FELICE ROMANI

FIRST PRODUCTION—MILAN, 1831

CAST

COUNT RUDOLPH.................*Basso*
TERESA, a miller.........*Mezzo-Soprano*
AMINA, adopted daughter of Terasa *Soprano*
ELVINO, betrothed to Amina........*Tenor*
LISA, innkeeper, in love with El-
vino ....*Soprano*
ALESSIO, peasant admirer of Lisa....*Basso*
A NOTARY......................*Tenor*

PLACE—Swiss Village.
TIME—19th Century

La Sonnambula

ACT 1

A Village Square. Men and maidens make merry over the forthcoming wedding of Amina and Elvino. But Lisa is sad, for she loves Elvino too. *"Sounds so joyful."* The future bride and groom appear and sign the contract. Duet: *"Take now this ring."* Suddenly into the midst of the throng a gallant stranger gallops. He says he is going to the castle and will remain at the inn that night, completing his journey next morning. He is introduced and is much impressed with Amina. He pays her considerable attention. He tells the peasants that in childhood he lived with the former lord of the castle and now brings news of the lord's son, who had disappeared. The peasants tell him, however, of a spectre that haunts the country. Chorus: *"When dusky nightfall."* The stranger makes light of their tale, and is shown to his room by Lisa, the innkeeper. When he departs the bridegroom is jealous, and rebukes Amina for her interest in the stranger. Duet: *"I envy those amorous toyings."*

ACT 2

The Stranger's Room. The stranger is well pleased with the evening's pleasure. Lisa enters and inquires if he is comfortable. She indicates that the villagers suspect he is none other than the Count Rudolph himself. With this information, the landlady departs, dropping her veil as she goes out. Now Amina, walking in her sleep, comes into the room. The Count is surprised at such conduct but quickly sees that the girl is not conscious of her act. But Lisa, peeping in, puts an uncharitable view on the thing and goes to summon Elvino. The Count departs via a window and Amina lies down on his bed. Elvino and the others enter, more than astonished to find Amina in the Count's bedroom and bed. She wakes now and is herself astonished. But Elvino, not understanding, repulses her. *Duet: "Not in thought's remotest dreaming."* Teresa, the adopted mother, is the only one who stands up for Amina.

ACT 3

Valley near the Castle. Teresa and Amina are going to the castle and induce the Count to clear up the situation that has so deeply involved the good name of Amina. They are met by the jealous Elvino, who again denounces Amina. This time he takes the wedding ring from her. The next scene shows the mill of Teresa. Elvino, seeking solace, has turned his attentions to Lisa and they are on their way to the church. The Count stops them and declares that Elvino was wrong and that Amina has done no wrong. But Elvino refuses to listen to explanations. Now Teresa, woman-like, shows him a veil that his new sweetheart, Lisa, must have dropped in the Count's room. He now believes that she too is unfaithful and is in despair over the infidelity of woman. But soon he is convinced of his error. Amina, walking in her sleep again, comes from a window in the mill. She climbs down the big wheel while all are breathless lest she slip and fall. She sings of her love for Elvino. *"Sweet flowers, tenderest emblem."* Finally she reaches the foot of the wheel safely. Elvino understands now how she came to be in the Count's room, and he joyfully embraces her as she awakens. *Duet: "Recall not one earthly sorrow."*

TALES OF HOFFMANN

OPERA IN THREE ACTS WITH A PROLOGUE
AND AN EPILOGUE
MUSIC BY JACQUES OFFENBACH
LIBRETTO BY JULES BARBIER, FROM THE
TALES OF E. T. A. HOFFMANN
FIRST PRODUCTION—PARIS, 1881

CAST

HOFFMANN, the poet..............*Tenor*
NICLAUS, his friend..............*Soprano*
OLYMPIA, the mechanical doll....*Soprano*
GIULIETTA, the courtesan........*Soprano*
ANTONIA ....*Soprano*

COPPELIUS ..
DAPERTUTTO { The Evil One in } *Baritone*
DR. MIRACLE { Various Guises }

LUTHER, inn-keeper.................*Basso*
SCHLEMIL, lover of Giuletta.........*Basso*
SPALANZANI, an apothecary........*Tenor*
CRESPEL, father of Antonia.........*Basso*

PLACE—Various Parts of Europe.
TIME—19th Century.

PROLOGUE

Luther's Tavern. Here the poet Hoffmann
and his companion Niclaus are warmly
greeted by Hoffmann's student friends. *Chorus: "Master Luther."* They all drink and

Tales of Hoffmann

sing. His friends accuse Hoffmann of being in love. He pleads not guilty, and in a dreamy mood agrees to tell the story of his three fantastic loves. Each of the three acts that follows is one of these queer stories.

ACT 1

Ballroom in Spalanzani's Home. Spalanzani is a mechanical genius who has constructed a life-size doll that looks and acts like a human being. He exhibits her, Olympia, as his beautiful daughter. Hoffmann comes along and Coppelius, the Evil One, sells him a pair of magic glasses. He falls deeply in love with Olympia. *Hoffmann: "'Tis she."* Olympia is not responsive, but she sings just as any lovely girl might do. *Olympia: "The birds in the trees."* Niclaus tries to persuade Hoffmann to give up his mad infatuation, but the poet will not be persuaded. But in the furious dance something goes wrong and the beautiful Olympia literally flies all to pieces. To Hoffmann it is an uncanny, tragic end to his amours.

ACT 2

Court by a Canal in Venice. Giulietta, the wondrously beautiful courtesan, is entertaining lavishly. Here the famous barcarolle is sung by Giulietta and Dapertutto: *"O, night of love."* The maidens and men also sing. *Chorus: "Those who weep."* Hoffmann meets and loves the courtesan, though Niclaus again tries to make him see things clearly. *Hoffmann: "The sky lends thee splendor."* Dapertutto, the Evil One in human form, owns the shadow, or soul, of Schlemil, who also loves Giulietta. He also hopes to obtain the soul of Hoffmann. The poet easily falls into the trap laid by Giulietta. She tells him that he may have the key to her bedroom if he challenges Schlemil, who now has it. Hoffmann challenges and kills Schlemil. But instead of winning Giulietta, he sees her sail off down the canal in Dapertutto's arms.

ACT 3

Home of Krespel. Here Hoffmann loves the sweet, delicate Antonia. The girl's mother was a great singer, and Antonia loves to sing though she knows it may overtax her lungs. Her father forbids her to sing, but Hoffmann wants to hear her. *Hoffmann and Antonia: " 'Tis a song of love."* Dr. Miracle, the Evil One, comes to the girl and shows her a vision of her mother who urges her to sing. She obeys the vision and the strain is too much. She dies in Hoffmann's arms.

EPILOGUE

Here Hoffmann finishes his stories. He has had three kinds of loves—one that comes from mere beauty, one that springs from lustful passion, and one based on pure motives. Now he has had enough. In the future his only love will be the Muse who never proves unfaithful. Dreaming of her, Hoffmann falls asleep.

* * *

TANNHAUSER

MUSIC DRAMA IN THREE ACTS
MUSIC AND DRAMA BY RICHARD WAGNER
FIRST PRODUCTION—DRESDEN, 1845

CAST

HERMANN, Landgrave of Thuringia..*Basso*
TANNHAUSER ....*Tenor*
WOLFRAM VON ESCHENBACH..*Baritone*
WALTHER VON DER VOGEL-
    WEIDE ....*Tenor*
BITEROLF ....*Basso*
HEINRICH, the writer.............*Tenor*
ELIZABETH, niece of the Land-
    grave ....*Soprano*
VENUS ....*Soprano*
A YOUNG SHEPHERD...........*Soprano*

PLACE—Thuringia and the Wartburg.
TIME—13th Century

ACT 1

The Venusberg. Here the lovely Venus loves the romantic Tannhauser and surrounds him with maidens and beautiful flowers. But he is melancholy. *Venus: "Art thou wavering?"* *Tannhauser: "For earth I'm yearning."* He wearies of the "soft chains of shame." Venus, infuriated, tells him to depart, but warns him that he will long to be back with her. Suddenly Tannhauser finds himself in a beautiful valley. Pilgrims to Rome pass him in procession. *Pilgrims' Chorus: "Almighty, praise to thee."* Tannhauser kneels in prayer. Here he is found by the Landgrave and his friends. The knights recognize him as their long-lost brother who departed because he was unsuccessful in song, and they joyfully receive him. Wolfram tells him that his, Tannhauser's, singing won the heart of Elizabeth. *Wolfram: "When for the palm in song."* At mention of Elizabeth's name Tannhauser agrees to enter the forthcoming song contest at the Wartburg.

ACT 2

Hall in the Wartburg. Elizabeth is happy, hearing of Tannhauser's return. *"O hall of song, I give thee greeting."* The unselfish Wolfram, who loves Elizabeth, leads Tannhauser to her and kneels at her feet. Soon all assemble for the contest. Landgrave addresses the throng. *"Minstrels assembled here."* Wolfram sings first—his eulogy of love. *Wolfram: "Gazing upon this assembly fair."* He sings of love as pure and ethereal. Tannhauser hotly replies, singing of the sensuous love he has known with Venus. *"O, minstrel if 'tis thus."* Other knights uphold Wolfram, and Tannhauser sings in praise of Venus. The knights are now infuriated and rush on Tannhauser with drawn swords. But Elizabeth saves him. *Elizabeth: "Away from him."* A distant song of pilgrims is heard. Tannhauser is penitent and decides to join them and go to Rome for forgiveness.

ACT 3

Valley of the Wartburg. Elizabeth kneels at a shrine in prayer. She questions returning pilgrims but can learn nothing of Tannhauser. She now gives up hope of his return and prays to the Virgin. *Elizabeth's prayer: "O, blessed Virgin, hear my prayer."* The noble Wolfram comes upon her and wishes to accompany her. She is grateful but departs, leaving him alone. Sadly he sings the lovely Song of the Evening Star: *"Like death's dark shadow."* Now Tannhauser comes in rags, unforgiven. As Venus had predicted, he longs for the Venusberg. He tells Wolfram of the Pope's failure to pardon him. *"Rome I gained at last."* Venus appears to the unhappy man in a vision. Wolfram reminds him of Elizabeth and again Tannhauser is penitent. Now a sorrowful company comes bearing the body of the dead Elizabeth. With a prayer to her as his saint, Tannhauser dies. But a budding rod tells that he has at last been forgiven.

* * *

THAIS

OPERA IN THREE ACTS BY MASSENET
TEXT BY GALLET
BASED ON THE NOVEL BY ANATOLE FRANCE
FIRST PRODUCTION—PARIS, 1894

CAST

ATHANAEL, a monk.............*Baritone*
NICIAS, a young Sybarite...........*Tenor*
THAIS, a courtesan..............*Soprano*
PALEMON, the head monk...........*Basso*
ALBINE, an abbess.........*Mezzo Soprano*
MYRTALE ..... { Slaves } ....*Soprano*
CROBYLE ..... { Slaves } ....*Soprano*
LA CHARMEUSE, a dancer

SCENE—Theban Desert and Alexandria, Egypt
TIME—Early Christian Era

Thais

ACT 1

Cenobite huts on the banks of the Nile. The monks are at supper and are offering prayers for the safe return of Athanael, who has journeyed to Alexandria to protest against the luxury and corruption of that city. While they are praying, he returns, weary and disheartened, having found that city given up to sin and ruled by Thais, a beautiful courtesson. He is anxious to return and convert her to his faith, but Palemon warns him not to venture there again. In his dreams that night he sees her half-clad in the theatre, posing before a crowd as Aphrodite. The people applaud, acclaiming her a goddess. Athanael awakens (*"Oh, shame! Oh, madness! Oh, eternal gloom!"*), and, calling the monks together, bids them farewell, although they try to dissuade him.

SCENE 2

Alexandria. Nicias' home. Athanael arrives, asking for Nicias, whom he knew years before when living in Alexandria. *Athanael:* *"Oh, dreadful city of doom."* Nicias greets him as an old friend. He questions Nicias about Thais, and he tells him that at present he is her accepted lover, but that he is paying extravagantly for the distinction. Athanael then unfolds his plan, which idea Nicias ridi-

[300]

cules, although promising to help him, and
invites him to a dinner that evening at which
Thais will be present. He accepts the invita-
tion and allows the slaves to cover his ragged
robes with a beautiful garment, and when
Thais presently appears amid cheering, she
is curious to know about him. Athanael
frankly tells his purpose, and she seeks to
allure him with her charms (*Thais: "Why
art thou so hard, so unyielding?"*) and when
she attempts to pose as in the dream, he flees,
horror-stricken. She bids him come to her
house and she will listen.

ACT 2

Thais' house. After the night's revelry she
returns home, fatigued. *"Alone at last."* She
prays to Aphrodite for a continuance of
beauty and awaits Athanael, whom she thinks
will be her next lover. Athanael, at first
spellbound at her loveliness, pauses at the
door, silently praying; then, advancing, tells
her (*"Thais, I love thee"*) that the love he
offers is from God. As she listens she places
incense in a burner and invokes Venus.
Thais: "Venus, enchantress, queen." The
voice of Nicias is heard, and Athanael departs, saying he will wait outside until the
dawn.

Thais

Outside her palace. Moonlight floods the
court, and through the windows come the
sounds of revelry. Thais slowly appears and
tells Athanael that she has decided to leave
all and follow him, and he tells her he will
take her to a monastery. He bids her destroy
all traces of her former life, and she asks to
take with her a little image of Eros (*Thais:*
"This little ivory image"), which he breaks
by throwing on the pavement. They set fire
to her house. The revelers from Nicias' home
now appear and sing and dance. *Duet: "She*
whose light steps turn hither." They try to
detain Thais, but Nicias, realizing the situation, appeases the crowd by scattering gold,
and she follows Athanael. As they are leaving, her palace burns.

ACT 3

An oasis in the desert. Thais, utterly fatigued, arrives with Athanael, who urges her
onward; but when she sinks down, fainting,
his compassion is aroused and he gets her a
drink from the well. *Thais, alone: "Oh, holy*
messenger." At this moment the nuns are
heard. *Chorus: "Pater noster, qui es in*
coelis." Athanael intrusts her in their care
and she bids him *"Farewell forever."*

[302]

SCENE *2*

The Cenobite dwellings. Athanael returns
and the monks congratulate him upon his
success. He is weighted down with sorrow
and confesses to them that he can think of
nothing but his love for Thais. Palemon,
pitying him, reminds him of his warning;
then leaves him to his prayers. Later, in a
vision, he sees Thais dying at the monastery,
and, grief-stricken, he rushes out into the
desert. *Athanael: "Thais must die."*

ACT 4

The garden of the monastery. Surrounded
by nuns, Thais lies dying. *Albine: "God
calls her and a shroud will veil her soon."*
Athanael enters inquiring for her. The nuns
lead him to her, and she reminds him of her
conversion. *Thais: "Heaven opens its gates.
Angelic forms I see."* Athanael begs her to
come back to him, his heart now filled only
with earthly love (*Athanael: "Come! Mine
are thou"*), but, looking toward Heaven, she
calls to God, and as she dies he falls to the
earth with a cry of despair.

TOSCA

OPERA IN THREE ACTS
MUSIC BY GIACOMO PUCCINI
LIBRETTO BY ILLICA AND GIACOSA, FROM THE
DRAMA OF VICTORIEN SARDOU
FIRST PRODUCTION—ROME, 1900

CAST

FLORIA TOSCA, an opera singer...*Soprano*
MARIO CAVARADOSSI, an artist....*Tenor*
BARON SCARPIA, chief of police..*Baritone*
CESARE ANGELOTTI, an escaped
  prisoner ....*Basso*
A SACRISTAN...................*Baritone*
SPOLETTA, agent of police.........*Tenor*
SCIARRONE, gendarme.............*Basso*
PLACE—Rome. TIME—1800

ACT 1

Interior of the Church of Sant' Andrea.
Mario is painting a Madonna. His model
has been an unknown worshiper who has
come regularly to the church to pray. Mario
loves Tosca, the singer, and notices that his
Madonna strangely resembles her. *Mario:*
"Strange harmony." Soon his old friend Angelotti rushes in. Held as a political prisoner, he has escaped. Mario hides him in
the chapel from whence he will escape in his
sister's clothing—his sister being the unknown

who has unconsciously been Mario's model. Tosca arrives and finds Mario ill at ease. At first she is jealous, but he dispels her worry. She is delighted at the thought of an excursion with him. *Tosca: "Now listen." Duet: "Our cottage secluded."* But again Tosca's jealousy returns when she sees the picture of the Madonna and recognizes in the face Angelotti's sister. But Mario swears that none but Tosca's eyes charm him. *Duet: "No eyes on earth."* Tosca departs and Mario aids the disguised Angelotti to escape. Soon Scarpia arrives. He is on the trail of Angelotti. He discovers a woman's fan, dropped by the prisoner and suspects that Mario had something to do with the escape. Tosca suddenly returns. Scarpia, who desires above all things to possess her, pays her a fine compliment. *"Divine Tosca."* She ignores him until he shows her the fan. Now she is in a jealous rage for she feels sure that Mario has been loving another woman. The Te Deum is heard as the curtain falls.

ACT 2

Apartment in the Farnese Palace. Scarpia has sent a note to Tosca telling her he has news of Mario. Meanwhile Mario has been captured. Angelotti escaped. The young painter is brought in and taken to the torture chamber when he refuses to tell where Angelotti is hiding. Tosca arrives and from her Scarpia discovers where Angelotti is. He has Mario tortured in the adjoining apartment, and unable to bear the groans of her lover, Tosca reveals the secret. Mario is now brought out and, though suffering greatly, rebukes Tosca for telling of Angelotti's hiding place. He is dragged off to prison. Now Scarpia bargains for Tosca. *Scarpia: "Venal, my enemies call me."* He will spare her lover if she will be his. *Tosca: "Love and music have I lived for."* She finally consents. Scarpia tells her that there will have to be a mock execution of Mario so as to make his escape possible. He now writes a passport that will enable her and her lover to leave Rome. As he finishes writing Tosca, with a quick lunge, stabs him. Scarpia falls and dies. Placing candles at his head and a cross on his breast Tosca goes out.

ACT 3

Terrace of San Angelo Castle at dawn. Mario is brought out to die. He writes a last note to Tosca. *Mario: "The heavens blaze with stars."* Tosca arrives suddenly, and tells Mario that his execution is only to be a mock affair. Then with her passport they will escape from the country. Both are

overjoyed. *Duet: "The bitterness of death."*
The soldiers come. Mario stands before them
and they fire. When they are gone Tosca is
horrified to discover that Scarpia's trickery is
complete—the execution was genuine. Learning now of Scarpia's murder, soldiers come
running to take Tosca. But she escapes them
by leaping to her death from the parapet.

* * *

TRISTAN AND ISOLDE

MUSIC DRAMA IN THREE ACTS
MUSIC AND DRAMA BY RICHARD WAGNER
FIRST PRODUCTION—MUNICH, 1865

CAST

KING MARK OF CORNWALL......*Basso*
TRISTAN, his nephew..............*Tenor*
ISOLDE, princess of Ireland........*Soprano*
BRANGAENE, friend of Isolde *Mezzo-Soprano*
KURWENAL, servant of Tristan...*Baritone*
MELOT, a courier..................*Tenor*
A SHEPHERD......................*Tenor*
A STEERSMAN....................*Baritone*

ACT 1

The Deck of a Vessel. Tristan, the knight,
is bringing Isolde from Ireland to Cornwall
to become the bride of King Mark, she hav-

ing accepted his proposal, made through Tristan. The sailors are joyous over the killing of Marold by Tristan, the former being the betrothed of Isolde. The deed has freed Cornwall from the domination of Isolde's father. Isolde, on the threshold of a loveless match, is attracted by Tristan whom she alternately loves and hates. Finally she decides that he shall die by poison and that she will die with him. She orders Brangaene to prepare the drug. But the faithful friend, dreading to see the Princess perish, prepares a love potion instead. This Tristan and Isolde drink. They are amazed and then embrace each other in ecstasy just as the ship reaches the shores of Cornwall.

ACT 2

Garden of the Palace. The King has left his bride and gone on a hunting expedition. But Brangaene tells Isolde that the King's departure is a ruse and that the Princess is being watched by the courtier Melot. She tells Isolde, too, about the substitution of the love potion for poison. *"Fatal folly."* But Isolde does not rebuke her, nor does she heed her warning about the crafty Melot. She declares that love's goddess was instrumental in her drinking the love draught. *Isolde: "They act."* Tristan, signaled to by

Isolde, finds the Princess and they are oblivious to everything except each other and their happiness. Kurwenal, Tristan's friend and servant, arrives to warn him of the danger. But it is too late now, for Melot and the King surprise the lovers. The King bitterly reproaches his nephew but despises the low trickery of Melot. Tristan draws his sword on the courtier but in the fight Melot inflicts a fatal wound.

ACT 3

Interior of Tristan's Castle in Brittany. Here the wounded knight has been brought by Kurwenal. Isolde has been sent for to use her healing arts in restoring Tristan to health. Her coming is announced from the ramparts. Tristan, delirious, tears off his bandages in his effort to go to Isolde. As she reaches him he dies in her arms. Following her come King Mark and Melot. The King has come to reunite the lovers. But Kurwenal, thinking they have come to kill and not to heal, attacks them. He slays Melot and is himself slain by Melot's soldiers. King Mark finds Isolde dying of grief by the dead Tristan. *Isolde's death song: "Mild and softly he is smiling."* As she expires King Mark prays over her body.

IL TROVATORE

OPERA IN FOUR ACTS
MUSIC BY GIUSEPPE VERDI
BOOK BY SALVATORE COMMANARO
FIRST PRODUCTION—ROME, 1853

CAST

LEONORA, a noble lady...........*Soprano*
AZUCENA, a gypsy..........*Mezzo-Soprano*
INEZ, attendant of Leonora........*Soprano*
MANRICO, the troubadore—in reality
   the brother of the Count di Luna...*Tenor*
COUNT DI LUNA, influential noble *Baritone*
FERRANDO, captain of the guard....*Basso*
RUIZ, soldier of Manrico...........*Tenor*
AN OLD GYPSY.................*Baritone*

PLACE—Biscay and Aragon
TIME—15th Century

ACT 1

Vestibule in the Count's Palace. Ferrando tells of the tragedy in the Count's family. His brother when an infant came under the evil spell of a gypsy-witch. The witch was burned at the stake but she commanded that the daughter, Azucena, avenge her death. This revenge began with the disappearance of the infant brother. The changing scene now shows the palace gardens. Here Leonora confesses her love for the troubadour Manrico.

[310]

"*My heart is his alone.*" But the Count loves her desperately and he appears before her window just as the serenade of Manrico is heard. *Manrico: "Lonely on earth abiding."* Leonora meets Manrico and the Count vents his rage. *Count: "Now my vengeance."* Manrico is his enemy condemned to death. They draw swords and in the duel Manrico is wounded.

ACT 2

A Gypsy Camp in the Mountains. Work begins and here the wonderful Anvil Chorus is heard. *Chorus: "See how the shadows."* Azucena has nursed Manrico back to health after his wounds received at the hands of the Count. She tells him how her mother was burned by the Count's father. "*Fierce flames are soaring.*" In revenge she seized the child she thought was the Count's brother and flung him into the fire. But in her frenzy she burned her own child, and Manrico, brother of the Count di Luna, was saved. She has reared him as her own son and he loves her as a mother. He tells her how in the duel he spared the Count's life. "*At my mercy.*" She urges him to vengeance, declaring he should kill the Count. A messenger arrives to tell Manrico Leonora believes he is dead and she will enter a convent.

[311]

Il Trovatore

Manrico hurries off to her. At the convent the Count plans to abduct Leonora before the ceremony of admission takes place. *Count: "Of her smile, the radiant gleaming."* But just as he is about to seize Leonora the troubadour appears. *Trio: Manrico, Leonora, Count: "O, blessed vision."* Leonora flees with Manrico.

ACT 3

Camp of the Count. The soldiers sing. *Chorus: "In the midst of conflict."* Azucena is captured and the Count learns that she is the one who burned his brother. When she confesses to being the mother of his rival, Manrico, his hatred is doubled. The scene changes to a castle. Manrico and Leonora sing a farewell and the former goes forth to meet the Count. *Duet: "The vows we fondly plighted."* News now comes that Azucena is to be burned. Manrico is in a frenzy for vengeance. *"Tremble ye tyrants."*

ACT 4

Exterior of the Palace. Manrico has been defeated and he and Azucena are imprisoned. Leonora comes to be near her lover. *Leonora: "In this dark hour."* Leonora, Manrico and chorus sing the celebrated Miserere, than which there is no more beautiful number in the entire realm of music. The Count refuses mercy. *Count and Leonora: "Let my tears implore thee."* Leonora now promises to wed the Count if he releases Manrico. *Leonora and the Count: "O, joy, he's saved."* They go into the prison to release Manrico. In the cell Manrico and Azucena sing, *"Home to our mountains."* When Manrico learns that Leonora has promised herself to the Count to secure his release, he accuses her of betraying his love. But suddenly he discovers that to cheat the Count, she has taken poison. He begs for forgiveness as Leonora dies. The Count is beside himself with rage on finding that death has robbed him of his bride. He orders Manrico to be executed immediately. As the Troubadour is beheaded the old Azucena tells the Count he has killed his own brother. Struck dumb with remorse, the Count falls senseless as the curtain descends.

* * *

LA TRAVIATA (VIOLETTA)

OPERA IN FOUR ACTS BY GIUSEPPE VERDI
LIBRETTO BY PIAVE
ADAPTED FROM DUMAS' "DAME AUX CAMELIAS"
FIRST PRODUCED, VENICE, MARCH, 1853

CAST

VIOLETTA VALERY..............*Soprano*
FLORA BELOIX.................*Soprano*

La Traviata

ANNINA, Servant..........*Mezzo Soprano*
ALFRED GERMONT..............*Tenor*
GERMONT AINE...............*Baritone*
GASTON DE LETORIERES........*Tenor*
BARON DOUPHAL...............*Baritone*
MARQUIS D'ORGIBNY..........*Baritone*
DR. GRENVILLE..................*Basso*

PLACE—Paris and Vicinity
TIME—About 1700

ACT 1

Drawing room of Violetta, a beautiful young queen of the Parisian demi-monde. She is already in the first stages of consumption. In the gay company she is entertaining there is Alfred Germont, a young man of excellent family. Invited to give a toast, he sings "We'll Drink to the Beauty," the guests joining in the chorus. When left alone with Violetta, Alfred declares his love. Violetta warns him against loving her in any other way than as a friend, but, discovering that his devotion is sincere, returns his love, giving expression to her happiness in the beautiful aria "Ah, Was It He?" Inspired by her new love, Violetta decides to abandon her life of pleasure and seek with Alfred the seclusion of country life.

ACT 2

Alfred and Violetta are living an ideal existence in a villa near Paris. Three months

[314]

have passed, when Alfred accidentally learns that Violetta is preparing to sell her home in Paris to defray the expenses of their country abode. He suddenly realizes the false position he is occupying and sees that he is neglecting the practical affairs of life. He decides to leave for Paris to get what money he can. No sooner has he left when Georgio Germont, his father, calls upon Violetta. Germont Senior pleads with Violetta to give up his son. He tells her he has a daughter who is about to be married and, that the joy of her coming marriage may not be shattered by scandal, asks Violetta to leave Alfred. He wins over Violetta and she promises him what he asks, and writes Alfred a letter of farewell, telling him she loves him no longer. Alfred suddenly returns, Violetta controlling her feelings, leaves him, pretending to go into the garden. Alfred reads the letter and realizes that Violetta has left him. He is not appeased by his father's remonstrances and flies to Paris, to seek her there.

ACT 3

The drawing room of Flora, one of Violetta's friends. The occasion is a masked ball. Violetta's companion is Baron Douphal, one of her former lovers. Alfred arrives and immediately begins to gamble and wins large sums. When Violetta enters on the arm of the Baron, Alfred in a fury of rage, hurls his winnings at her feet, asking the company to witness that thus he pays back the money she has spent on him. Violetta is fainting when Germont, Sr., enters and upbraids his son for his heartless conduct. He suddenly realizes that Violetta still loves him, and is in despair over the insult he has heaped upon her.

ACT 4

Violetta's bedroom, where she lies asleep. She is desperately ill. At her side is Annina, who has been faithful through all her sorrows. Dr. Grenville comes and assists Violetta to sit up. He informs Annina that her mistress has but a few hours to live. Broken hearted, Annina tries to cheer Violetta in her last hour. A letter from Germont, Sr., brings word of Alfred's return. He has learned of the sacrifice she has made for him. Violetta, however, bids adieu to hope as the end approaches. Annina then tells her Alfred has already come. He rushes in and Violetta clasps him in her arms. All the old love springs up afresh in both hearts. Alfred promises never to leave her again. The sudden joy is too much, however; she sinks

rapidly, and after giving Alfred her portrait
by which he is to remember her, she dies in
his arms.

DIE WALKURE

MUSIC DRAMA IN THREE ACTS
MUSIC AND DRAMA BY RICHARD WAGNER
FIRST PRODUCTION—MUNICH, 1870

CAST

SIEGMUND ....*Tenor*
HUNDING ....*Basso*
WOTAN, the god.................*Baritone*
SIEGLINDE ....*Soprano*
BRUNNHILDE ....*Soprano*
FRICKA, wife of Wotan.........*Contralto*

"Die Walküre" is the second of the series
of the Niebelung Ring. Wotan has learned
from Erda, the earth goddess, that if Alberich, the dwarf, secures the ring, the gods
will perish. The union of Wotan and Erda
results in the Valkyries, who ride with the
slain heroes to Walhalla, home of the gods.
The revived heroes defend Walhalla against
attack from the Niebelungs. But to regain
the ring from the giants there must be a
hero capable of any deed of daring. Hoping
to bring forth such a one, Wotan contracts
another union the result of which is Siegmund and Sieglinde. But when young, the

hunter Hunding finds their home, kills the mother, carries off Sieglinde and leaves Siegmund alone in the world.

ACT 1

Hunding's Hut in a Forest. Utterly fatigued, Siegmund rushes into the strange hut and falls half fainting. Here Sieglinde finds him and gives him reviving refreshments. Hunding arrives and recognizes in Siegmund his mortal enemy. The latter shall enjoy the hospitality of the hut; on the morrow he shall die. But in preparing Hunding's evening drink, Sieglinde puts a sleep-producing drug into it. She is attracted by Siegmund and returns to him. Siegmund sings to her the lovely Liebeslied. *"Winter storms have waned."* Sieglinde shows Siegmund a great sword that has been thrust into the tree around which the hut is built. There Wotan thrust it on her marriage day. It belongs to him who has the power to withdraw it. Siegmund, with a great effort, withdraws the sword. Sieglinde now recognizes her brother, the hero, and together they flee into the forest.

ACT 2

Rocky Pass in the Forest. Wotan commands his favorite Valkyrie, Brunnhilde, to ride in defense of Siegmund. *"Make ready thy steed."* Brunnhilde now summons the Valkyries. *"Ho, yo, to, ho."* But Fricka declares that Siegmund must be punished for the union with his sister, Sieglinde. Wotan protests but finally assents. He again instructs Brunnhilde, this time to protect Hunding. Hunding catches up with Sieglinde and Siegmund and battles Siegmund. Brunnhilde disobediently aids Siegmund. But Wotan, carrying out Fricka's wish, protects Hunding, who slays Siegmund. Brunnhilde carries Sieglinde away on her aerial steed. Wotan, completing the destruction, slays Hunding.

ACT 3

Summit of the Rock of the Valkyries. Tumultuously the Valkyries come riding on the clouds. Brunnhilde is frightened by her father Wotan riding after her. But her sisters will not aid her against him. Now Brunnhilde sends Sieglinde off into the forest, predicting that she will bear a son who will be the hero Siegfried. *Brunnhilde: "Fly then swiftly."* *Sieglinde: "O marvelous sayings, maiden divine."* Brunnhilde now awaits the furious Wotan. The gods tells her she will fall into a sleep and shall be awakened by and claimed by the first man who comes on her. But Brunnhilde pleads for mercy against his debasement. *"Was it so shameful?"* Wotan, moved to pity, now decrees that she shall be won only by a hero who can penetrate the flames by which she will be surrounded. *Wotan: "Farewell, my brave and beautiful child."* He tenderly places her on the rocks and fire breaks out all around the summit. The opera ends with Brunnhilde sleeping on the crags.

* * *

WERTHER

OPERA IN THREE ACTS
MUSIC BY JULES MASSENET
TEXT FOUNDED ON GOETHE'S NOVEL
FIRST PRODUCTION—VIENNA, 1892

CAST

WERTHER ....*Tenor*
THE BAILIFF ....*Basso*
CHARLOTTE, his eldest daughter..*Soprano*
SOPHIA, Charlotte's sister...*Mezzo-Soprano*
ALBERT, betrothed to Charlotte...*Baritone*
SCHMIDT, the bailiff's friend.........*Basso*
YOHANN, another friend...........*Tenor*

PLACE—Wetzler. TIME—18th Century

ACT 1

Terrace before the Bailiff's Home. The Bailiff sings a carol with his younger children: *"Holy night."* Charlotte, the eldest daughter, is preparing for a ball to be given in the village. To the house comes Werther, a young man who is more or less a stranger in town. *Werther: "How sweet to dwell here."* Charlotte appears and the happy children throng around her. Before going she gives them all their supper. Werther meets Charlotte and is so struck with her that he wishes to go with her to the ball. She consents. When they have departed, Albert, Charlotte's fiance, appears, having just come back from a long journey. He learns that Charlotte is out for the evening and he departs. Charlotte and Werther return, each enamored of the other. *Werther: "Joy must be told."* Charlotte tells him that it was her mother's dying wish that she marry Albert, and that she must fulfill this wish regardless of her feelings. Werther leaves in despair.

ACT 2

Square in Front of the Inn. Albert and Charlotte have been married for some little time. They pass through the square and enter the church. Werther despairingly watches them from a distance. *Werther:*

"*Another is her husband.*" Later Albert meets Werther and greets him in a friendly way. Werther expresses his thanks for this feeling. Soon Sophia, the young sister, comes with flowers. *Sophia: "At early morn."* She tries to cheer Werther but he is still despondent. Albert throws out the hint that Werther would meet with better fortune if he devoted his attention to Sophia. But this he cannot do, loving only Charlotte. He feels sorry for Sophia, who he sees loves him, and determines to be a man and conquer his love for Charlotte. *"I will be a man."* By this time Charlotte has convinced him that she loves her husband and is true to him. Sophia, seeing the hopelessness of her love, is found weeping.

ACT 3

Rooms in Albert's Home. Charlotte is alone reading Werther's passionate letters. She realizes now that she loves only him and cannot love her husband. As she continues reading her emotions overpower her. *Charlotte: "I am stifling."* Werther appears and they reveal their souls to each other. *Duet: "Am I awake."* Werther pleads passionately with Charlotte and she admits that she loves him. But tearing herself from his arms, she rushes off into another room. Werther de-

parts in the very depths of despair. Albert
returns home and finds his wife distraught.
Presently he receives a letter from Werther
requesting the loan of a pistol, the explanation being that he is going to travel and will
need it. Albert makes Charlotte give the pistol to the messenger. The next scene shows
Werther's room. Charlotte knows what the
loan of the pistol means and has hurried
off to save Werther. But he has already shot
himself and lies fatally wounded. Charlotte
finds him near death and embraces him.
Duet: "Away with dread and fear." Knowing now that she carries only his image in
her heart, Werther expires in the girl's arms.

* * *

WILLIAM TELL

OPERA IN FOUR ACTS
MUSIC BY GIOACCHINO ROSSINI
LIBRETTO FROM SCHILLER'S DRAMA
FIRST PRODUCTION—PARIS, 1829

CAST

WILLIAM TELL ....*Baritone*
HEDWIGA, Tell's wife............*Soprano*
JEMMY, Tell's son...............*Soprano*
ARNOLD, suitor of Matilda........*Tenor*
MELCTHAL, Arnold's father........*Basso*

William Tell

GESSLER, governor of Schwitz and
  Uri ....*Basso*
MATILDA, Gessler's daughter......*Soprano*
RUDOLPH, captain in Gessler's
  guard ....*Tenor*
WALTER FURST..................*Basso*
LEUTHOLD, a shepherd............*Basso*
RUODI, a fisherman...............*Tenor*
PLACE—Switzerland. TIME—13th Century.

ACT 1

Tell's Home on the Shores of Lake Lucerne. *The fishermen are singing: "Come hither, my dearest love."* A horn-blast announces the Shepherds' Festival. Arnold is dejected for he loves Matilda, daughter of the tyrant Gessler. Tell plans to overthrow Gessler and seeks Arnold's aid. *Duet: "Vain is all dissembling."* Halting between duty and love, Arnold finally decides to join Tell and departs to bid Matilda farewell. The festival is held and men and maidens are married as is the custom. But suddenly from the mountains rushes Leuthold, a shepherd, who has killed one of Gessler's guards for wronging his daughter. He begs to be rowed across the lake. All fear Gessler's wrath, but Tell takes the oars and rows him out of danger. Infuriated, the soldiers burn the village. *Chorus: "Let the flames rage."*

ACT 2

Valley in the Alps. *Huntsmen's chorus:*
"Let the horns sound." Here Matilda meets
Arnold and they declare their love. *Duet:*
"Forgive my love." Arnold agrees to renounce
his patriotic tendencies for Gessler's daughter. But Tell finds him and tells him that
the tyrant's soldiers have murdered his father. Now Arnold drives thoughts of Matilda from his mind and determines to battle
for freedom. *Trio: Tell, Arnold, Furst:*
"His life the tyrant wickedly hath taken."
The Swiss gather and swear to battle for liberty. *"To arms, to arms!"*

ACT 3

A Square Showing Gessler's Castle in the
Background. Here Gessler and his barons
watch the ballets that are given for their
entertainment. *Chorus: "Hail to thee."* On
a pole Gessler has a cap placed and all must
bow to it, thus recognizing his power. But
William Tell declines to bow. Gessler has
the patriot brought before him and is enraged to discover in him the man who aided
Leuthold to escape. Tell's little son is with
him. Wishing to have unique sport at Tell's
expense, Gessler orders him to shoot an apple from the boy's head at a considerable

distance. The patriot-marksman holds himself under perfect control and draws his bow. The arrow flies straight through the apple. But in Tell's coat is found another arrow. This he declares he saved for the tyrant should the first arrow have killed the boy. Matilda saves the boy, but Tell is bound and taken off to prison.

ACT 4

By the Burned Village. Arnold, now determined to fight for liberty, returns to say farewell to his old home. He finds the village in ashes. *"O, blessed abode."* A company of patriots arrive and tell Arnold of the imprisonment of Tell whom they are going to rescue. A change of scene shows another part of the lake. Tell's wife is on her way to demand of Gessler the release of her son and her husband. She is met by Matilda who has saved the boy from her father's wrath. She declares Tell is imprisoned. But Tell suddenly appears, having made his escape. He has also freed his country by shooting dead the tyrant Gessler. A storm breaks overhead displaying the peaks of the Alps in all their grandeur. The patriots joyously sing of their new-found freedom. *Chorus: "Let us invoke with hearts devout."*

ZAMPA

OPERA COMIQUE IN THREE ACTS
MUSIC BY LOUIS J. F. HEROLD
LIBRETTO BY MELESVILLE, FOUNDED ON
"THE STATUE BRIDE"
FIRST PRODUCTION—PARIS, 1831

CAST

ZAMPA, a pirate.....................*Tenor*
ALPHONSO, his brother.............*Tenor*
CAMILLA, betrothed of Alphonso..*Soprano*
DANIEL, mate of Zampa..........*Baritone*
RITA, companion of Camilla *Mezzo-Soprano*
DANOLO ....*Basso*

PLACE—Sicily.   TIME—17th Century.

ACT 1

A Gothic Vestibule. The maidens are examining the wonderful gifts for Camilla who is to be the bride of Alphonso. Camilla's father has gone to meet a convoy from Smyrna. Now Alphonso arrives with the news that Zampa, the pirate, has been captured, thus minimizing the danger that had threatened Camilla's father. Camilla urges her fiance to pray to the statue of Albina. *Camilla: "Like the roseate blush of morning."* The statue is of a girl who was wronged and it is held in veneration by all the countryside.

[327]

Zampa

When the story is told Alphonso realizes and
confesses that Albina was deceived by his
brother. Suddenly Danolo arrives with a
story of a desperate stranger he met in the
forest. In a short while the stranger (Zampa,
the pirate) himself comes on the scene. He
brings a message that Camilla's father has
been taken prisoner by Zampa and that a
ransom must be sent. Now Zampa is joined
by Daniel who tells him that Alphonso also
is a prisoner. The pirates congregate and
drink. *Zampa: "When the wave we are dancing o'er."* Zampa's attention is called to the
statue of Albina, whom he wronged. Intoxicated, he places a ring on the statue's finger
and promises to wed her next day. When he
tries to remove the ring to give it as a pledge
to Camilla for her father's safety, the marble
hand closes on it. The pirates are frightened.

ACT 2

Country by the Seaside. Sea, showing a
Chapel. *Chorus: "If our earthly hope should
fail us." Zampa: "Like the bee I fondly
rove."* Zampa proposes that Camilla shall
be his bride as ransom for her father. He
has been warned that he may be captured,
but, fascinated by the girl, he scorns all warnings. Camilla is forced to accept the pirate.

[328]

Zampa: "*Maidens who are longing for a faithful lover.*" Alphonso, released by the pirates, comes to claim Camilla. He learns that she cannot wed him because she must save her father. Preparations are made for the wedding. Just before the ceremony a vision of the figure Albina appears to Zampa from the tomb and threateningly shows the ring on the finger. He is unnerved but determines to wed Camilla. Alphonso stops him on his way to the chapel and challenges him to fight for possession of Camilla. But at this moment a messenger arrives with a pardon for Zampa if he and his band fight for Sicily against the Turks. Now the people know who the prospective bridegroom is. But Camilla's father is in his power and, half-fainting, the girl enters the chapel with him.

ACT 3

A Room. Zampa and Camilla are now husband and wife. Alphonso comes serenading, "*Gondolier, stay, nor bid farewell.*" He then enters the room and begs Camilla to flee with him. Zampa arrives and Alphonso hides. Now Zampa reveals to Camilla that he is a count and brother of Alphonso. She is astounded at this revelation. Alphonso is

caught in the house and Zampa, despite pleadings, orders his execution. But before this
order can be carried out the statue of Albina
appears. The marble arms gather Zampa in
a terrible embrace and carry him off in a
flash of fire.

* * *

ZAZA

OPERA IN FOUR ACTS
LIBRETTO ADAPTED FROM SIMON AND BERTON
MUSIC BY RUGGIERO LEONCAVALLO
FIRST PRODUCTION—MILAN, 1900

CAST

ZAZA, a concert hall singer........*Soprano*
ANAIDE, her mother........*Mezzo-Soprano*
FLORIANA, a concert hall singer....
............................*Alto-Soprano*
NATALIE, Zaza's maid........*Comprimaria*
SIGNORA DUFRESNE........*Comprimaria*
MILIO DUFRESNE................*Tenor*
CASCART, a concert hall singer....*Baritone*
BUZZY, a journalist................*Baritone*
MALARDOT, the proprietor of the con-
cert cafe.......................*Alto Tenor*
LARTIGNON, a monologue artist.....*Basso*
DUCLOU, stage manager.............*Basso*
MICHELIN, a journalist.............*Tenor*

[330]

MARCO, valet of Signor Dufresne....

..............................*Alto Basso*

TIME—Present.

PLACE—Paris.

ACT 1

The stage is set in two sections; the dressing room of Zaza being at one side, at the other side a stage setting. Zaza, a concert hall singer, loves Dufresne and brags to Buzzy, a journalist, that she will make him love her in return. Exerting all her charms, Zaza finally makes Dufresne succumb to her fascination.

ACT 2

The reception room of Zaza's home. Zaza is informed by Dufresne that he is forced to leave her, as he must go to America for several months. Pleading with him not to go, Zaza induces him to postpone his trip, but he tells her he must go to Paris at once on business. An old lover of Zaza's, Cascart, enters and arouses Zaza's jealousy by hinting that Dufresne may have other reasons for the trip and tells of seeing him in Paris with another woman. Zaza announces her intention of following him to Paris.

ACT 3

A room in Dufresne's home in Paris. Zaza enters with her maid. Discovers a letter addressed to Signora Dufresne, realizing thereby that he is married. His little girl enters and finally Signora Dufresne herself. She gazes with astonishment at the visitor. Zaza in explanation states that she has mistaken the house for another and leaves.

ACT 4

Zaza's house in the suburbs. Cascart, having learned of Zaza's visit to Paris, begs her to give up Dufresne. She laughs at the idea and is sternly reminded by Cascart that it is a matter of duty. As Cascart leaves, Dufresne is announced. In spite of his affectionate greetings, Zaza tells him of his marriage, but that she forgives the deception. She tells him that she has informed Signora Dufresne of their intimacy, in which he curses her in a rage. He is sent away by Zaza, who cries that she is cured of her love, after telling him that her first story was untrue and that his wife knows nothing of the affair.